TYPES OF
THEMATIC STRUCTURE

TYPES OF THEMATIC STRUCTURE

The Nature and Function of Motifs in
Gide, Camus, and Sartre

BY EUGENE H. FALK
with an Introduction by Bernard Weinberg

THE UNIVERSITY OF CHICAGO PRESS
CHICAGO & LONDON

LIBRARY OF CONGRESS CATALOG CARD NUMBER: 67-16775

THE UNIVERSITY OF CHICAGO PRESS, CHICAGO & LONDON
THE UNIVERSITY OF TORONTO PRESS, TORONTO 5, CANADA
© 1967 BY THE UNIVERSITY OF CHICAGO
ALL RIGHTS RESERVED. PUBLISHED 1967
PRINTED IN THE UNITED STATES OF AMERICA

TO EUGÈNE VINAVER

When I give, I know what
you have given, and my
giving then becomes a
deed of thankfulness and
of esteem.

Acknowledgments

I wish to thank Professor Robert Garapon of the Sorbonne and Professor Harry T. Levin of Harvard, who read an earlier draft of the manuscript and offered valuable suggestions. I am particularly grateful for the encouragement I received from Professor Bernard Weinberg of the University of Chicago, whose introductory essay to this book offers a significant perspective for thematic studies. I also wish to express my sincere appreciation for the support I received from Dr. Leonard Rieser, Dean of the Faculty and Provost of Dartmouth College. Finally, I wish to thank Éditions Gallimard for their generous permission to use copyright material from Gide's *La Symphonie pastorale,* Camus' *L'Etranger,* and Sartre's *La Nausée.*

E. H. F.

Dartmouth College
Hanover, New Hampshire

Contents

CHAPTER 3

La Symphonie pastorale

CHAPTER 4

L'Etranger

CHAPTER 5

La Nausée

CHAPTER 6

Introduction

Thematism, or the approach to literary study through the study of themes, has sometimes been a useful form of literary criticism; more often than not, it has remained distant from the central preoccupations of criticism. I think that we may say that thematism has been coincident with criticism whenever it has served to emphasize and clarify structural features of a given work and that it has been non-critical whenever it has tended to lead away from the work and toward historical or biographical generalizations. In this sense, the practice of thematism by American critics has frequently been a profitable adjunct to the arts of criticism, whereas the European (and especially the French) thematists have for the most part failed to bring their approach into contact with the real problems of analysis and evaluation.

This divergence in the use and application of thematism has been symptomatic of the general tendencies discernible in the two traditions of literary study. The American tradition, in this century, has moved progressively away from literary history and toward literary criticism—or, in some cases, to a useful combination of the two disciplines. If we have renounced an exclusive faith in the historical techniques inherited from Europe by those who founded literary scholarship in this country, it is because we have felt that those techniques were taking us constantly farther from literature itself and from the disciplines that we thought of as properly literary. We had had enough of facts and dates, of sources and influences, of classifications and movements that told us many things about other things but very little about the works that we were reading. We wanted to return to the text, to the poem whether a novel or a drama or a lyric. We had had enough of the biographical curiosity that centered its efforts upon the poet and that found the poem interesting and pertinent only as a biographical document. For we found the poem interesting in itself and pertinent only to the special artistic delights that it was capable of giving us. We wanted to learn how to read it and understand it, to penetrate its meaning and discover its form, to evaluate it, to extract from it the maximum pleasure for which it was the instrument and the potential.

If we have had, on this continent, a "new criticism," it has been largely a result of our wish to return to the text. That wish has been pursued in many ways and to various ends. Upon these ends have depended the orientations of the divers groups and schools of criticism that have flourished in recent decades, and from them have derived multiple methods and approaches. Some of the methods were such as to lead deeply into the text and remain there, producing conclusions and judgments relevant exclusively to the poem as a poem. Others, while they returned to the text as an initial step in their inquiry, soon turned from it again to investigate matters of an external nature; their conclusions and judgments necessarily bore on those matters. Thematists and thematic approaches have been conspicuous in both categories; for a theme may be considered either as a structural element at one level or another within the poem or as a non-structural element that serves only to relate the poem to other works or to biography or to history. I shall speak shortly of the ways in which Eugene Falk, in his *Types of Thematic Structure,* has expanded the whole concept of the use of thematic considerations for the analysis of texts and for the arrival at structural conclusions.

European critics have not been insensitive to the need for a new criticism, one that would supplement the old historical and biographical methods with new insights of a more sensitively literary sort. Hence the French have also had their "nouvelle critique"—a relatively recent development—and they have had their thematists who have attempted to find the new insights through the study of literary themes. But I believe it not incorrect to say that neither the "nouvelle critique" nor French thematism (and to a certain extent the two have been coextensive) has displayed any urge to return to the text; or, when either has done so, it has been for brief visits that were way stations on the road to further biographical or historical generalizations. French curiosity about literature remains basically a curiosity about universal man or about the poet as a man, not about the poem as a work of art. It has therefore tended to seek its solutions in philosophical speculation or in psychiatric delving rather than in aesthetics. It has followed the line of Sainte-Beuve and Lanson, crossed with the line of everyman's Freud; but it has scrupulously desisted from any probing into the nature of the poetic art, from such probing as might give preference to the return to the poem over the flight to the poet.

Two practitioners of thematism in France typify the dangers and the deficiencies of an approach having such orientations as these. The first is Georges Poulet. In the sense that his high literary sensitivity frequently leads him to the passing insight that illuminates a detail in a work, he belongs to the tradition of Sainte-Beuve and Lanson; but he is more like the latter than the former since his curiosities are historical rather than biographical. Poulet uses the concept of theme as a kind of link between the history of literature and the history of philosophy. Yet because of certain peculiarities of his approach, the application of this concept brings results that are as unliterary as they are unphilosophical. He thinks of theme as a subject matter or a *topos* that appears and recurs either in the various writings of a single author or in many authors over a period of time. The themes that most attract him are such universals as time, space, the circle —themes that he can seek and find in almost any period of any literature. What interests him about any theme is precisely its universality, since he wishes to use it as a touchstone by means of which he may assay the state of the human spirit as manifested in given men in successive centuries.

The chronological ordering of Poulet's *Etudes sur le temps humain,* and only the chronological ordering, accounts for its pretensions to history. In the introduction, Poulet outlines these pretensions through a rapid tracing of the theme of "human time" in philosophy and literature across the Middle Ages and the whole of the French written tradition. But from the first words of the introduction, it is clear that the history will only be nominally and superficially such. Instead of developing a narrative proposition forward from a point of beginning to a point of ending, it will work backward from a culminating point in the present to all the past preparations for that present culmination. On the assumption that the highest conception of time is found in existentialist time, Poulet will give us "une histoire du temps existentialiste depuis nos jours jusqu'aux origines," a reverse history making for a reverse thematism. Essentially, the theme itself is important only as an auxiliary to and a manifestation of a certain kind of total human sensitivity, a global way of vibrating to the problem of human existence. Hence from the outset the theme of time will shade off into the related themes of existence, liberty, the *moi* and the *néant,* others that belong to the central preoccupations of the existentialists. The thematism itself is dubious.

When the theme becomes a state of feeling rather than an idea, the work that treats its vicissitudes falls out of the domain of philosophy. For any properly philosophical approach must deal primarily and always with ideas, not as isolated and distinct but in the context of the arguments and the developments and the methodological presuppositions that give them their meaning. An idea ripped from such contexts is either meaningless or has any meaning that the writer wants to give it. Poulet's procedure both isolates passages containing his theme and its by-themes from their significant contexts and endows these passages with meanings that will serve the demonstration under way—this probably not through a deficiency of intellectual honesty but rather through an excess of partisan zeal. He is frequently, as in the case of his study of Descartes, not interested in philosophical texts at all but rather in the states of soul—as he reconstructs them from primary or secondary sources—that are alleged to have produced the philosophical text. The chapter on Descartes, entitled "Le songe de Descartes," reconstructs and interprets an episode of Descartes' youth. It concludes thus: "C'est au contact d'épisodes comme ceux-ci qu'on saisit le mieux les rapports qui existent entre les inquiétudes de l'âme et les spéculations de l'esprit, et qu'alors s'éclaire jusque dans son fond ce qui fait une philosophie: œuvre non seulement de la partie purement intellectuelle de l'être, mais de l'être tout entier." Perhaps so. But this is a statement, as the whole chapter is a chapter, about the man rather than about his work or his philosophy; it is devoted to genetic rather than to analytical considerations; and it shows to what extent the theme of time (which has here entirely disappeared) was merely a device for the discovery of the man.

In his discussion of poets—unfortunately I cannot say of poetry—Poulet exploits a thematic method that is equally disruptive of texts and destructive of poems. Each study of a poet asks what kind of conception of time is present in his works, seeks and collects the fragments of poems that contain the theme or its by-themes, organizes them into an answer that may fit into the total demonstration. The beginning of the chapter on Racine, "Notes sur le temps racinien," may illustrate the approach:

> C'est par *La Thébaïde* que s'ouvre le théâtre de Racine. Or, dès les premiers vers s'y pose un problème si urgent, si fondamental, que tout le théâtre racinien ne fera presque rien d'autre que le remettre en question:
>
> > O toi, Soleil, ô toi qui rends le jour au monde,
> > Que ne l'as-tu laissé dans une nuit profonde!
>
> C'est le problème de l'existence, mais posé par rapport à la continuation de l'être, et non directement quant à son origine. La double réalité que suscitent et enferment ces vers, les premiers où frémisse l'authentique accent racinien, est celle d'un Soleil qui rend le jour au monde, et d'un monde qui a mérité que le jour ne lui fût pas rendu. Pourquoi le pouvoir créateur consent-il à recommencer une œuvre qui s'est avérée défectueuse et monstrueuse? pourquoi consent-il à prolonger d'un jour présent la série des jours passés qui, d'eux-mêmes, tombaient dans la "nuit profonde"? Problème d'autant plus inexplicable, que la création d'un nouveau jour n'implique pas seulement, comme celle du jour premier, la création d'un être encore pur et digne de Dieu; mais cette fois l'invention d'un être qui

a déjà eu une existence et qui, en raison de cette existence passée, loin de mériter une existence présente, aurait dû être "laissé dans la nuit." A moins donc d'imaginer cette chose absurde: la création perpétuelle d'un monde chaque fois radicalement nouveau, et qui serait effacé à chaque instant pour être "rendu" dans l'instant suivant à sa virginité première, il n'y a, une fois l'existence du mal acquise, et l'indignité de la créature reconnue, point d'autre solution possible pour Dieu, que de cesser de créer, ou que de créer alors quelque chose qui se continue, et qui continue précisément un passé où le mal s'est introduit. . . . Tel est l'aspect caractéristique que prend le problème de l'existence pour Racine.

The passage from *La Thébaïde,* torn untimely from the play, is used by Poulet as the basis for a meditation on being, existence, good and evil, God and creation, in which he himself is obviously passionately involved but which has nothing to do with Racine's tragedies or even with the by-theme that he is treating. The two lines are outrageously misread in order to force upon them a thematic content. We need to read them more simply and poetically, for what they say in themselves and for what they are in the drama to which they belong. Jocaste is speaking. She has just learned that, with the coming of day, the opposing forces of her sons, the "enemy brothers" Etéocle and Polynice, are about to do battle outside the walls. The grieving mother regards that battle as unnatural and monstrous; she wishes that the day that must see it had never dawned, that the night that might have prevented it had lasted forever; in these lines she says so. She refers to earlier statements where she had expressed her long concern over the fraternal enmity, where she had spoken of awaking after a night of sleep during which the criminal opposition had been prepared:

> Mes yeux depuis six mois étaient ouverts aux larmes,
> Et le sommeil les ferme en de telles alarmes!
> Puisse plutôt la mort les fermer pour jamais,
> Et m'empêcher de voir le plus noir des forfaits!

The two verses that Poulet quotes belong in a situation at the beginning of a tragedy; they are spoken by one of the personages involved in the action and they express her emotions relevant to it; they are meaningful only in terms of their poetic context.

But for Poulet there are no contexts because there are no poems. There are only passages that contain themes and themes that are symptomatic of the soul of the poet or of the sensitivity of his times. Since both soul and sensitivity are predetermined, and since there is an over-all pattern into which a given man or a given time must fit, one selects passages at will and one interprets them as one wills, without regard to the poetic circumstances that give to a given passage or line or word, at a given place and time in the poem, its particular function and its necessary meaning. Thematism so conceived and so practiced results in the destruction of poetry.

If thematism as exploited by Georges Poulet is a device for the construction of historical generalizations about the progress of the human spirit, thematism in Jean-Pierre Richard is an instrument for the reconstitution of the psyche of the individual poet. The same processes of isolation and detachment of the theme or word or phrase are employed; but rather than seeking a single theme in many texts and many authors, Richard seeks within the total written residue of a single writer, all those themes that may serve him—because they are the most frequent and the most prominent—in reconstructing the "imagination" or the "sensibilité" of the writer. In his *L'Univers imaginaire de Mallarmé,* his purpose is to detach from all the writings of Mallarmé, whether poems or poems in prose, articles or letters, stories or fragments of any kind, all the major themes; then to arrange them as they fall into natural categories or as they relate to known biographical data; then to fit together the pieces of what must have been Mallarmé's innermost soul and to give that soul a development and a history. Thematism becomes the means by which the man who made the poems is made to rise again from the dust of the poems he made.

Richard is aware of the fact that he might be reproached with reducing poems to dust and with studying only the particles resulting from the destruction. Yet he does not foresee the true nature of the reproach and its real implications. In his introduction to *Mallarmé* he says: "Ces remarques peuvent mener à une autre question: vous négligez, nous dira-t-on, les alentours de l'œuvre, mais cette œuvre elle-même, votre analyse la respecte-t-elle dans sa figure, dans l'aspect extérieur sous lequel elle s'offre à nous? Ne compromet-elle pas son visage le plus familier? Ne nie-t-elle pas sa réalité d'œuvre d'*art?*" From the way in which he asks the questions that supposedly will be asked of him, Richard must think that those who are concerned with art and the work itself, with its figure and form, are only fearful of the destruction of an external form. He uses, as equivalent to "l'œuvre elle-même," three other formulas, "sa figure," "l'aspect extérieur," and "son visage le plus familier." This means that he himself can conceive only of the superficial, the external, the immediately perceptible aspects, and that for him these are its form. He does not so much as recognize the possibility of an "essential" or "intimate" form, of a principle of organization or structure in the individual work, far below the visible and apparent surface, that accounts for its external form as well as for its ultimate effectiveness.

Because of these shortcomings in his general conception of art, Richard (continuing the paragraph that I have been citing) proposes the following answer to his hypothetical objection:

> Il est certes bien vrai que toute lecture profonde choisit ses points d'affleurement, qui ne coïncident pas forcément avec le relief externe du poème. Celui-ci peut alors en paraître négligé, parfois même rompu. Sa structure formelle se trouve détruite et cette destruction doit être déplorée, même si elle s'exerce finalement au profit de l'œuvre dont elle nous aura permis de saisir la structure interne. . . . Un tel reproche risque de nous être adressé par la critique anglo-saxonne, à qui importe avant tout, on le sait, la réalité architecturale et objective des œuvres isolées.

From the development of these ideas later in the text, it becomes evident that when he speaks of a "lecture profonde," Richard means two kinds of "downward" penetration into the work: linguistic penetration, down to the deepest private and special meaning of the word that it has through its association with the whole of the writer's private and special lexicon; and psychological penetration, down to the innermost operations of the spirit or the psyche or the imagination that had given rise to the word in its special meaning. That is, Richard's analysis in depth is a dual process which first takes the word out of the text and puts it into the context of all the writer's linguistic habits, then transforms the word into a psychological act that reflects a new context of spiritual pattern and operation. In a word, expression and the state of soul expressed.

Analysis in depth so conceived is a thematic mode that moves from the poem to the word to the psyche, with the theme as the vehicle of passage. But the passage constantly takes one farther away from poems and texts. The internal structure that Richard conceives is first the structure of a personal language, last the structure of an individual soul. It is never the structure of a work of art, as work of art, having within itself an internal *raison d'être,* explicable in terms of an architecture of its parts that is independent, now, of its psychological origins and of other works manifesting the same linguistic context. The analysis in depth that would discover it, even if it were to use thematic devices, would have to move constantly deeper into the poem and its form, rather than out from it and away from it. Richard's pretensions at so doing are unjustified. For nowhere in his book does he consider a theme—or any other element—as a constitutive part of the whole poem, as subordinated to its total structure, and as contributory to an effect that depends as well upon all the other parts. He is interested in the man and his language rather than in the poem and he uses thematic approaches to serve those interests.

If I have insisted as I have done on the "centrifugal" nature of the thematism practiced by Poulet and Richard, it was so that I might clarify the "centripetal" nature of Eugene Falk's thematic approach. The center is of course the work of art, the poem (in the broadest classical sense). As Poulet and Richard "flee the center," they move outward in the direction of philosophical generalization, or of linguistic explanation, or of psychological reconstitution. They travel on the theme, which takes them constantly farther away from the point of departure in the text; and there is no point of return. Eugene Falk, on the contrary, always "seeks the center." Indeed, it might be said that he seeks the center of the center. For, remaining always within the work, he moves constantly inward from the superficial form (the only one that Richard understands) to the intimate form, from the word (used by Richard for his linguistic excursions) to the object signified by the word and to the place of that object in a structure of objects. He travels on the theme, but it takes him progressively in the direction of those central organizing elements of the structure that give the poem its artistic integrity and its aesthetic efficacy.

Falk's title, *Types of Thematic Structure,* is itself revelatory of his intentions and his hopes. He will be dealing with themes and thematism; but thematism will at all times be related to the structure of works. He will be discussing, at any given time, a given work, with a view to finding what themes, rising to the surface, may be used as instruments for the discovery of links and relationships within that work. He will approach each work without presuppositions, neither seeking a given predetermined theme of interest to him for special historical or philosophical reasons nor trying to find again the themes that have appeared in other works by the same author. The work will be abstracted from all such contexts—as it must be for proper structural study—and will itself provide the whole of the context for the thematic investigation. It will give what themes it has. Nevertheless, there is a sense in which Falk goes beyond the isolated work; he uses it as a basis for generalizations about the *types* of themes and of thematic linkings that he finds within the individual work or in a group of works studied in the same way. As he studies the work, he makes discoveries about the powers of his thematic approach for the illumination of other poetic structures. Hence his subtitle, "The Nature and Function of Motifs."

The thematic technique that Eugene Falk uses is posited on a double supposition: there are some themes within any work that recur or are repeated in approximately the same form, and there are other themes that grow and develop as they appear in successive parts of the poem. Both types serve to link parts of the work with one another and with the whole, and they thus become elements of the "structure" or the "fabric." While the first establish static relationships within the work—elements of constancy and repetition—the second establish dynamic relationships within the work—elements of progression and development. But even the static themes, to the extent to which they may contribute to a developing plot or story, are in their turn linked to the dynamic themes. All become structuring components, building the poem in both its spatial and its temporal dimensions.

In a sense, Falk distinguishes themes on two levels, on the level of the objects represented—actions or persons or things or even informing ideas—and on the level of the words through which the representation is made. He himself does not so divide them, but it is evident both from the theoretical discussion and from the practical applications that he alternates between substantive or material considerations and the verbal expression of substance or matter. Thus his concern with the "linking image" or the "linking phrase" is a concern with the single word or with the formula that recurs or reappears. This is verbal linking, but there is a thing represented by the word or the image or the phrase; and the thing remains constant while the word may suffer variations. Things are more overtly involved in those "repetitious labels" which signify factors in a situation, conditions and circumstances that serve as causes for the action. Similarly, the motivations and purposes of the personages who act, recurring as they must at points where the action needs to be prepared or justified, constitute themes of an essentially substantive nature. Action itself, or the acts of which it is composed, is material rather than verbal, and the themes that it carries—or that carry it—are the ones that could least readily be reduced to verbal considerations.

Themes may therefore be seen as comprising the whole of the action in a fictional work, or the causes of that action that reside in individual motivations and purposes, or the causes that are to be found in situation and circumstance or in the thoughts and feelings and passions that link (at an intermediate level) persons with their acts. Themes are also seen in the descriptive elements through which objects of all kinds are identified and presented. In this wide range of themes—reduced now to their substantive rather than to their verbal form—those relating to action itself are the only really dynamic ones, since the only thing that moves forward and changes within the fictional complex is the action or the plot. Hence these are developing themes while the others, which state or restate the constant causes, are recurrent or repetitive themes. Whether they are dynamic or static, related to action proper or to the causes of action, all themes are particular to the work in which they are found. They belong to the structure or the fabric of the individual work and have only such meanings as the work gives them.

For Eugene Falk, then, the practice of thematism is the practice of a brand of formal or structural analysis. Whether he is dealing with the single theme that he traces through a poem or with the whole complex of themes from which he deduces the body of relationships within the poem, he is concerned with structural elements, with the part or the parts and the links that are established between the parts and the whole. The theme is a device for the progressive penetration into the workings of the poem. When he speaks of the themes to be found in action or in plot, he is of course treating the major structural element in a narrative or a dramatic work; he is inquiring into that dynamic factor which accounts for the order of the work as well as for its basic unity and to which all other factors are ultimately related. Moreover, since he thinks of causal links between themes of character or themes of thought on the one hand and themes of action on the other hand, he insists on the formal principle of internal or poetic causation that effectively relates the parts. It is through this principle that the static parts are made operative in the dynamic whole and that the spatial relationships within the whole are transmuted into the temporal relationships that organize the whole.

Thematism of this kind differs from an integral formalism only in two ways: in the fact that formalism distinguishes the terms that it applies to the different qualitative parts of the work, whereas Falk uses the term "theme" for all the parts (hence the necessity for the epithets that identify the intended parts); and in the fact that a complete formalism wishes always to go beyond the individual "part" or "theme" to the predominant structuring element that gives its *raison d'être* to each auxiliary part and each contributory theme. That is, thematism and structuralism may coincide on the level of the individual and separate part, may trace it through its appearances and reappearances in the work, may discover its relationships to the other static or repetitive parts or to the major dynamic or progressive part. But while this may be a final and self-sufficient procedure for the thematic critic, for the formal critic it must always remain an intermediate and insufficient procedure. The formal critic will always wish to move from the subordinated part to the subordinating part, from any part to the whole—and then back from the whole to each of the parts in the light of the totality of the relationships that link all the parts. The form is always a whole and formal analysis can be satisfied with no less than the discovery of the whole.

As he applies his thematic method to the practical analysis of the three works that he studies, Eugene Falk does pass beyond the study of the individual theme, to kinds of structural examination that involve the whole of the poetic form. On the practical as well as on the theoretical side, his fundamental interest in the essential form of the literary work moves him constantly closer to formal criticism.

BERNARD WEINBERG

1

Types of Structural Coherence
and Definitions of Motifs,
Leitmotifs, and Themes

In his remarks[1] on *The Magic Mountain*, Thomas Mann urged that his book be read twice: "The way in which the book is composed results in the reader's getting a deeper enjoyment from the second reading." The word "composed," says Mann, was used designedly to point out "the strong formative influence" of music on his style. "To me the novel was always like a symphony, a work in counterpoint, a thematic fabric; the idea of the musical motif plays a great role in it . . . I followed Wagner in the use of the leitmotif, which I carried over into the work of language. Not as Tolstoy and Zola use it, or as I used it myself in *Buddenbrooks*, naturalistically and as a means of characterization—so to speak mechanically. I sought to employ it in its musical sense . . . that is why I make my presumptuous plea to my readers to read the book twice. Only so can one really penetrate and enjoy its musical association of ideas. The first time, the reader learns the thematic material; he is then in a position to read the symbolic and allusive formulas both forwards and backwards."

I am not concerned with Thomas Mann's statement as a key to *The Magic Mountain*, but I am concerned with two assumptions his statement implies. The first is that our awareness of the structural coherence of the thematic fabric increases and intensifies our pleasure; the second, that because leitmotifs, by effecting an association of ideas from one theme to another, may perform an important function in the composition of the thematic fabric, our awareness of its structural coherence depends upon our grasping the relationship between themes and leitmotifs. The second assumption invites a closer scrutiny of what is actually meant by leitmotif

---

[1] "The Making of *The Magic Mountain*," in H. T. Lowe-Porter's translation of *Der Zauberberg* (New York: Alfred A. Knopf, 1953).

in a narrative and of how the term "theme" should be understood when the structural coherence of the thematic fabric is under consideration. It should prove useful to identify and make appropriate distinctions between the different motifs to which the term "leitmotif" has been applied[2] and to indicate others to which it could be applied. It is even more important to explore the way in which themes may be compositionally relatable with or without the use of the so-called leitmotif as an agent of relatedness. Before turning our attention to the variety and function of leitmotifs and to thematic relatedness that may be effected without their use, however, we must first determine the meaning of the term "theme" as it will be used in this study and then consider the earlier assumption that our awareness of the structural coherence of the thematic fabric increases and intensifies our pleasure.

General Definitions of the Terms "Theme" and "Motif"

Various meanings have been attributed to theme. This term is sometimes applied to the topic that indicates the materials. Thus the topic may be, for example, the hero's class, his religion, his profession, or his relation to society: the peasant, the soldier, the rebel, the prodigal son. The topic may be the hero's dominant characteristic: the miser, the adventurer, the sentimentalist. It may be the main event or situation: conspiracy, war, delinquency, the murder of brothers, unrequited love. Or it may be the complex of features and situations associated with certain figures: Oedipus, Don Juan, Faust. The theme as topic marks out a salient feature of the materials.

But the term "theme" may also be assigned to the ideas that emerge from the particular structure of such textual elements as actions, statements revealing states of mind or feelings, gestures, or meaningful environmental settings. Such textual elements I designate by the term "motif"; the idea that emerges from motifs by means of an abstraction, I call the theme.

Before we proceed, we must establish the distinction between a theme as topic and a theme emerging from a motif. In saying that the topic indicates the materials, we have classified under materials the hero's class, his relation to society, his dominant characteristic, the main event, the main situation, or, finally, the complex of some of these features and situations. All these materials may be thought of without regard for the particular textual elements by which they are manifested in the narrative.

---

[2] See Oskar Walzel, *Das Wortkunstwerk* (Leipzig: Verlag Quelle und Meyer, 1926); see especially the essay "Leimotive in Dichtungen."

When we think of themes as topics, we conceive of them as generalizations drawn from dominant motifs, but apart from the motif structure within which they achieve concrete textual existence. Themes as topics are mere indications of classificatory divisions, unrelated to the mode of the textual constellation of motifs.

On the other hand, themes emerging from motifs are ideas with which textual elements are pregnant within their contextual, structural coherence. Since the term "theme" is used to designate the ideas carried by motifs, it should be understood that we are here concerned only with meanings emerging from the context, with meanings emerging from motifs by virtue of the coherence in which they appear.

Sometimes the message a work is intended or supposed to convey is considered to be the theme. A message, however, is the result of reflections in which motifs are not under immediate consideration. The theme is a "first intention," whereas the message is a conception obtained through reflection upon a previous conception gained by abstraction from the motifs themselves. A message is thus a "second intention"; and when we confuse a message with a theme we do so at the risk of assuming wrongly that a work is a preconceived embodiment of a "philosophy."

Awareness of Structural Coherence as a Source of Pleasure

We may now proceed to examine the assumption that awareness of the structural coherence of the thematic fabric intensifies our pleasure. Our examination should be based on the following questions: What are some of the significant modes of structural coherence of the thematic fabric? Under what circumstances and by what means does structural coherence enter our awareness? What sort of pleasure results from such an awareness?

The structural coherence of the thematic fabric may be conceived as a linear or sequential coherence of themes. Or it may be conceived as a generative or causal coherence between themes. It may also be conceived as a generic coherence of themes which exhibit a certain affinity and thus a structural relatedness.

One view of the importance of coherence for our appreciation of the aesthetic qualities of structure was expressed by Aristotle,[3] for whom every whole made up of parts must present a certain order in its arrangement of parts if it is to be recognized as beautiful (see p. 23). The incidents must be "so closely connected that the transposal or withdrawal of any of them

---

[3] All quotations are taken from Ingram Bywater's translation. *Aristotle on the Art of Poetry* (Oxford: The Clarendon Press, 1909).

will disjoin and dislocate the whole" (p. 27). Furthermore, a whole must "also be of a certain magnitude. Beauty is a matter of size and order" (p. 23; see also p. 27). A certain coherence, as well as size (which is one condition for our perception of a whole), is thus necessary to perceive "beauty," or, as we should prefer to say, to feel the pleasure of an artistic presentation. What kind of coherence is meant by the statement that incidents need to be so closely connected that either the transposal or the withdrawal of any would disjoin and dislocate, or, as I should prefer to say, disrupt the coherence of the whole? (The implied emphasis is here obviously on coherence and not on wholeness, for there is no whole without coherence.) The notions of transposal and of withdrawal provide the clue. The connection of incidents whose transposal affects the coherence of the whole is, I believe, a connection based on the probable order in which the incidents follow one another, that is, on a sequential order. The connection of incidents whose withdrawal would affect the coherence of the whole must be a connection based upon the necessary order in which incidents are causally related to one another, that is, upon a cause-effect relationship. Aristotle's statement implies the requirement of sequential and of causal coherence for the perception of beauty.

Probability as the Principle of Order in the Linear Coherence of the Story; Necessity as the Principle of Order in the Causal Coherence of the Plot

In discussing the principle underlying the manner in which incidents should be connected and the unity of action maintained, Aristotle speaks of two kinds of connection: probable and necessary. "In writing an *Odyssey*, he [Homer] did not make the poem cover all that ever befell his hero —it befell him, for instance, to get wounded on Parnassus and also to feign madness at the time of the call to arms, but the two incidents had no probable or necessary connection with one another—" (p. 25). Again, in another context, he states: "From what we have said it will be seen that the poet's function is to describe, not the thing that has happened, but a kind of thing that might happen, i.e., what is possible as being probable or necessary" (p. 27). Thus, possibility is based upon either probability or necessity. And finally: "I call a plot episodic when there is neither probability nor necessity in the sequence of its episodes" (p. 29).

Before we examine the generic coherence of the thematic fabric—based on an affinity of themes regardless of their actual disposition in the sequential order, regardless of their causal connection, regardless of whether they

4

occur in episodic units—we shall first continue to examine the thematic fabric based on sequential and causal coherence.

Here the term "story"[4] will be used to indicate the chain of coherent events in their sequential order, and the term "plot" to indicate the chain of coherent incidents in their causal order. Coherence in the story rests on the probable succession of incidents. The story (more readily than the plot) can be divided into segments of sets of incidents which, to a certain degree, have a recognizable, relatively self-contained course and outcome. As we read, our perception of the story as a whole is actually preceded by our perception of its segments; hence the perception of the story as a whole is the cumulative effect of our perception of its segments. When we analyze, we perceive the sequential or causal coherence within a given segment more easily than that within the whole story or within the entire plot. Thus, the segment is a basic unit the size of which affords a ready perception of order.

Probable sequential coherence, arousing our curiosity[5] and creating suspense, satisfies us with each passing incident. Under the spell of a first reading, we are primarily concerned with what happens next. But we do not consciously conceive of probability as the agent of coherence in the sequential order until we have gained a certain perspective. We are satisfied with an impression of coherence without realizing that it is imparted by probable sequence. This impression of sequential coherence remains essentially unaffected even when a "time-shift" disposition of incidents or when multiple focusing disrupts direct linear progression.

Sequential coherence depends upon probability. This statement, however, in no way implies the dependence of sequential coherence upon causal coherence. Probability is not necessarily the result of cause-effect relationships. In a cause-effect relationship we judge the effect from the cause, whereas we accept any incident as sequentially probable if we can conceive of it as possibly relatable—in time and circumstance—to its antecedents, if we can *grasp* it as part of a possible, a conceivable, sequence of incidents that have no generative effect on one another.

Causal coherence arouses our suspense as we seek to assess what is potentially realizable in view of given or implied causes, or it arouses our curiosity about the causes—the driving forces—underlying the inci-

---

[4] I am borrowing E. M. Forster's terms, "story" and "plot," because his use of this terminology in his *Aspects of the Novel* (New York: Harcourt, Brace & Co., 1927) is most applicable to the classification that can be derived from Aristotle. Forster defines the story as "a narrative of events arranged in their time sequence" and the plot also as "a narrative of events" but with "the emphasis falling on causality."

[5] See Forster, *Aspects of the Novel*, p. 215.

dents. Causal coherence satisfies our need for understanding developments brought about by an interaction of forces.

Emotional and Intellectual Involvement in Story and Plot; Distanciation

In order to perceive and to appreciate necessity in the causal coherence of incidents and probability in their sequential coherence, we must to a certain degree reduce our primarily emotional involvement in story and plot and supplement it by a measure of primarily intellectual involvement induced by inquiry. What distinguishes these two kinds of involvement is the perspective we achieve through a measure of "distanciation." By distanciation I mean the process whereby we gain a perspective by displacing the focal point of our vision. Although a certain measure of detachment is the consequence of this process, since emotional involvement is weakened to the extent to which distanciation occurs, nevertheless distanciation should not be equated with detachment. Intellectual involvement, which is the result of inquiry, depends upon a measure of distanciation. Both forms of involvement afford pleasurable experiences, but they are not the same.

In the course of an analysis we at first perceive only certain phases of causal coherence: the necessary cause-effect relationships of individual incidents. Similarly, as we follow the sequential coherence, we do not at one time embrace more than a few successive incidents in their probable linear continuity. As we aim at encompassing a greater number of sequentially coherent incidents or as we seek to perceive their causal coherence in its wider ramifications, we must effect a gradually increasing distanciation. The wider the area within which we perceive sequential or causal coherence, the greater becomes our interest in the meaningful cohesion of sequentially or causally coherent thematic units. We no longer seek to discover what happens next, or what incident was the cause of another; instead, our inquiry turns toward the meaning of sets of sequentially coherent incidents, the meaning of the nature of their causes, and the meaning of their direction.

Increasing distanciation thus brings about first a shift from our involvement in incidents and their causes to our perception of their linear and generative coherences, and then from this perception of coherences to the meanings—themes—emerging from them. At an ideal point of distanciation from which we perceive, in a comprehensive manner, linear and generative coherences, we achieve what we may call a distanciated vision of the thematic coherence in story and plot.

6

Because this vision provides a pleasurable experience of its own, we must, on the one hand, distinguish the pleasures derived from an emotional involvement in incidents from those of the primarily intellectual involvement in their linear or causal coherence, and on the other, distinguish these pleasures from those derived from a consciously sought distanciated vision of the thematic coherence in story and plot. The keener and more encompassing our awareness of the thematic coherence in story and plot, the less do we feel those other pleasures derived from the depth of our emotional involvement and from the intellectual inquiry into the probable or necessary coherence of incidents. From these reflections it follows that coherence induces our emotional involvement through our grasp of probable and our understanding of necessary continuity; but it also follows that if we are to resist the impact of our involvement, we must attain an intentional and increasing distanciation so that we may appreciate the art by which our experience of involvement was effected, gain pleasure from such an appreciation, and gain in the distanciated vision of thematic coherence yet another pleasure from the structure of story or plot.

There is no intention here to maintain or even to imply that sequentially startling and causally seemingly unrelated incidents may not also induce our involvement. In our daily lives, we often encounter experiences in which we are shocked by surprise and to which we remain riveted by shock and surprise. When such incidents are used in a coherent narrative, they may elicit a strong reaction; seen, however, from that point of distanciation from which sequential or causal coherences are perceived, such incidents may serve to break with the convention of a sequential or causal order, but are probably intended primarily to point to a different kind of coherence, independent of sequential or causal coherence, that is, generic thematic coherence, which we shall discuss later. However gripping our involvement in such incidents, we still seek to relate them to a larger context.

While we recognize the enjoyment we derive from the experience of involvement, we also realize with Thomas Mann that a deeper, and we should add, indeed a different kind of enjoyment results from the awareness and appreciation of composition and coherence. Foreshadowing the discussion of Sartre's *La Nausée,* we may state that one reason a narrative is superior to what it depicts is that it affords an opportunity not only for emotional and intellectual involvement, but also, and particularly, for a distanciated vision of various coherences. What we but rarely seek in life and what life so seldom suggests, the art of the narrative invites us to seek, namely, the perspective opened up in the process of distanciation and the awareness of the perceived relationships of probably or necessarily coherent parts within a readily recognizable coherent whole, or of the random grouping of parts in what proves to be generically a coherent whole. The incidents of our lives afford many opportunities for emotional involvement in elemental shreds of chaotically fragmented experiences that we fail to relate to a larger context unless—if ever—we view them in retrospect from the distanciated vision effected by the passage of time. Emotional or intellectual involvement, then, is not an experience which art alone can offer; but the perception of the means that induce it and the awareness of multiple coherent interrelationships are experiences which the art of the narrative does offer in a most comprehensive manner.

Definition of Generic Coherence of Themes; Definition of Component Motifs and Correlative Themes

Turning our attention to motifs that have been termed "leitmotifs," we may first wish to remind ourselves that they are considered to effect an association of ideas from one theme to another. It is necessary, then, to distinguish the linear relatedness of themes in the story and the causal coherence of themes in the plot from the reciprocal relatedness of themes independent of probable sequence and causal coherence. This reciprocal relatedness of themes constitutes their generic coherence and is based on their affinity of similarity or of contrast. We shall call generically coherent themes "correlative themes," and the motifs which carry them "component motifs." The primary function of a leitmotif is to draw our attention to the component nature of the motifs in connection with which it occurs and thereby to alert us to the correlative quality of the themes the component motifs carry.

A necessary and obvious feature of a leitmotif is its recurrence in connection with component motifs. It is by virtue of its recurrence that it alludes to the component nature of motifs and hence to the correlation of their themes. But neither the recurrence of the leitmotif in a text nor its main function of establishing contextual coherence of those parts of the narrative in which it occurs suffices for an adequate definition. These features do not describe the variety of leitmotifs or the different functions they perform. Even before describing their variety and functions, we can state that they are an integral part of the generic coherence of themes. Their very recurrence assures their component quality and consequently the correlation of their themes. Some leitmotifs, as we shall see, are component not only with each other but also with the motifs in connection with which they occur.

The Nature and Variety of Functions of Different Leitmotifs

In order to distinguish various leitmotifs on the basis of their nature and the variety of their functions, it is necessary to introduce some new terms by which different leitmotifs may be more readily identified.

The simplest and most obvious recurring motif, often called a leitmotif, may properly be called a *repetitious label*. It is a gesture, a word, or a phrase used to underscore some particular trait of a character. In *La Symphonie pastorale*,[6] the pastor repeatedly described Gertrude, the blind orphan he takes into his home, in a crouching position indicating her animal posture:

> . . . je pus distinguer, accroupi dans l'âtre, un être incertain, qui paraissait endormi . . . (p. 15).

> . . . j'étais reparti, emmenant blotti contre moi ce paquet de chair sans âme . . . (p. 18).

> . . . mais lorsque j'avançai vers elle une chaise, elle se laissa crouler à terre, comme quelqu'un qui ne saurait pas s'asseoir; alors je la menai jusqu'auprès du foyer, et elle reprit un peu de calme lorsqu'elle put s'accroupir . . . (pp. 20–21).

> . . . En voiture déjà elle s'était laissé glisser au bas du siège et avait fait tout le trajet blottie à mes pieds (p. 21).

> . . . Je veillerai pour entretenir le feu auprès duquel dormira la petite (p. 26).

With a similar end in mind, he describes her eating habits during the initial period of her stay in the parsonage:

> Ma protégée . . . dévora goulûment l'assiette de soupe que je lui tendis (p. 26).

> Cette bouderie ne cédait qu'à l'approche du repas, que je lui servais moi-même, et sur lequel elle se jetait avec une avidité bestiale des plus pénibles à observer (p. 31).

To achieve the same purpose, the pastor describes Gertrude's inexpressiveness in similar terms:

---

[6] All page references are to André Gide, *La Symphonie pastorale* (Paris: Gallimard, 1960 edition).

L'expression indifférente, obtuse de son visage, ou plutôt son inexpressivité absolue ... (p. 31).

... ses traits semblaient durcir; ils ne cessaient d'être inexpressifs ... (p. 31).

Gide's use of these three repetitious labels, describing in various but similar terms the initial impressions made by Gertrude on the pastor, has the obvious function of emphasizing the blind girl's characteristic features at the beginning of the story and of carrying the theme of Gertrude's animality.

But Gide then exploits the cumulative effect of these repetitious labels in order to project vividly—as in relief—the contrasting depiction of the sudden change in Gertrude's character resulting from a changed situation.

> Le 5 mars. J'ai noté cette date comme celle d'une naissance. C'était moins un sourire qu'une transfiguration. Tout à coup ses traits *s'animèrent,* ce fut comme un éclairement subit, pareil à cette lueur purpurine dans les hautes Alpes qui, précédant l'aurore, fait vibrer le sommet neigeux qu'elle désigne et sort de la nuit; on eût dit une coloration mystique; et je songeai également à la piscine de Bethesda au moment que l'ange descend et vient réveiller l'eau dormante. J'eus une sorte de ravissement devant l'expression angélique que Gertrude put prendre soudain ... (p. 41).

Again, in contrast to Gertrude's earlier voracious devouring of food, her later equally voracious craving for knowledge, expressed in similar and therefore already familiar terms, owes its emphasis to this very similarity in phrasing; and it owes its further significance to another effect of the similarity in phrasing, that is, it recalls the totally different "avidité bestiale": "C'est aussi ques ses progrès furent d'une rapidité déconcertante: j'admirais souvent avec quelle promptitude son esprit saisissait l'aliment intellectuel que j'approchais d'elle et tout ce dont il pouvait s'emparer, le faisant sien par un travail d'assimilation et de maturation continuel" (p. 63).

If we consider the functions of these repetitious labels prior to the further purpose which Gide has made them serve, prior to the depiction of characteristics in contrast to previous ones, we realize that the basic function proper to repetitious labels is to emphasize characteristic features. Their use in the depiction of new contrasting situations[7] and for the

---

[7] Walzel deals with the wording of a few lines at the beginning and at the end of Goethe's *Faust*. Gretchen expresses the keenest anguish and pain at the beginning, and with a slight variation in wording she expresses the height of bliss at the end.

simultaneous recall of previous situations brings us to the consideration of a leitmotif whose function differs from and transcends the basic function of the repetitious label. By themselves, these sequentially separated and changed situations may, at first glance, fail to impress the reader as being related by contrast; therefore the function of a recurring wording or phrase—which I call the *linking phrase*—is to bring their relatedness to our attention. But situations connected by a linking phrase need not be related only by contrast; they may be related by similarity. Every time, for instance, the pastor suspects Gertrude of being unhappy because of her inability to see with her own eyes the beauty she imagines, he consoles her in almost identical terms:

Ceux qui peuvent y voir ne les [the birds] entendent pas si bien que toi, ma Gertrude ... (p. 45).

Ceux qui ont des yeux, dis-je enfin, ne connaissent pas leur bonheur (p. 54).

Je te l'ai dit, Gertrude: ceux qui ont des yeux sont ceux qui ne savent pas regarder (p. 88).

But Gide is not content here to use the linking phrase solely to relate similar situations, scattered in the sequence of events; the emphasis derived from repetition also has the purpose of reinforcing the pastor's belief that blindness does indeed protect Gertrude's happiness. Later in the story the ironical rejection of this notion—that the imagination of the blind is an adequate or even a superior substitute for the experience of beauty that sight alone can provide—receives its full weight in great part from the previous emphasis achieved by the repeated use of the linking phrase. The pastor, still believing that blindness assures happiness, questions the desirability of the operation that may restore Gertrude's sight: "Au surplus, n'est-elle pas heureuse ainsi?" When, after her successful operation, Gertrude does perceive the beauty of the world, the falsity of the pastor's previous beliefs need not even be mentioned. Gertrude's enthusiasm about the beauty she is able to behold is in itself a sufficient expression of her disagreement and disapproval: "Quand vous m'avez donné la vue, mes yeux se sont ouverts sur un monde plus beau que je n'avais rêvé qu'il pût être; oui vraiment, je n'imaginais pas" (pp. 135–36).

Linking phrases relate similar or contrasting sequentiatially scattered situations whose connection becomes more readily apparent because of the similarity of the phrasing. The repetitious label refers to characteristic traits; its function is primarily epithetic and its purpose is emphasis. The

11

linking phrase has a certain associative quality because of the context in which it is first used. It carries the association to each situation in connection with which it reappears. But this association would appear, so to speak, suspended if the situations themselves were not relatable by the similarity or the contrast of their respective themes. The primary function of the repetitious label, then, is to emphasize the theme it itself carries—a theme descriptive of character, whereas the primary function of a recurring linking phrase is to allude by its recurrence to the similarity or the contrast of themes in connection with which it appears in sequentially separated situations. The repetitious label as such is thus not a thematic link, whereas the linking phrase is. The preceding example has shown, however, that a repetitious label may function as a linking phrase and consequently as a thematic link.

The linking phrase should be distinguished from another thematic link which we may call the *linking image*. Like the linking phrase, the linking image also relates themes in situations scattered in the text, but the manner in which the linking occurs is different. The very first entry in the pastor's diary begins: "La neige qui n'a pas cessé de tomber depuis trois jours, bloque les routes" (p. 11). Although the first entry is a record of events written when the pastor was forcibly confined to his home and out of touch with the world, the events themselves actually took place two and one-half years earlier, in the month of August, and refer to his discovery of Gertrude, whose blindness had kept her soul walled in almost without any communication with the outside world. The next entry, seventeen days later, begins thus:

> La neige est tombée encore abondamment cette nuit. Les enfants sont ravis parce que bientôt, disent-ils, on sera forcé de sortir par les fenêtres. Le fait est que ce matin la porte est bloquée et que l'on ne peut sortir que par la buanderie. Hier, je m'étais assuré que le village avait des provisions en suffisance, car nous allons sans doute demeurer quelque temps isolés du reste de l'humanité. Ce n'est pas le premier hiver que la neige nous bloque, mais je ne me souviens pas d'avoir jamais vu son empêchement si épais (pp. 28–29).

The pastor then reports his complete failure to reach Gertrude's mind because of what he calls, in a different context, her "engourdissement profond." Some time thereafter, the pastor expresses his delight at Gertrude's surprisingly rapid progress:

> Certainement un travail se faisait en son esprit durant le temps que je l'abandonnais à elle-même; car chaque fois que je la retrouvais, c'était avec

une nouvelle surprise et je me sentais séparé d'elle par une moindre épaisseur de nuit. C'est tout de même ainsi, me disais-je, que la tiédeur de l'air
et l'insistance du printemps triomphent peu à peu de l'hiver. Que de fois
n'ai-je pas admiré la manière dont fond la neige: on dirait que le manteau
s'use par en dessous, et son aspect reste le même. A chaque hiver Amélie
y est prise et me déclare: la neige n'a toujours pas changé; on la croit épaisse
encore, quand déjà la voici qui cède et tout à coup, de place en place, laisse
reparaître la vie (pp. 42–43).

Finally, the first entry in the second notebook is introduced by yet another
reference to the snow which, we are given to understand, kept the village snowbound while the first notebook was being written: "La neige
avait enfin fondu, et sitôt que les routes furent redevenues praticables, il
m'a fallu m'acquitter d'un grand nombre d'obligations que j'avais été forcé
de remettre pendant le long temps que notre village était resté bloqué" (p.
95). Thereupon the pastor reveals the new insight he has gained and finally
recognizes the evidence of his previously unavowed love for Gertrude.
Also, in this second notebook, the incidents of the story pertain to Gertrude's successful operation, her vision, and her new awareness.

In the first two instances, in which the snow is described as blocking
the roads, the reasons for mentioning it have on the surface no direct
connection with the events recorded. In the third instance, the imper-
ceptibly melting snow is described as an image reflecting the process by
which Gertrude's torpor yields to the concealed activity of her mind. It
is at this point that the heavy snow mentioned previously clearly appears
as an allusion to Gertrude's blocked mind. In the fourth and last instance,
the pastor reports that the snows have finally melted, and there follows
the description of the reasons that have for so long kept hidden from
him the evidence of his love, at last unveiled for him.

It was the actual comparison between the concealed activity of Gertrude's mind and the almost imperceptible melting away of the layers of
snow hidden below the surface that drew our attention to the function
of the motif of the blocking snow, in the first instances of its occurrence,
as a linking image of subsequent themes, and then again to the function
of the motif of the already melted snow as a linking image of themes
in the second notebook. Without that allusion these leitmotifs might have
appeared as motifs recurring in self-contained and relatively insignificant
variations, the only function of which was to place the pastor's recollec-
tions in a setting conducive to the task he has set for himself, that of
recording the events preceding the diary he is about to begin. The allusion to the significance of these motifs, effected by a comparison, revealed

to us that the themes of these motifs were, in a way, calls in expectation of a response: that the responses were to be sought, in the first two instances, in motifs carrying the theme of Gertrude's mind blocked by physical blindness as well as in motifs carrying the theme of the pastor's growing intellectual blindness, and in the last instance, that the responses were to be sought in motifs carrying the themes of the new awareness which the pastor and Gertrude ultimately reach.

The blocking snow is a linking image relating the themes of Gertrude's physical and intellectual blindness and of the pastor's blindness to his own feelings as well as to the feelings of others. The melting snow is a linking image relating the themes of Gertrude's and the pastor's awakening to a new awareness.

There is another significant example of a linking image in *La Symphonie pastorale* which pertains to the motivation and purpose governing the pastor's consciously pursued endeavor. It is the image of the lost sheep. In an effort to explain and justify his actions, the pastor declares to his family: "Je ramène la brebis perdue." After Amélie has repeatedly reproached him for spending an inordinate amount of time in his preoccupation with Gertrude and has shown herself incapable of understanding the charity which motivated his pious endeavor, the pastor enters the following reflection in his diary:

> J'ai souvent éprouvé que la parabole de la brebis égarée reste une des plus difficiles à admettre pour certaines âmes, qui pourtant se croient profondément chrétiennes. Que chaque brebis du troupeau, prise à part, puisse aux yeux du berger être plus précieuse à son tour que tout le reste du troupeau pris en bloc, voici ce qu'elles ne peuvent s'élever à comprendre. Et ces mots: "Si un homme a cent brebis et que l'une d'elles s'égare, ne laisse-t-il pas les quatre-vingt-dix-neuf autres sur les montagnes, pour aller chercher celle qui s'est égarée?"—ces mots tout rayonnants de charité, si elles osaient parler franc, elles les déclareraient de la plus révoltante injustice.
>
> Les premiers sourires de Gertrude me consolaient de tout et payaient mes soins au centuple. Car "cette brebis, si le pasteur la trouve, je vous le dis en vérité, elle lui cause plus de joie que les quatre-vingt-dix-neuf autres qui ne se sont jamais égarées". Oui, je le dis en vérité, jamais sourire d'aucun de mes enfants ne m'a inondé le cœur d'une aussi séraphique joie que fit celui que je vis poindre sur ce visage de statue … (pp. 40–41).

The same linking image recurs after the description of Gertrude's and the pastor's excursion to Neuchâtel, where they attend a concert and hear Beethoven's *Pastoral Symphony*. Upon their return, Amélie again reproaches her husband for spending more time with Gertrude than he has ever done with his own children, and the pastor—still convinced that he is motivated by charity alone—reflects: "C'était donc toujours le même grief, et le même refus de comprendre que l'on fête l'enfant qui revient, mais non point ceux qui sont demeurés, comme le montre la parabole ..." (p. 59).

It is worth noting that this linking image is used to point out only the conscious motivation that guides the pastor and that it is intended to reinforce his belief that charity is his only concern. Consequently, this linking image at the same time serves the purpose of allowing the pastor's subconscious motivation—his love and his delight in Gertrude's happiness, which he considers his own creation—to remain repressed, or hopefully concealed, once he is confronted with the evidence of self-recognition.

In a more indirect fashion the image also presents for the pastor an explanation of Amélie's continued reluctance to follow him on his path of charity, and it contributes to the blindness that prevents him from realizing that his wife is aware of the shift in his motivation from charity to love.

Although both the linking phrase and the linking image relate thematic materials, they differ in one significant respect: the linking image reflects in a perceptual manner, as an image, the themes it relates. Furthermore, it does not recur every time in connection with every situation the themes of which it reflects, but is placed focally so that its diverging rays reach situations in the text and so that themes carried by these situations converge upon it. As thematic links, both these leitmotifs are structural devices. They themselves, however, are also theme carriers, and as such they contribute also to the total thematic fabric; nevertheless, these leitmotifs have primarily the special function of pointing out and of relating textually separated parts of the thematic structure.

If leitmotifs are not used, it is conceivable for motifs to appear to be thematically unrelated even if they are in textual proximity. In the case of materially similar motifs, their connection is more readily recognized, but the thematic relatedness of materially different motifs may remain unnoticed. Whether motifs are materially similar or different, their textual concreteness forces them into a sequential order and we perceive each separately from any other, even if we are aware of their relatedness. Motifs, as such, cannot be perceived simultaneously, whereas two relatively distinct melodies can be perceived simultaneously in a contrapuntal arrangement. The closest approximation to counterpoint can be achieved only on the level of themes. The theme lingers on in our awareness beyond the range of the motif which carries it, and may combine or blend with another theme with which it is related by similarity or by contrast. The linking phrase and the linking image have in common the function of affecting our simultaneous perception of related themes. Hence our recognition of these leitmotifs contributes to the pleasure we derive from our awareness of the structural coherence to which they draw our attention.

The recurring linking phrase consists of materially similar motifs which, at each recurrence, carry the same theme. In relation to one another, then, they are component motifs and their themes are correlative. The linking image also consists of materially similar motifs, but here, in spite of the similarity, there is far greater variability than in the linking phrase, which remains almost unchanged every time it recurs. Here too, however, it is by virtue of its similarity at each recurrence that this leitmotif forges the link between themes.

Materially Similar Parallel Component Motifs

There are materially similar component motifs which are not leitmotifs, whose function is not to allude to the component quality of other motifs, and which therefore are not thematic links. These motifs appear at the least in pairs, the sequentially later revealing the allusive quality of the one preceding. Their parallelism clearly points to the correlative nature of their themes. Striking examples of materially similar parallel component motifs can be found in La Symphonie pastorale, and we shall draw seven examples from a single passage.

A prominent place in the pastor's diary is given to a report of Doctor Martins' encouragement and advice. To make the pastor persevere in his undertaking, Martins relates the case of Laura Bridgeman, a deaf-mute blind girl, whose mind did finally respond to the patient care of her doctor.

> 1. Et durant des semaines, il n'obtint aucun résultat. Le corps semblait inhabité. Pourtant il ne perdait pas confiance (pp. 34–35).

Three themes are contained in this statement: Complete failure in the early stages of the doctor's undertaking, the apparent lack of any response of the mind, and the doctor's confident perseverance. The first and second themes recall sequentially preceding correlative themes in statements describing the pastor's own experiences, similar except in that they occur in conjunction with the contrasting theme of frustration and discouragement:

16

> . . . j'étais reparti, emmenant blotti contre moi ce paquet de chair sans âme . . . (p. 18).

> Oui, vraiment, j'avoue que les dix premiers jours j'en étais venu à désespérer, et même à me désintéresser d'elle au point que je regrettais mon élan premier et que j'eusse voulu ne l'avoir jamais emmenée (p. 32).

A similar correlative theme of confident undeterred perseverance is carried by a motif which follows sequentially:

> Il y fallut, dans les premières semaines, plus de patience que l'on ne saurait croire, non seulement en raison du temps que cette première éducation exigeait, mais aussi des reproches qu'elle me fit encourir. . . . Ce que je lui [Amélie] reprochais plutôt c'était de n'avoir pas confiance que mes soins pussent remporter quelques succès. Oui, c'est ce manque de foi qui me peinait; sans me décourager du reste (pp. 38–39).

> 2. Je me faisais l'effet de quelqu'un, racontait-il, qui, penché sur la margelle d'un puits profond et noir, agiterait désespérément une corde dans l'espoir qu'enfin une main la saisisse. Car il ne douta pas un instant que quelqu'un ne fût là, au fond du gouffre, et que cette corde à la fin ne soit saisie (p. 35).

The theme of faith in the existence of intellect and soul, and therefore in the potential communication between minds, expressed in this passage, is sequentially preceded by a similar theme carried by the following parallel motif expressed in the course of the pastor's reflections:

> Tout le long de la route, je pensais: dort-elle? et de quel sommeil noir . . . Et en quoi la veille diffère-t-elle ici du sommeil? Hôtesse de ce corps opaque, une âme attend sans doute, emmurée, que vienne la toucher enfin quelque rayon de votre grâce, Seigneur! (p. 18).

> 3. Et un jour, enfin, il vit cet impassible visage de Laura s'éclairer d'une sorte de sourire; je crois bien qu'à ce moment des larmes de reconnaissance et d'amour jaillirent de ses yeux et qu'il tomba à genoux pour remercier le Seigneur. Laura venait tout à coup de comprendre ce que le docteur voulait d'elle; sauvée! (p. 35).

Here the theme of pious gratitude for a successfully accomplished task alludes to the same feeling expressed by parallel motifs after the pastor's first positive result:

> Les premiers sourires de Gertrude me consolaient de tout et payaient mes soins au centuple. . . . Oui, je le dis en vérité, jamais sourire d'aucun de mes enfants ne m'a inondé le cœur d'une aussi séraphique joie que fit celui que je vis poindre sur ce visage de statue certain matin où brus-

quement elle sembla commencer à comprendre et à s'intéresser à ce que je m'efforçais de lui enseigner depuis tant de jours.

Le 5 mars. J'ai noté cette date comme celle d'une naissance. C'était moins un sourire qu'une transfiguration. Tout à coup ses traits *s'animèrent,* ce fut comme un éclairement subit ... J'eus une sorte de ravissement devant l'expression angélique que Gertrude put prendre soudain, car il m'apparut que ce qui la visitait en cet instant, n'était point tant l'intelligence que l'amour. Alors un tel élan de reconnaissance me souleva, qu'il me sembla que j'offrais à Dieu le baiser que je déposai sur ce beau front (pp. 40–42).

4. A mere juxtaposition of the two following statements, the first in reference to Laura Bridgeman, the second to Gertrude, reveals their parallelism:

A partir de ce jour elle fit attention; ses progrès furent rapides; elle s'instruisit bientôt elle-même ... (p. 35).

Autant ce premier résultat avait été difficile à obtenir, autant les progrès sitôt après furent rapides. ... il me semblait parfois que Gertrude avançât par bonds comme pour se moquer des méthodes (p. 42).

5. ... chacune de ces emmurées était heureuse, et sitôt qu'il leur fut donné de s'exprimer, ce fut pout raconter leur *bonheur* (p. 36).

Although the pastor becomes increasingly sensitive to what he suspects to be Gertrude's sadness at not being able to see the beauty of the world he describes, we nevertheless realize that her reactions are those of joy and happiness:

Je me souviens de son inépuisable ravissement lorsque je lui appris que ces petites voix [of the birds] émanaient de créatures vivantes, dont il semble que l'unique fonction soit de sentir et d'exprimer l'éparse joie de la nature (p. 45).

... je connais le bonheur d'entendre (p. 54).

Pasteur, est-ce que vous sentez combien je suis heureuse? (p. 54).

6. The following is the significant passage in which the doctor defends the happiness based on ignorance of evil:

... l'âme de l'homme imagine plus facilement et plus volontiers la beauté, l'aisance et l'harmonie que le désordre et le péché qui partout ternissent, avilissent, tachent et déchirent ce monde et sur quoi nous renseignent et tout à la fois nous aident à contribuer nos cinq sens. De sorte que, plus volontiers, je ferais suivre le *Fortunatos nimium* de Virgile, de *si sua mala nescient,* que du *si sua bona norint* qu'on nous enseigne: Combien heureux les hommes, s'ils pouvaient ignorer le mal! (pp. 36–37).

Contrary to his original intention not to shield Gertrude from the knowledge of evil, the pastor does in fact try to protect her illusion of a world in which happiness and joy remain free of evil and sin:

> Et cette parole du Christ s'est dressée lumineusement devant moi: "Si vous étiez aveugles, vous n'auriez point de péché." Le péché, c'est ce qui obscurcit l'âme, c'est ce qui s'oppose à sa joie. Le parfait bonheur de Gertrude, qui rayonne de tout son être, vient de ce qu'elle ne connaît point le péché. Il n'y a en elle que de la clarté, de l'amour. . . . Je me refuse à lui donner les épîtres de Paul, car si, aveugle, elle ne connaît point le péché, que sert de l'inquiéter en la laissant lire: "Le péché a pris de nouvelles forces par le commandement" . . . (p. 103).

7. Finally, the parallelism between the attitude expressed in *The Cricket on the Hearth* in Dickens' Christmas books and the pastor's reflections after hearing Beethoven's *Pastoral Symphony:*

> Puis il me parla d'un conte de Dickens, qu'il croit avoir été directement inspiré par l'exemple de Laura Bridgeman et qu'il promit de m'envoyer aussitôt. Et quatre jours après je reçus en effet *Le Grillon du Foyer,* que je lus avec un vif plaisir. C'est l'histoire un peu longue, mais pathétique par instants, d'une jeune aveugle que son père, pauvre fabricant de jouets, entretient dans l'illusion du confort, de la richesse et du bonheur; mensonge que l'art de Dickens s'évertue à faire passer pour pieux, mais dont, Dieu merci! je n'aurai pas à user avec Gertrude (p. 37).

It is true that the occasion and the circumstances in which the pastor's views are expressed do differ from those in Dickens, but the attitudes are essentially the same: ". . . je réfléchissais que ces harmonies ineffables peignaient, non point le monde tel qu'il était, mais bien tel qu'il aurait pu être, qu'il pourrait être sans le mal et sans le péché. Et jamais encore je n'avais osé parler à Gertrude du mal, du péché, de la mort" (pp. 53–54). Actually, this motif carries in relation to its component motif two correlative themes: one similar, the other in contrast to the pastor's declared intention of not wishing to deceive Gertrude by pious delusions.

Materially Different Parallel Component Motifs

This example, in which the parallelism of motifs rests on a somewhat unsubstantial similarity of materials, leads us to the consideration of component motifs which are materially different and which turn out to be component only after their themes have proved to be correlative. Indeed, if we do not seek to establish their coherence on the level of themes, they may appear only loosely connected in the sequential order of the story, and their function may, at times, seem limited to purely descriptive ends. It should suffice to note one particular example of these materially different parallel component motifs whose themes are correlative. Thematically the description of the pastor's trip to the cottage of the dying woman is significant in several respects, but the description of the cottage in which he is about to discover the blind girl provides an especially striking example of a motif which is materially different but thematically correlative by similarity to a subsequent motif: ". . . ma jeune guide m'indiqua du doigt, à flanc de coteau, une chaumière qu'on eût pu croire inhabitée, sans un mince filet de fumée qui s'en échappait, bleuissant dans l'ombre, puis blondissant dans l'or du ciel" (p. 13). Then, later, in the description of Gertrude, we find a passage (already quoted in another connection) carrying a similar theme: ". . . ce paquet de chair sans âme et dont je ne percevais la vie que par la communication d'une ténébreuse chaleur" (p. 18). Just as the cottage, mysteriously shrouded in dusk and silence, would seem uninhabited and abandoned were it not for the smoke significantly rising to the sky in hues that change from dark to light, so too would Gertrude's body seem uninhabited were it not for its warmth engendered by life and for a soul waiting to rise from the shadows of blindness to the light of perception.

So far our attention has been directed to leitmotifs as well as to parallel component motifs, and we have seen that leitmotifs are primarily devices by which allusion is made to the component quality of textually more or less scattered motifs. Leitmotifs are consequently pointers that draw our attention to certain aspects of generic coherence of the thematic fabric. The extent to which themes revealed to be correlative by the use of leitmotifs also have affinities with themes of such other motifs to which leitmotifs make no allusion may vary. The pervasiveness of their effect upon the thematic fabric as a whole is therefore an indication of their relative significance and therefore also of the structural importance of the leitmotifs used to manifest their correlation. Similarly the significance of parallel component motifs depends upon the relatedness of their themes to other themes in the thematic fabric. This relatedness is frequently less obvious than the correlation of the themes which parallel component motifs carry. The themes of the materially different component motifs last mentioned do, for instance, relate to a pervasive aspect of the whole thematic fabric: the aspiration of Gertrude's soul toward moral and spiritual goals. By virtue of this relatedness, these particular parallel component motifs also serve incidentally as linking images that reflect significant elements of the thematic fabric.

2

Motifs and Themes within the Structure of Story and Plot

Incidents as Motifs in Story and Plot

We have already stated that the probable sequence of incidents by itself imparts sequential coherence to the story. In seeking the thematic coherence of the story we establish a linear progression of incidents regardless of whether the structure of the story is linear or not. Before we can turn our attention to the relatedness of themes based on the sequential coherence of incidents in the story and to the relatedness of themes based on the causal coherence of incidents in the plot, we must make a distinction between incidents in story and plot. In the story incidents are actions as well as conditions and situations in which actions take place or which result from actions. In the plot incidents are only actions, that is, statements, deeds, or gestures to which characters are prompted by more or less conscious motivations directed at more or less clearly perceived purposes. In the story we are concerned with the course and outcome of the actions; in the plot, on the other hand, actions are seen from the point of view of the underlying motivations and purposes from which they derive their direction. Incidents in story and plot constitute the motifs of each.

Theme and Motif in Iconography and Iconology

It is useful for us to turn to the terms "theme" and "motif" in the visual arts, which in spite of important differences can shed some light on our use of these terms in story and plot. In the chapter entitled "Iconography and Iconology: An Introduction to the Study of Renaissance Art" in Erwin Panofsky's *Meaning in the Visual Arts*,[1] the author distinguishes three kinds of meaning.

The first he calls the "primary or natural meaning." The second is the "secondary or conventional," and the third is the "intrinsic meaning or

---

[1] New York: Doubleday Anchor Books, 1955.

content." Primary meanings actually consist of two different meanings: the *factual meaning* in which we identify forms with objects and actions or events that we know from experience, and the *expressional meaning* which we apprehend, again from our own experience, as the particular mood with which the object or event is endowed. The forms which are carriers of primary, that is, factual and expressional meanings, are called artistic motifs.

The second kind of meaning, called the "secondary or conventional," furnishes an answer to different kinds of questions. The primary meanings provided answers to questions we may try to formulate in the following manner: With what objects in our practical experience can we identify the form we are perceiving, and what expressional quality, what psychological nuance, does the pose or gesture convey to the sensitivity we have derived from our own practical experience? To reach the next level of meaning we would have to ask: What does the particular presented object or event represent? What cultural pattern or custom does the event have as its origin? Is the object a representation identifiable with individuals or objects, historical or legendary, belonging to a particular tradition? Obviously, such questions are not dictated by practical experience, but by our understanding of the significance of phenomena as representations of a culture of which we have knowledgeable awareness.

In seeking answers to these questions "we connect artistic motifs and combinations of artistic motifs (compositions) with themes or concepts. Motifs thus recognized as carriers of a secondary or conventional meaning may be called *invenzioni;* we are wont to call them stories and allegories. The identification of such images, stories and allegories is the domain of what is normally referred to as 'iconography'."[2] In the domain of iconography, artistic motifs carry on one level factual and expressional meanings, on another level—as images, stories, and allegories—they carry themes or concepts. A motif carries a theme when as an image it conveys the idea of "concrete and individual persons or objects." The motif as a story carries the concept of events in which persons participate. A motif as an image also carries a theme when it is a personification or a symbol conveying "abstract and general notions such as Faith, Luxury, Wisdom, etc." The motif as an allegory also carries a concept, that is, a combination of personifications and symbols. In summing up we may state that themes are either ideas of concrete and individual persons or objects, or abstract and general notions conveyed by personifications or symbols. Themes are distinguished

---

[2] *Ibid.*, p. 29.

from concepts, which are either events in which persons participate or combinations of personifications and symbols.

Finally, the third kind of meaning is the "intrinsic meaning or content." We are offered the following general definition: "It may be defined as a unifying principle which underlies and explains both the visible event and its intelligible significance, and which determines even the form in which the visible event takes shape."[3] This means that the intrinsic meaning underlies, determines, and explains the artistic motif. Furthermore, the particular configuration of the motif, the mood it conveys, the object and the cultural significance of the event it represents are understood as symptomatic manifestations of a culture. While no single motif manifests comprehensively the culture and the philosophy that determine it, these are implicitly inherent in every motif they determine. The intrinsic meaning "is apprehended by ascertaining those underlying principles which reveal the basic attitude of a nation, a period, a class, a religious or philosophical persuasion—qualified by one personality and condensed into one work."[4] In relation to these extrinsic determining forces, which endow the motif in its various functions with an intrinsic meaning, the motif is interpreted as a "symbolical" value of what it implicitly manifests, as a "particularized evidence" of such forces. Consequently, the intrinsic meaning is intelligible and explicable in terms of extrinsic forces. "The discovery and interpretation of 'symbolical' values (which are often unknown to the artist himself and may even emphatically differ from what he consciously intended to express) is the object of what we may call 'iconology' as opposed to 'iconography'."[5]

Neither the concept of this study nor the use of terminology, in spite of identical terms, leads us to recognize a close analogy with all procedures and objectives of iconography or iconology; nevertheless, differences need to be established and similarities discovered. In summing up the foregoing presentation, we find that the first level of iconographical, or rather pre-iconographical, interpretation is concerned with the identification of artistic motifs with objects, events, and moods in our natural practical experience; on the second level of iconographical interpretation one is concerned with the identification of motifs as carriers of themes and concepts relating to a particular cultural tradition; and on the third level, in the course of an iconological interpretation, one seeks to establish the intrinsic meaning of motifs as "symbolical" values of extrinsic determining forces. Let us now

---

[3] *Ibid.*, p. 28. [4] *Ibid.*, p. 30. [5] *Ibid.*, p. 31.

consider a possible application of these insights to the investigation of the meaning of theme and motif in story and plot.

The linear progression of a story (the unfolding of individual incidents) —when perceived apart from the plot—makes us aware of the particular existence of incidents in the story, of the details constituting their identity: (*a*) the nature, course, and outcome of actions; (*b*) the nature of relations between characters; (*c*) the nature of (and the changes in) moral, intellectual, and physical conditions; and (*d*) the nature and transitions from one stage to another of moods or states of mind which invest the actions of characters and affect conditions and situations. By thus identifying the incidents of the story individually in sequentially coherent segments, we become aware of their factual meaning as well as of their expressional meaning in a way similar to that by which one becomes aware of artistic motifs by identifying them in a pre-iconographical study. In the story these identifications yield the themes carried by the motifs of the story.

On the second level of iconographical interpretation the theme of the artistic motif as an image is derived from our recognition of the motif as a representation of concrete and individual persons or objects belonging to a particular cultural tradition. A combination of such motifs is the motif as a story, which carries concepts of the events in which the persons participate.

What insights would one gain if one limited himself to this kind of interpretation? First we would identify the factual meanings of persons, objects, and incidents and recognize them on the basis of our personal practical experience or as representations of persons, objects, and incidents belonging to a particular culture. Assuming that we assign the term "theme" to both theme and concept, we could say that the identification of single motifs and compositions (that is, persons, objects, and incidents in the story) as representations of extrinsic materials amounts to the determination of their themes. This means that if we recognize in the motifs representations of extrinsic materials known from a personal practical experience or as belonging to a certain culture, we thereby establish the themes these motifs carry. But in this sense the motifs carry only the meaning of being subject matter; their theme is then the theme as a topic: The motifs (as images) may represent the worker, the lawyer, the businessman, or similarly, may be personifications of jealousy, patriotism, avarice. The motifs (as stories) may portray conspiracy, a homeward journey, or social strife. Or the motifs (as images and stories) may represent persons, objects, and incidents known from history or legend: Oedipus, Don Juan, or Faust.

It is one thing to seek the expressional meaning that invests the actions

24

of characters and affects conditions and situations, but it is a very different undertaking to seek one dominant trait with which a character is especially endowed. In the latter case we seek in statements and actions characteristics that permit us to identify a character primarily as a type. In the former, we search for psychological nuances in the course of their changing manifestations in order to capture their signification, that is, what they reveal about characters and about the characters' material and intellectual conditions in the linear progression of the story. Here a particular incident is a motif that carries a theme of an attitude or a mood in its development and in its relations to other similar or contrasting expressional meanings within one work. *This is the thematic significance which we derive once we have established the details constituting the identity of the incidents of the story.* In order to perceive this thematic significance of motifs, it is necessary to see them not only individually and segmentally but also from the point of view of their total sequential structure. This means that a certain distanciation must be effected. The objective of this distanciation is a vision of unfolding traits of characters and conditions derived from sequential coherence. It is worth noting that Wolfgang Kayser[6] states that the theme of Goethe's *Werther* is the sensitive young man and the theme of the *Iliad* the wrath of Achilles; we must realize, however, that these are by no means the only themes of these works and that we could under no circumstances place such themes in the same category with some others Kayser mentions in the same breath—for example, the theme of Odysseus' journey home as the theme of the *Odyssey*.

On the next level, we find intrinsic meanings with which iconology is concerned and in which one seeks "the basic attitude of a nation, a period, a class, a religious or philosophical persuasion—qualified by one personality and condensed into one work." In the course of this interpretation "we deal with the work of art as a symptom of something else." Actually the work of art, as a "particularized evidence" of extrinsic forces, may in the course of this kind of interpretation become a document used for the primary purpose of detecting the forces determining its nature, an interpretation advocated by Sainte-Beuve and Taine. The themes which a work yields on the basis of this interpretation may also be understood as Ernst Robert Curtius has conceived of them: "Thema ist alles, was das originäre Verhalten der Person zur Welt betrifft. Die Thematik eines Dichters ist das Register seiner typischen Reaktionen auf bestimmte Lagen in die ihn

---

6 Wolfgang Kayser. *Das Sprachliche Kunstwerk* (Bern and Munich: Francke Verlag, 1959), p. 79.

das Leben bringt. Das Thema gehört der Subjektseite an. Es ist eine psychologische Konstante. Es ist dem Dichter mitgegeben."[7]

There is, however, one particular distinction we should make while considering the thematic significance of the intrinsic meaning of a work which is symptomatic of extrinsic determining forces: if we find that certain ideas are directly expressed, or certain issues are represented through actions, and we know that the same ideas are held and the same issues are debated in the culture which the work reflects, we can say that while the ideas and issues are inherent in the incidents within the work, they are at the same time symptomatic of ideas and issues which are the concern of the culture. Thus to the extent to which the "intrinsic meaning" is inherent in the incidents, that is, in the motifs, it is a theme, an inherent theme. To the extent to which the intrinsic meaning is symptomatic of phenomena outside the work, it may be considered as a theme only in the sense in which a topic is a theme.

A grasp and understanding of forces operative in a culture may help us recognize the inherent thematic significance of incidents and, in certain instances, may prevent misinterpretations. In thematic interpretation, however, we do not consider extrinsic forces as points of reference, nor do we consider motifs as mere documentary particularized evidence of extrinsic forces; the motifs themselves are the points of departure, and the recognition of forces operative outside the work is useful only as a possible control device. In thematic interpretation the motif is not a symptom of something else; it is the concrete manifestation of general characteristics of human experience within the world of the work itself. The recognition of the relationship between the motifs in the work and the extrinsic phenomena is not the end of thematic interpretation—as in iconology—but only a useful or occasionally a necessary antecedent for the interpretation of certain works.

Distinction between Themes of the Story and Themes of the Plot

An analysis, analogous to pre-iconographical interpretation, seeks to establish in the sequential order of the story the identity of motifs and those of their traits in which we perceive concrete and particular manifestations of universal qualities which are the themes the motifs carry.

In observing the transitions from one incident of the story to another and from one state of mind or mood to another, we do not limit our interest to

---

[7] Ernst Robert Curtius, *Kritische Essays zur europäischen Literatur* (2d rev. ed.; Bern: Francke Verlag, 1954); see pp. 165–66 for his distinctions between theme and motif, which, he feels, are not interchangeable terms.

their identity and sequential coherence, or to that distanciated vision from which universal meanings of sequentially coherent particulars are revealed; we also wish to understand the forces—within the work—that have set the sequence of incidents in motion and which may largely account for the course, the transitions, and the outcome of the actions of the plot. These forces are motivations and purposes which also underlie and explain the actions. This is a parallel procedure to that employed in iconological interpretation except that iconology is concerned with extrinsic forces underlying and explaining motifs.

From the point of view of thematic interpretation, motivations and purposes (1) bring about the coherence of actions in the structure of the plot, (2) explain the origin and direction of actions, and (3) invest the actions with the meaning they have—not as mere symptoms of these forces, but as effects thereof. Actions conceived in terms of motivations which engender them and in terms of purposes they fulfill are the motifs of the plot, and motivations and purposes are the themes they carry. We may conclude that actions are carriers of two kinds of themes: in the story their meanings lie in their nature, course, and outcome as well as in the moods and states of mind which invest them; in the plot they are motifs carrying the themes of motivations and purposes.

Distinction between Motivation and Purpose

Motivation needs to be distinguished from purpose. A conscious motivation provides an impetus as well as a sustaining force for an action, but the action may serve only a vaguely perceived purpose and therefore fail to reveal consistent direction. A subconscious instinctive drive may similarly induce and sustain an action the real purpose of which may not be perceptible; in fact, it may be effectively repressed and another apparent purpose substituted. A clearly perceived purpose may kindle a latent motivation, and such a motivation with a clearly perceived aim may give impetus, sustenance, and direction to a chain of consistent actions like those that characterize the initial segments of the plot in *La Symphonie pastorale*. On the other hand, a purpose may be completely lacking, the actions may not be directed and concerted with any ultimate aim in the character's mind: a brief satisfaction of emerging desires brought to a subliminal or to a conscious level of awareness by motivating instincts or habits may be the only discernible purpose of some actions, as for instance in the first half of *L'Etranger*. Purposes and motivations, when simultaneously operative, are mutually stimulating and determine the emergence and direction of actions.

It is clear that the particular manifestation of an action does not depend solely upon motivations and purposes, and it is also clear that if one were to explain the various reasons for a particular manifestation a broader interpretation, akin to that of iconology, would be necessary; within the framework of differing cultural patterns the same motivation or purpose may be objectified by different kinds of action. As in the case of motifs in the story, however, we are concerned only with inherent themes and not with the reasons for a particular manifestation of an action.

The Contingent Incident

Besides intrinsic and extrinsic forces, there is yet another force operative within a work, and its effect on an action must be taken into consideration: it is the contingent incident. Whereas motivation and purpose are determinants of an action, a contingent incident is not; it is a catalyst setting into motion actions to which a character is predisposed by inclination or conviction. At times a contingent incident may give direction to or reorient actions already in motion. The pastor's decision to take the orphaned Gertrude to his home is due not only to what he believes is divine inspiration, it is also brought about by the death of the old woman in whose cottage he finds Gertrude. This contingent incident provides at least the occasion for an action for which there exists a latent motivation. Gertrude's sudden attempt at suicide offers a more striking example. Her attempted suicide is only vaguely motivated by her despair of ever becoming Jacques' wife; it is actually prompted by the shock of perceiving in the face of the pastor's wife the torture of barely endured jealousy and by the guilt the girl herself suddenly feels at having been the cause of Amélie's suffering. This recognition and her subsequent decision are contingent on her perceiving Amélie's anguished smile upon her return.

Difference between the Distanciated Vision of Motifs and of Themes

The thematic fabric of the plot as a whole is carried by the actions and interactions of all characters involved in the chain of events and linked in an order of causal or generative coherence. We have noted that a degree of distanciation is needed to perceive causal coherence and that the predominantly intellectual involvement induced by inquiry diminishes the emotional involvement induced by our curiosity in the progression of individual incidents. In following the story we look so to speak forward; in trying to understand the coherence of the plot, we look back. We also have to bear in mind that there is a difference between the focal point of distanciation from which the coherence of motifs is perceived and that from which our perception is directed at the relatedness of themes in the thematic fabric. The sequential coherence of motifs in the story is perceptible in the course of a distanciation which seeks to encompass the sequential structure governed by probability. The causal coherence of actions in the plot is revealed in the course of a distanciation which seeks to encompass their causal structure governed by necessity. In both instances distanciation aims at a structural feature of motifs—at a probable or at a necessary coherence of incidents. A different kind of distanciation is necessary to perceive the relatedness of themes in story and in plot. This relatedness is, of course, closely tied to the coherence of motifs, for it is they that carry the themes. But the distinguishing feature of a distanciation aimed at the revelation of themes in story or plot is that orientation of our perception which seeks universality in the particular. In the same manner in which themes emerging from the story are universal traits particularized by unfolding incidents invested with changing psychological nuances, the themes of the plot—motivations and purposes—also derive their meaning from their universality.

3

La Symphonie pastorale

Linear Progression of Incidents in the Story

We may now seek to establish the thematic significance of the incidents in *La Symphonie pastorale,* and we should therefore briefly recall their linear progression in the story.

The pastor brings the orphaned, blind Gertrude to his home. Amélie, his wife, reproaches him for his lack of consideration. While still convinced of the righteousness of his move, he is discouraged to the point of despair by his failure to communicate with Gertrude and by his disgust with her animal demeanor. Reassured by a doctor, however, he resumes his task of teaching Gertrude and of reaching her mind, unshaken by Amélie's doubts and unmoved by her reproaches. He is determined not to use pity and not to create false illusions. His first success in reaching Gertrude's mind fills him with delight as he beholds her radiant expression. He is grateful to find his charitable endeavor justified. Gertrude's progress is rapid; in fact, she outstrips his intended pace. To her great delight he describes a world of joy, harmony, and happiness. She soon suspects the pastor of concealing the real beauty with which her lively imagination endows the world, and she rejects his pity. But the pastor conceals only evil, suffering, discord, and notions of sin, which he fears may distort her image of the world's harmony that protects her happiness. Before long Gertrude detects this protectiveness and begs him not to mislead her. Indeed, she is aware of Amélie's grief and suffers because of the reproaches Amélie heaps upon her husband for neglecting his family.

The pastor's son, Jacques, a student of theology, has also helped Gertrude in her studies. To the pastor's surprise Gertrude has secretly accepted the young man's respectful affection. In a violent confrontation, the pastor learns of his son's intention to marry Gertrude and forbids Jacques to see her.

The pastor is surprised to find his wife pleased with their son's candid expression of his intention in spite of the misfortune she believes the marriage would cause. In vain Amélie tries to alert the pastor to his own sinful inclinations. Neither his jealousy of his son nor the allusions of his wife to his passion succeed in unsealing his blinded eyes.

Having perceived the pastor's anxiety and jealousy, Gertrude reassures him of her gratitude, her loyalty, and her innocent love. She also tries, without reaching his mind, to make him see the need of confidence and love, the lack of which has caused him to send his son away and to make him suffer. When told of Jacques' intention to marry her, Gertrude offers to dissuade him and the pastor eagerly assents.

A reading of his diary makes the pastor realize the true nature of his feelings for Gertrude, but he believes that nobody is aware of his secret. He therefore continues to misjudge both his wife and his son, considering their animosity to be a result of their narrow-mindedness, which does not permit Amélie to appreciate his dedication to his task and prevents Jacques from understanding his father's concept of Christianity as a faith in which love—not coercion—elicits devotion and creates happiness. In comparison with their views and attitudes, Gertrude's naïveté seems to him a far more pleasing trait. He considers her blindness a desirable protection against the torments induced by knowledge of coercive rules, as well as against views which thwart enthusiasm and imagination. Much to his surprise, the pastor is told that a successful operation on Gertrude's eyes is feasible.

Before the operation, to which he gives his somewhat reluctant consent, the pastor learns from Gertrude that she is deeply disturbed by their guilt in causing Amélie's suffering and by her suspicion that her own innocence and happiness may be mere illusions which he has fostered. Though she betrays an interest in whether Jacques may still be in love with her, she does confess her love for the pastor. Torn between fear of sin and the love that renders him helpless, the pastor awaits the outcome of the operation. Upon her return, Gertrude attempts to commit suicide. Before her death, she confesses to the pastor her reasons: having perceived with her own eyes the pain she had caused Amélie, she saw no other solution. Also, when she was able to see Jacques, she knew that she loved him and not the pastor. She reproaches the latter for having prevented her marriage to Jacques, who after his secret conversion had decided to become a priest. While she was at the hospital, Jacques read to her those parts of the Scriptures that made her grasp the meaning of guilt and sin. After her death, the pastor learns that it was his weakness and example that led to his son's and Gertrude's conversion.

Thematic Units of the Segments of the Story

On the basis of the linear outline of the story we are able to distinguish in the line of progression six segments with identifiable thematic units:

1. An act of charity leads the pastor to the recognition that self-denial is required of him as well as of his wife. Although he prevails over Amélie's resistance in spite of her aversion to the tasks involved in the care of Gertrude, he himself also experiences repugnance and discouragement. When assured of possible success, however, he overcomes his own sense of defeat and proceeds with his plan to reach Gertrude's mind and to endow it with awareness without any false notion of pity, and hence without recourse to deceit. With charity rekindled, the pastor makes a determined effort in his pious cause, with courage and intended integrity.

2. Gertrude begins to respond to his teaching and the pastor is overjoyed with his success which justifies his efforts. She makes rapid progress, but he succeeds in maintaining her joy and her happiness—as well as his delight with his own achievement—only by concealing evil, suffering, and sin, and by implanting in her mind an image of a beautiful, joyful, and harmonious world. But Amélie's unconcealed resentment of the pastor's absorbing concern awakens Gertrude's suspicion that sorrow and discord do exist, and begs the pastor not to mislead her. We see then that pure charity and sincerity yield to the delight of creating joy and happiness, in favor of which illusions are made to replace crude reality while suspicions of a reality that destroys illusions are calmly dismissed.

3. In a spirit of self-righteousness that barely conceals his jealousy, the pastor angrily refuses his consent to his son's intended marriage. He does not understand his wife's approval of Jacques' intention, or her allusions to his own unconscious feelings for the blind girl. He also fails to grasp Gertrude's reassurance of her loyalty to him as an indication of her insight into his own feelings and as an appeal to him to save his affection for his son. The pastor's self-righteousness and unconscious sinful inclination block his awareness, blunt his self-knowledge, and distort his understanding of others.

4. Although a reading of his diary reveals to the pastor his love for Gertrude, he still believes himself to be beyond suspicion. He adheres steadfastly to his intellectual and spiritual protection of Gertrude and finds in her naïveté and kindness proof that his teaching is right, that blindness protects happiness, and that his wife's and son's notions of sin, guilt, and of the necessity of coercion are wrong. Since innocence and goodness are the results of ignorance of evil, sin, and suffering, unawareness appears as desirable, concealment as justified. The protective screen of blindness appears as a necessary safeguard against awareness which may result in anguish, guilt, and coercion.

5. Before her operation Gertrude shows a growing awareness of her

own as well as of the pastor's guilty inclinations. She suspects her happiness is based on ignorance of the suffering she is causing. Both Gertrude and the pastor stand torn between love and guilt. They are prey to these conflicting feelings, the irreconcilability of which is still hidden from them because of his spiritual and her physical blindness. Because of their blindness they are prevented from submitting to the demands of a divine order, of human compassion and responsibility.

6. After the operation Gertrude returns to see with her own eyes the anguish of Amélie. She has learned from Jacques to appreciate the weight of human responsibility, to recognize in her awakened awareness of sin the measure of guilt which the pastor and even she herself have incurred. In this state of mind, and without hope of marrying Jacques, she rejects the pastor, tries to commit suicide, and dies. Once the veil of blindness was rent, despair followed in the wake of the recognition of the destruction wrought by unfettered emotions.

Central Themes of the Story

The first of these thematic units, in which pious charity is pursued with courage and integrity, stands as a contrasting background to the themes carried by the other segments where joy and happiness appear good in themselves. If joy and happiness cause a selfish disregard for anguish, pain, and suffering, they are still considered justifiable when such harm is caused in a state of innocence protected by unawareness. But immediacy of perception, awareness of the pain caused to others by "innocent" self-indulgence, destroy untrammeled bliss. In the face of sinfulness and guilt, salvation and happiness appear attainable only through submission to demands that impose limitations on freedom and deny man's right to innocence. Knowledge, awareness, insight—the very conditions of intellectual existence—deprive man of the bliss of freedom in blind innocence, dispel his illusion of paradise which his blindness seeks to recapture, and force him to see himself in his nakedness.

This formulation of the themes of the story does not aim at stating the purpose the story is supposed to serve. Such a judgment should properly follow upon reflection on the theme, as a "second intention." It is true that Gide wrote in a letter that he depicted through the pastor the danger to which his own doctrine can lead rather than the doctrine itself.[1] We may then accept the fact that the work is intended to carry such a message, but the message, as we have already stated,[2] is a conception obtained through

---

[1] Mischa M. Fayer, *Gide, Freedom and Dostoevsky* (Burlington, Vt.: Lane Press, 1946).

[2] See chapter 1, page 3.

reflection upon a previous conception gained by abstraction from the motifs themselves.

Turning our attention to the thematic significance of the stages of transition, we note a transition from blindness to awareness, and another from awareness to blindness, the one marking the stages of Gertrude's intellectual and spiritual growth, the other the stages in which the pastor succumbs to his passion to the point of making his intellect and his spiritual loyalties assume the modifications enforced by his emotions. This thematic feature of *La Symphonie pastorale* endows the work with a structural equilibrium. These transitions from one extreme to another are accompanied, and in some way complemented, by the transitions in attitude and outlook we note in Amélie and Jacques. Amélie begins on a tone of harsh recriminations, self-righteously and aggressively, but under the impact of her own defeat and the pastor's pathetic decline, her attitude turns to resignation and compassion. In a way these transitions parallel those of the pastor: from an awareness approximating foresight, Amélie resigns herself to an assumed blindness intended to protect the pastor from an insight she fears would shatter his illusion of righteousness on which she believes his moral stand to rest. Jacques, on the other hand, in his ascent to awareness of moral principles, of sin and guilt—an awareness he shares in the end with Gertrude—offers a striking contrast between his own firmness and rigidity at the height of what to him is ultimate insight, and the pastor's spiritual breakdown in helpless blindness.

A chain of component motifs helps us determine yet another of the central themes of the story—one that captures the transitions of alternating confidence and diffidence in the mood of the pastor's entire undertaking and marks it with a stamp of ironic futility. At the end of *La Symphonie pastorale* the pastor kneels down and begs his wife to pray for him because he is in need of divine help. Haltingly Amélie recites the Lord's Prayer, with long silent pauses filled with their implorations. Then the diary records these words: "J'aurais voulu pleurer, mais je sentais mon cœur plus aride que le désert" (p. 140). It is on this note of futility that the work ends. It is noteworthy that at the beginning of the story we find a component motif the theme of which is correlative by contrast with the preceding one: not knowing what to do with Gertrude, the pastor suddenly realizes—as if by revelation ("il m'apparut soudain que Dieu")—while kneeling in prayer by the bed of the dead woman that God had placed on his path a duty he could not shirk. His inspired decision to take Gertrude to his home fills him with a sense of victory over diffidence. On his way home he implores God again. He prays that he be permitted to free Gertrude's soul of its dreadful darkness: "Hôtesse de ce corps opaque, une âme attend sans doute, emmurée, que vienne la toucher enfin quelque rayon de votre grâce, Seigneur! Permettrez-vous que mon amour, peut-être, écarte d'elle l'affreuse nuit?" (p. 18). Then, much later in the story, just before Gertrude's operation, the pastor implores God once again. This time he seeks assurance that his love is not sinful, and he prays for divine light that may dispel the confusion and the darkness into which he is sinking:

> Je ne peux plus prier qu'éperdument. S'il est une limitation dans l'amour, elle n'est pas de Vous, mon Dieu, mais des hommes. Pour coupable que mon amour paraisse aux yeux des hommes, oh! dites-moi qu'aux vôtres il est saint.

> Je tâche à m'élever au-dessus de l'idée de péché; mais le péché me semble intolérable, et je ne veux point abandonner le Christ. Non, je n'accepte pas de pécher, aimant Gertrude. Je ne puis arracher cet amour de mon cœur qu'en arrachant mon cœur même, et pourquoi? Quand je ne l'aimerais pas déjà, je devrais l'aimer par pitié pour elle; ne plus l'aimer, ce serait la trahir: elle a besoin de mon amour ...

> Seigneur, je ne sais plus ... Je ne sais plus que Vous. Guidez-moi. Parfois il me paraît que je m'enfonce dans les ténèbres et que la vue qu'on va lui rendre m'est enlevée (pp. 124–25).

That his prayers were not granted, that his desperate call for divine pity remained unanswered, that his offer to renounce his love in order to save Gertrude's life proved vain, the brutally crushing incidents reveal in their precipitous rush toward the final catastrophe. The component motifs of prayers, whose cumulative thematic significance is the ironic futility of his spiritual aspirations, lead first from humility to self-confidence and grati-tude, then from a yearning for freedom from guilt and sin to a contrite imploration for pity and to a desperate and vain penitence. In the end, the pastor turns to his wife so that she may offer prayers on his behalf, for at the depth of his despair he can neither pray nor cry.

These component motifs carry the theme of the ironic futility of man's inspired endeavors—if man is human, if he has not entirely overcome his weakness of yielding to a yearning for his own happiness and joy of which his spirit may disapprove and which his conscience actually rejects as reprehensible. The course and especially the outcome of the incidents of the story clearly condemn the pastor, but Amélie's pity for her misguided and crushed husband reveals equally clearly that only the pastor, not the man, may be condemned, for man is "neither angel nor beast," and the judgment he deserves must be attenuated by a charitable "indulgence," for man does err, may not be constantly and firmly on guard, and his best intentions to raise himself above himself may indeed prove futile. Otherwise he has the alternative of a cautious withdrawal from involvement, as represented to a large extent by Amélie, or of a rigid and gloomy self-coercion, as represented by Jacques. Neither of these choices appears in this work unequivocally preferable.

We have thus established the central themes of the story as seen on the basis of the course and outcome of incidents, of transitions from one stage to another of the states of mind and moods that invest actions and affect relations between characters, and finally on the basis of a focally placed recurring motif which carries the theme of the changes in spiritual aspirations.

Themes of the Plot

As a preliminary step to an examination of the plot structure, it is necessary to identify in a pre-iconographical sense some of the more salient traits of the characters whose actions carry the themes of the plot. Their basic dispositions and views affect not only the manner in which motivations become operative and the clarity with which purposes become defined, but also the relevance and the intensity of their responses which determine interactions between characters. *La Symphonie pastorale,* written in the form of a diary, presents all characters mostly from a single point of view. Some implications of that procedure are not without significance in the formulation of basic traits of character, but they are not relevant to the purposes of this study.

Although sensitive to his surroundings, to the physical existence perceptible to his senses, the pastor shows a marked lack of consideration for the feelings of others and an equal lack of understanding and even of awareness of their judgments. He conceives their statements and actions without proper regard for motivations and intentions, but primarily as disturbing or pleasing to himself. Consequently, he repeatedly misjudges the cognitive as well as the volitional states of conscience in others and is frequently surprised and disappointed by their actions and reactions. He is capable of awareness, empathy, and understanding only when he is confronted with a projection of his own beliefs and feelings onto a receptive mind. To the extent to which the emotional and intellectual make-up of other characters reduces the degree and scope of their uncritical receptiveness, the pastor's unawareness, misunderstandings, and disappointments increase.

Happiness and joy are for the pastor the ultimate purposes in life, and he

36

believes that happiness and joy can be the results only of boundless love and of complete harmony among men. His notion of love excludes selfishness and jealousy, and his belief in the boundlessness of love is such that any limitation of it by others elicits his sometimes regretful but usually censorious deprecation. The limitations of his own love—his own selfishness and jealousy—evade his consciousness, because he assumes that his feelings are directed by his convictions, which do not admit of either selfishness or jealousy. And his notion of harmony is sustained by his concept of love which cannot hurt others, nor can it be hurt, for it is selfless. Since the one sinful evil the pastor recognizes is the suffering inflicted by selfishness, his notion of love which excludes selfishness necessarily also excludes the possibility of sin. It creates harmony by leading to willing submission without coercion. But since the pastor remains unaware of his own selfishness, he also remains unaware of his own sin—of the suffering he himself causes.

The vital point in the pastor's view, to which the view of his son Jacques stands in sharp contrast, is that happiness is the ultimate and "obligatory" purpose in life, that it is inseparably bound up with joy, and that boundless love is the condition for its existence. Happiness without joy is inconceivable to him. This, then, is a happiness of ecstatic delight, of carefree enjoyment, of unbounded freedom, of unlimited expectations, of spontaneous actions, and of unconcern—a happiness to which man has the right and the "obligation" to aspire. To place any obstacle on man's path to such a happiness is not only contemptibly ungenerous but actually sinful. Furthermore, if no obstacles such as selfishness and anguish are placed by others on the path of him who aspires to such happiness, he need not be concerned with them; but if his happiness should thus be threatened, then innocence in self-indulgence should be protected and justified by a blind unawareness of obstacles and, if necessary, by a self-righteous disregard for them. The *story,* of which this concept of happiness is one of the central themes, gives an account of the incidents which carry the theme, but the *plot* explains the concept and tries to justify it—not merely excuse it; it also explains the reasons for the pastor's increasing blindness and Gertrude's deepening insights, as well as the futility of the pastor's prayers—the other central themes of the story.

The pastor feels securely set in the ideas to which his pastoral beliefs and duties have taught him to adhere. We find him steeped in his work, somewhat regretfully aware of his intellectual and emotional isolation amidst the daily cares of the household which absorb his wife and amidst the preoccupations of his children, who leave him estranged as they withdraw from his influence. He considers all his thoughts and emotions so imbued with his convictions that any deviation seems inconceivable to him; he sincerely and even self-righteously believes that any emotion that may stir his heart or any thought that may enter his mind is in perfect accord with his pastoral beliefs and functions. He lives with the illusion of having reached the stage of arrested mutability and therefore of an existence beyond suspicion. The pastor could not have been depicted more appropriately if Gide had wished to cast his character in a role exemplifying Pierre Bayle's view of man almost never acting consistently in accordance with his principles and following his "natural inclination to pleasure" regardless of the knowledge with which his mind is filled. From his wife the pastor expects generous submission to his plans and actions, so convinced is he of his righteousness and of her sincere willingness to submit once she has recognized the merit of his endeavors. He is grieved over what he believes to be her selfish hesitations but confident that she will ultimately follow his example. From his children he expects obedience, and he elicits it by an appeal to their conscience and to his rightful authority.

Coupled with his assurance is an apparently humble yet haughty assumption of having been singled out—he, the pastor—for a special task: "Béni soit le Seigneur pour m'avoir confié cette tâche." His assumption of being guided by God supports even if it does not directly engender the naïveté which disposes him to spontaneous acts without forethought. His lack of a realistic imagination deprives him of insight and foresight while freeing him to indulge in hopes, yearnings, and dreams of a blissful existence in harmony, happiness, and joy toward which he believes it to be his function to lead men by freeing them through unbounded love from the fear of doing evil and from the dread of sin.

His first impulse to take Gertrude to his house is prompted by inspired *caritas,* by the love of man for the love of God; it is a willingly assumed obligation. His initial failure to reach Gertrude's mind, the encouragement he receives from Dr. Martins, and Amélie's lack of confidence in his success bring about a change in his motivation: to awaken Gertrude's dormant intellect becomes a challenge. As soon as his success is assured and Gertrude's awakening actually occurs, her pleasure, joy, and happiness prove that the challenge has been met. Although *caritas* remains a conscious motivation, the attainment of Gertrude's growing delight with her achievements becomes his primary purpose, superseding the original one of simply awakening her mind and of permitting her to develop into a human being in spite of her blindness. His own joy of beholding her ecstatic happiness becomes the impelling force that drives the pastor to seek consciously Gertrude's ever-increasing joy through visions of beauty and harmony and unconsciously to seek his own delight of reveling in the joyful happiness he is creating. His initial resolution to refuse to foster illusions for the sake of happiness by concealment and deception is brushed aside and forgotten, and the creation of joyful happiness becomes the purpose.

That the pastor's purpose with regard to what he had been aiming to achieve for Gertrude has changed from sober contentment to ecstatic happiness is textually evident, but so is the change in motivation from charitable to hedonic impulses and ultimately to a passionate love of Gertrude whose happiness becomes his happiness; and the loved one becomes confused with, or identified with, the pleasure her joy engenders. It is this new motivation, this gradually emerging agonistic theme of the plot, that sustains the new purpose.

In the course of his efforts to maintain Gertrude's happy disposition, the pastor anxiously conceals his disagreements with his wife, for disagreements may belie Gertrude's carefully nurtured illusion of pervasive harmony. He resolutely opposes his son's influence on Gertrude for fear that Jacques' stern principles of morality may reveal to her a world in which suffering caused by man may be allayed only by abnegation, a world in which man can be delivered from the sin of causing suffering only by self-denial sustained by fear and by humble submission to coercive commandments—whereas according to the pastor's teaching unbounded love alone should lead to submission, and such a love precludes suffering and sin. He opposes his wife's petty and selfish unconcern for his worthy task of charitable dedication and blames her for her inability to rise with him to his pure and lofty joy of raising a soul from darkness to the heights of bliss. He accuses his son of preferring the torment of a soul tortured by guilt to the blissful soul inspired by generous love.

But he can blame his wife and son so self-righteously only as long as he himself remains unaware of his own subconscious motivation, of his love of Gertrude which causes suffering to Amélie and Jacques, only as long as his deepening unawareness shields him from the knowledge of his own guilt and sin. It never occurs to him to ask at what price of suffering caused to others he maintains his notion of unbounded love and joyful happiness; and it does not occur to him to bestow and to teach a happiness which flows from self-denial, the happiness which consists of the sorrowful yet gratifying knowledge of not indulging in one's own pleasures—of sacrificing them because of one's truly unbounded love, unbounded by blind egotism and selfishness.

39

In order to justify his efforts on behalf of Gertrude before his wife and before his own conscience, he clings with increasing determination to his initial genuine and righteous course of following the example found in the parable of the lost sheep. It is this course, on which he decided prior to his new and unconscious motivation, as well as Amélie's opposition, which she has maintained from the outset, that remain in his awareness and prevent him from becoming conscious of the shift in his motivation and from realizing Amélie's new reasons for her opposition based on her understanding of that shift.

In his efforts to maintain Gertrude's happiness, he fosters her illusions of a joy that pervades nature, which the birds herald in their song, the butterflies in their colors, the mountains in their splendor, and music in its harmony. The world of man with its cares and sorrows, of which Gertrude is slowly becoming conscious, is explained away by the pastor as a regrettable inability, a spiritual blindness, which afflicts man whose head bows under the weight of self-inflicted worries born of selfish and petty concerns. But he succeeds in maintaining Gertrude's illusion of an all-pervasive joy and harmony only as long as she does not realize Amélie's sorrow and painful opposition, as long as she does not feel the pastor's jealousy of Jacques, and the latter's sad withdrawal. And as long as she does not gain her eyesight, he succeeds—however precariously—in maintaining his own illusion of safeguarding Gertrude from what he believes to be the destructive influence of Amélie, Jacques, and her own deepening insights; he succeeds because of his wife's and son's dutiful and sensitive charity which prevents them, if not from opposing his actions and opinions, at least from unsealing his eyes and from making him face the fact of his intellectual and spiritual decadence. And he owes his illusion of maintaining a hold on Gertrude's heart to her gratitude, love, and pity which prevent her, if not from concealing her understanding of the true nature of their love and guilt, at least from abandoning him by drawing her own conclusions about having been made a victim of the deceptions which she still attributes to his love.

It is due to his unconscious hedonic motivation that the pastor relinquishes the integrity with which he had intended to lead Gertrude and feeds her imagination with visions of beauty, her mind with the peace of harmony, and her heart with joy and happiness. It is due to his yet unconscious passion that he opposes her marriage to Jacques, forbids his son any communication with Gertrude, and eagerly accepts her consent to refuse Jacques' expressions of affection. When he is told that Gertrude may undergo a successful operation, he gives his consent only reluctantly, for he fears—forewarned by her suspicions of what he may have concealed as well as by the affection for Jacques which she has never overcome—that she may fully realize that her happiness has been safeguarded by her blindness and that her love of the pastor may have endured only because of her inability to compare the features of the father with those of the son. Gertrude's blindness suddenly appears to him preferable to the vision which may destroy her carefree joyful happiness. He does not actually visualize the particular dangers that threaten her happiness and peace of mind; his anxiety is vague, but it is induced by his controversy with his son and by the knowledge that he has carefully omitted from her readings such disturbing notions as evil, guilt, and sin that seemed to him—concerned as he was with the perfect equanimity that served Gertrude as a protective shield for happiness—unfounded and untenable. Gertrude's final insights before her death spell out the dangers of which the pastor is only vaguely apprehensive: that she may find out that she was without sin because she was blind—"If ye were blind, ye should have no sin."[3] And she may learn that while "there is nothing unclean of itself,"[4] once we consider with awareness and insight that something is wrong and evil, it becomes so because we consider it to be so; that sinning is denying evil wherein we have recognized evil to be; that to indulge in unawareness, to ignore our beliefs by not acting according to them, is to deny our sinfulness, to deceive ourselves, and to have no truth in us; that to remain free of the sin the pastor does recognize—that of endangering the happiness of others—one must be and remain intentionally conscious of what it is that endangers the happiness of others; and finally, that it may be impossible to safeguard one's happiness if one is determined not to commit the sin of destroying the happiness of others, unless one considers one's happiness to be that of freedom from guilt and that of contentment which the mastery of one's own emotions brings.

Within the story we have found, among other themes, some that are central, such as the theme of blindly innocent joyful happiness, the theme of salvation through submission and self-coercion, the themes of transitions from awareness to blindness and from blindness to awareness, and the theme of the ironic futility of the pastor's spiritual aspirations.

The plot has revealed the theme of the pastor's changed motivations from charitable to hedonic love; the theme of his changed purposes from leading Gertrude to consciousness and a realistic acceptance of life to the creation of a happiness based on illusions; the theme of Amélie's

---

[3] John 9:41.   [4] Romans 14:14.

purposes which do not change in essence although the increasing restraint in her opposition weakens her antagonism; the theme of Jacques' increasingly rigid commitment to purposes guided by his awareness of religious principles; and finally, the theme of Gertrude's increasing antagonism to a blindly innocent self-indulgence as her sense of guilt and sinfulness emerges from her awakened consciousness and from her aroused conscience.

Relationships between Themes of the Story and Themes of the Plot

The question before us is the following: What is the relationship between themes of the story and themes of the plot? To begin with, the pastor's initial motivation, *caritas,* and his initial purpose have the function of maintaining, in the first notebook, his notion of his conscious endeavors while the repressed subconscious motivation and the changing purpose gradually rise to the threshold of his awareness. In the second notebook, the pastor proclaims charity—his original and commendable motivation—as his driving force, in the hope of concealing his new hedonic motivation, the purpose of which is Gertrude's blindly innocent happiness and his own delight. His original purpose of awakening Gertrude's intellect, largely achieved early in the work, is replaced by an equally commendable continuing obligation of solicitude for the blind girl. But this apparently simple purpose, which he believes cannot but be approved, is in reality subordinate to the primary purpose of preserving Gertrude's innocent happiness and his own pleasure. It is evident, then, that the theme of blindly innocent happiness in the story is at the same time the theme of a purpose in the plot—the purpose which the pastor's new hedonic motivation seeks to achieve.

The other theme of the story, the theme of happiness and salvation through submission and self-coercion, presents the intellectual and spiritual contrast to the theme of blindly innocent happiness. This theme is equally a theme of a purpose in the plot, of the purpose Jacques has espoused and to which he clings with increasing steadfastness. It also becomes the purpose of Gertrude after she has recognized under Jacques' influence her own as well as the pastor's guilt.

Changes in motivations and purposes also account for the transitions from awareness to blindness and from blindness to awareness. The manner in which textual elements are used to introduce these transitions is worth noting. We find two materially different contingent[5] incidents

---

[5] See chapter 2, page 28.

placed at the very points at which the pastor and Gertrude make the transition from blindness to awareness. These contingent motifs, in spite of their material difference, are thematically correlative in so far as both reveal situations with which the characters suddenly find themselves confronted and in which they are forced to behold their identity as it emerges from the confrontation; both motifs lead to self-recognition and self-awareness. The first of these contingent motifs marks the point at which the pastor rereads the entries in his diary and realizes his own previously unavowed inclination toward Gertrude as well as her love for him. The other contingent incident marks the point of Gertrude's return from the hospital with her eyesight restored. Both incidents bring to the surface subconscious or barely conscious states of mind and the recognition of conditions the full nature of which has been concealed. We may now consider how the transitions from blindness to awareness are governed in the plot by motivations and purposes after being introduced and placed into perspective by the two contingent motifs.

Despite his revealing insight, it does not occur to the pastor that his previous convictions do not determine his emotions, that in the meantime his emotions have molded his convictions and have led him to accord his original charitable impulses with what he has come to recognize as an equally charitable view of human happiness. Preoccupied with Gertrude's religious instruction, he develops interpretations on the strength of selections from the Scriptures chosen to support his teaching and to protect her joyful happiness. The pastor's changed purpose causes him to foster ignorance and naïve innocence, to refuse doctrines and precepts which appear to him disturbing, and to prefer spiritual blindness for the sake of an unhindered illusion—consciously only for Gertrude but by unconscious adaptation for himself also. With mounting anxiety and in a last desperate attempt to save what he erroneously still believes to be Gertrude's peace of mind, the pastor begins also to cherish her physical blindness, by which, incidentally, he hopes to keep her love. Thus the incidents that follow the pastor's momentary self-recognition show him preoccupied with new commendable purposes while his subconscious motivations remain repressed as a result of his confidence in his unerring righteousness.

Gertrude's transition from blindness to awareness is at the same time physical, intellectual, and spiritual. Her ascent from blindness to insight reaches its high point upon her return from her successful operation. Her love, gratitude, and pity, which previously helped to allay her suspicions, turn under the impact of the startling evidence perceived with her own eyes to disappointment, indignation, repugnance, guilt, and despair.

Altered by suspicions, fearful and resentful of her dependence, Gertrude aspired long before her operation to knowledge, insight, and certainty. She objected repeatedly and resolutely to the pastor's pity because she suspected that it was intended to keep her happy within the limitations of blindness, whereas she was intent on being freed by insights that surmount physical bounds. She refused to be spared suffering and the knowledge of suffering, for it was by such knowledge that she had come to feel an intellectual and spiritual strength that helped her in surmounting her confining debility. With ever increasing intensity she felt that her happiness made the night of her blindness darker and that her joy was the effect of deception. Thus happiness and joy, which the pastor struggled to preserve as the ultimate purposes in life, become finally reduced in her own mind to worthless palliatives used to mitigate the anguish of blindness. Hence the pastor's purpose is conclusively superseded by Gertrude's submission to Jacques' coercive principles toward which her intellectual growth has evolved. Indeed the last and decisive blow by which Jacques' antagonistic purpose dispels illusory and blindly joyous happiness is represented by Gertrude's rejection of all the pastor's purposes. Before deciding on whatever message one may be tempted to derive from this conclusion, it should be noted that while Gertrude's rejection of the pastor's purposes occurs at the height of her intellectual insight, it also occurs at the height of her feverish agitation. The motifs as actions, gestures, and expressions indicate the supremacy of one theme over the other, but the motifs as conditions and circumstances preclude such a clear-cut resolution.

Finally, the theme of the ironic futility of the pastor's spiritual aspirations is also put into perspective by the purposes in the plot, and the reason for the ironic futility is explained by the pastor's subconscious motivation and erroneous assumptions. The pastor's good intentions have a disappointing outcome, and Gide has chosen several incidents with the intention of emphasizing the theme of the ironic futility. For instance, Jacques might have become merely a convert to Catholicism instead of becoming a priest, but the latter was necessary to point out, by placing an unsurmountable obstacle to Gertrude's marriage, the futility of any hope of undoing the harm the pastor had caused. Gertrude's suicide attempt, after her perceptual discovery of human suffering and her full realization of the guilt she and the pastor have incurred, provides the final proof not only of her rejection of his purposes but also of the futility of his prayerful hopes. But there lies an even deeper irony in that after the shift from a conscious to a subconscious motivation the pastor's prayer ceases to be a supplication for inspiration and becomes a prayer for condonation of his aberrations. The futility of his aspirations is deeply rooted in his blind assumption of the feasibility of creating happiness without awareness of the basic selfishness which a consistent pursuit of joyful happiness presupposes, and consequently without regard for the reality of conflicting emotions. The irony of his aspirations is made even more manifest by the forbearance shown to him by his wife, who in spite of her opposition to his purposes shows generous compassion and pity— qualities which the pastor feels have determined every one of his own moves and with which he only grudgingly credits his wife. Similarly, the irony is also emphasized by Jacques' respectful restraint. In spite of his uncompromising stand, he himself refrains from accusing and condemning his father. Finally, the irony is painfully brought to light by Gertrude's affection and pity and by her desperate and ultimately un-successful attempt at concealing her angry contempt.

Generic Coherence of Themes

What distinguishes linear, causal, and generic coherence of themes is the manner in which themes are related to one another. We have al-ready noted that the generic coherence of themes is independent of linear or causal coherence and that it is based solely on their affinity of similarity or contrast. The motifs which carry correlative themes may occur any-where in the text. The textual disposition of linking phrases is important because their presence alerts us to the component quality of the motifs in connecton with which they appear. The textual disposition of linking images is also important, for in them we see the reflection of previous and succeeding themes. Textual proximity is an advantage of similar parallel component motifs; it is indispensable in the case of materially different parallel component motifs because their discovery depends upon the lingering quality of their themes which have to be recognized as correlative before their materially different motifs prove to be com-ponent.

We have already established the generic coherence between the themes of several component motifs in *La Symphonie pastorale,* and we have noted that two of the central themes of the story (the theme of blindly joyful happiness and the theme of happiness through submission and self-coercion) are correlative by contrast. We have also noted the corre-lation between the antagonistic motivations and purposes in the plot, and we shall now turn our attention to some of the more outstanding instances of thematic correlation based upon recurring motifs and upon textual contiguity.

Although the pastor's hedonic motivation does not become apparent until his delight with the happiness he creates awakens his desire to renew that experience, a vague thematic allusion to his predisposition to relive a sentimental experience is embedded early in the text. Commenting on his journey to the dying old woman, the pastor writes:

> Je croyais connaître admirablement tous les entours de la commune; mais passé la ferme de la Soudraie, l'enfant me fit prendre une route où jusqu'alors je ne m'étais jamais aventuré. Je reconnus pourtant, à deux kilomètres de là, sur la gauche, un petit lac mystérieux où jeune homme j'avais été quelquefois patiner. Depuis quinze ans je ne l'avais plus revu, car aucun devoir pastoral ne m'appelle de ce côté; je n'aurais plus su dire où il était et j'avais à ce point cessé d'y penser qu'il me sembla, lorsque tout à coup, dans l'enchantement rose et doré du soir, je le reconnus, ne l'avoir d'abord vu qu'en rêve (pp. 12–13).

There are nostalgic references to a time in his life when, without cares and duties, he was free to move about and enjoy his youth. The enchantment and the mystery of that life from which his pastoral duties have kept him away now appear as unreal as if he had only known them from dreams.

Much later in the story, he returns once again to memories the theme of which is correlative to that which we have just described in that it conveys a similarly inspired nostalgia. He remembers the freedom of his youthful enthusiasm and the bold and generous aspirations in which his young bride, Amélie, was hopefully to lead the way. Comparing his daughter Sarah with his wife, he states:

> Elle ressemble non point, hélas! à ce que sa mère était à son âge, quand nous nous sommes fiancés, mais bien à ce que l'ont fait devenir les soucis de la vie matérielle, et j'allais dire la culture des soucis de la vie (car certainement Amélie les cultive). Certes j'ai bien du mal à reconnaître en elle aujourd'hui l'ange qui souriait naguère à chaque noble élan de mon cœur, que je rêvais d'associer indistinctement à ma vie, et qui me paraissait me précéder et me guider vers la lumière—ou l'amour en ce temps-là me blousait-il? ... (p. 111).

The first thematic allusion foreshadows the pastor's hedonic motivation, the latter seems intended to justify it in retrospect.

The theme of charity is supported by motifs of blindness, darkness, night, and apprehension which underlie the pastor's pity. Motifs of light, warmth, song, and happiness underlie his delight at the revelations of Gertrude's blissful insights. These insights as well as her suspicions that she is not being told of all the beauty there is to behold cause the pastor's charitable pity, directed at dispelling the darkness of blindness, to turn into a hedonic desire for the initially unexpected effects of his charity: the luminous joy of blindness.

> Sa surprise et sa *crainte* d'abord, dès qu'elle avait quitté la maison, me laissèrent comprendre, avant qu'elle n'eût su me le dire, qu'elle ne s'était encore jamais hasardée au dehors. Dans la chaumière où je l'avais trouvée, personne ne s'était occupé d'elle autrement que pour lui donner à manger et l'aider à ne point mourir, car je n'ose point dire: à vivre. Son *univers obscur* était borné par les murs mêmes de cette unique pièce qu'elle n'avait jamais quittée; à peine se hasardait-elle, les jours d'été, au bord du seuil, quand la porte restait ouverte sur le grand *univers lumineux.* Elle me raconta plus tard, qu'entendant le *chant des oiseaux,* elle l'imaginait alors un pur *effet de la lumière,* ainsi que cette chaleur même qu'elle sentait caresser ses joues et ses mains, et que, sans du reste y réfléchir précisément, il lui paraissait tout naturel que *l'air chaud se mît à chanter,* de même que l'eau se met à bouillir près du feu. Le vrai c'est qu'elle ne s'en était point inquiétée, qu'elle ne faisait attention à rien et vivait dans un engourdissement profond, *jusqu'au jour où je commençai de m'occuper d'elle.* Je me souviens de son inépuisable ravissement lorsque je lui appris que ces petites voix émanaient de créatures vivantes, dont il semble que l'unique fonction soit de sentir et d'exprimer *l'éparse joie de la nature* (pp. 43–45.)[6]

Motifs of night and darkness carrying the theme of intellectual and spiritual blindness recur significantly at the beginning of the story in reference to Gertrude, and at the end in reference to the pastor. It is worth noting that when these motifs are used in reference to Gertrude, they appear often in conjunction with motifs of light ("aurore," "sommet neigeux," "sort de la nuit," "moindre épaisseur de nuit"), whereas when they are used in reference to the pastor, they are chosen to express his plunging into darkness.

> J'ai projeté d'écrire ici tout ce qui concerne la formation et le développement de cette âme pieuse, qu'il me semble que je n'ai fait sortir de la nuit . . . (p. 12).

> Tout le long de la route, je pensais: dort-elle? et de quel *sommeil noir* . . . (p. 18).

> Je me faisais l'effet de quelqu'un . . . qui, penché sur la margelle d'un *puits profond et noir,* agiterait désespérément une corde dans l'espoir qu'enfin une main la saisisse (p. 35).

---

[6] Italics are mine except where otherwise indicated.

Tout à coup ses traits *s'animèrent,* ce fut comme un éclairement subit, pareil à cette *lueur purpurine* dans les hautes Alpes qui, précédant l'*aurore,* fait vibrer le *sommet neigeux* qu'elle désigne et *sort de la nuit* . . . (p. 41). (The word *"s'animèrent"* is italic in the text.)

. . . car chaque fois que je la retrouvais, c'était avec une nouvelle surprise et je me sentais séparé d'elle par *une moindre épaisseur de nuit* (p. 43).

Seigneur, je ne sais plus . . . Je ne sais plus que Vous. Guidez-moi. Parfois il me paraît que *je m'enfonce dans les ténèbres* et que la vue qu'on va lui rendre m'est enlevée . . . (p. 125).

Dans quelle abominable *nuit je plonge!*
Pitié, Seigneur, pitié! (p. 128).

While motifs of darkness or light allude to some of the central themes, it would be wrong to conclude that every such motif contributes to the generic coherence of the thematic fabric, for they are sometimes used for purely descriptive purposes.

In two succeeding entries in his diary the pastor recalls first Gertrude's delight upon being told that the voices she heard were those of birds and not the effects of light; then in the following entry he reverts to earlier incidents so as to recapture the initial difficulties he encountered in the course of the instruction given to Gertrude, especially the difficulty of making her understand the concept of colors. To all appearances, the time shift has the purpose of reestablishing the linear sequence of seemingly only pedagogically interrelated incidents and of filling in the reader by summarizing in a routine fashion Gertrude's progress. Then at the height of his effort to minimize the importance of his account, the problem of explaining colors is described with calculated underemphasis. The impression that the reader is directed toward the thematic significance of the motifs rather than toward the motifs themselves is inescapable. He explains the song of birds as the expression of joy that pervades nature, and colors as inscribed by joy on the wings of butterflies. In contrast to this the pastor reflects, in a mood similar to that experienced after the concert at Neuchâtel, on man's dull and numb incapacity to rise to a liberating experience of unfettered happiness—a clear allusion to Amélie and to the rigidity that marks his son's intellectual stand.

The themes of the materially very different motifs which deal with the problem of explaining colors do not readily reveal their correlation with the themes of the previous motifs, especially since the time shift purposely separates the two sets of motifs. While the pastor has been immediately successful in bringing delight into Gertrude's world by filling it with joyful birds and butterflies and the frolicsome play of nimble squirrels, he has difficulties in making her grasp the distinction between a color and its numerous shades from the brightest to the darkest. After the concert at Neuchâtel, however, at which they hear Beethoven's *Pastoral Symphony*, the pastor is able to draw a parallel between the different qualities of a given sound when played on different instruments and the different shades of a given color. "Une sorte de ravissement intérieur vint dès lors remplacer ses doutes." The use of this linking phrase, so similar to "Je me souviens de son inépuisable ravissement," used when the revelation of the song of birds made Gertrude happy, alerts us to the possibility of there being a potential thematic correlation to explore. The song of birds and the many shades of color on butterflies are heralds of a pervasive joy that finds free expression through a vast range of sounds and a multiplicity of shades. Joyful happiness can express itself only through free and spontaneous manifestations of mobility, and is therefore endowed with innumerable nuances. The notion of there being only solid colors is due either to blindness or to the weight of unimaginative and constrained earthbound rigidity which is the source of numbness (the expression "engourdissement" is used in reference to Gertrude's early stage of development) and of sadness that force the mind into paths bounded by rigid lines of demarcation. We do already see that these correlative themes clearly allude to two of the central themes of the story—the free and joyful happiness, and the sad contentment through submission to rigid coercion.

Although Gertrude is delighted with the revelation of pervasive joy through the free and unbounded field of colors and sounds, through imperceptible transitions from nuance to nuance, she is suddenly struck by the problem of conceiving the notion of black and white. Just as at the end of the story and at the point of the unfolding conflict in the plot Gertrude will first question and finally reject the pastor's belief and purpose, she already questions at the beginning of her intellectual growth the very basis of his assumptions: If any color is manifested only in one of its many shades, then what does white look like? According to his theory, she feels, white is unimaginable and consequently so is black. In a figurative sense, this is exactly the stand the pastor will take in his arguments with his son. Gertrude's convertibility to the belief in good and evil, to a black and white in ethical matters—and consequently to a rejection of a joyful happiness based on the most elusive concepts of morality—is long foreshadowed by her rejection of the pastor's theory according to which black and white are mere notions to which there is no counterpart in reality. Using the pastor's own means of explanation, she points out that a tone produced on any instrument remains distinct from the same tone produced on a different instrument regardless of how high or how low the tone may be. The objection leaves the pastor perplexed, and though he does not mention the implication—in fact he seems to repress it by pointing merely to his difficulties in teaching Gertrude—it is nevertheless clear that consequently black and white, and in fact any color, do exist in the particular shade in which they appear. Though there may be no single black or white or blue in itself, there is nevertheless a black, a white, a blue, namely, the one that one has recognized as such. But Gertrude's insight fails to unseal the pastor's eyes, nor will they be unsealed much later by the words from Romans (14:14): "that there is nothing unclean of itself: but to him that esteemeth any thing to be unclean, to him it is unclean." However, any disturbing polarity such as that between black and white, good and evil, innocence and guilt or sin, the pastor simply surmounts by elimination, by an intuitive denial of their reality. At most he concedes their virtuality but never without perceiving them as contingent on man's sad inability to soar to joyous flights of imagination toward harmony. This is why Beethoven's *Pastoral Symphony* has for the pastor so great an appeal. This was played at the concert to which he took Gertrude to make her feel the pleasure he knew was within her reach.

The "harmonies ineffables" of Beethoven's Sixth Symphony depict for the pastor the world not as it is, but as it might be were it not for evil and sin, and also for the knowledge of death. This view of harmony emanates from a yearning for the simple, the uncomplicated, the utopian relationship between man and nature. In this view, man is free from fears, for he knows no tomorrow; he is blind to the future and does not know death. Harmony exists because there is no discord, because there are no constraining distinctions or relationships. Here, ideally, man owes nothing and expects nothing from man, except what man gives as a spontaneous expression of happiness. In this utopian isolation of man from other men, man has no obligation, no guilt, no sin. His heart, as Rousseau has said, is at peace, and wretchedness is beyond his imagination. He lives in the present and for the present, and his immediate aim is joy. If he does associate with others, his moral unawareness does not threaten their joy, because his "natural pity"—as Rousseau understood it—acts as a natural force of moderation. Where such harmony prevails, there is no need for commandments and there is no need for coercion.

It seems that Gide has made his pastor follow the lost sheep so as to make him discover through the soul of a free human being, untouched and unspoiled by society, the joyful happiness of which in his natural state man may be capable for as long as his blindness shields him from realizing that he is not alone, that he is part of a human flock, and that this flock lives and moves in an order determined by mutual dependence, in an order where natural pity is not a sufficient safeguard against the indolence of joyful happiness.

4

L'Etranger

The Themes in the Linear Coherence of the Story

In considering the linear coherence of the story in Camus' *L'Etranger*,[1] we find that the first chapter consists of four segments: Meursault's preparation for his journey and his trip to Marengo following the announcement of his mother's death; his meeting with the director and the caretaker; the wake; and finally, the funeral.

A precipitous sequence of incidents follows Meursault's receipt of the telegram informing him of his mother's death. In preparation for his journey, he has to consider and carry out a number of tasks that require adhering to established procedures or at least to a timetable. The break in his routine, his concern with proper attitudes and with visible symbols of mourning, the unaccustomed formal sympathy of friends, the distraction, the haste in catching the bus, all end in Meursault's physical exhaustion, sleep, unconscious indolence (he is leaning in his sleep on the shoulders of the soldier who sits next to him in the bus), and indifference (when he wakes, he barely acknowledges the soldier's polite and kindly attempt to strike up a conversation).

In his dealings with the caretaker and with the director at Marengo, Meursault encounters established and formally regulated orderly procedures of a public welfare organization. A careful observance of properly functioning procedures assures the maintenance of efficient service and a regard for humane concerns. The director makes Meursault realize that existing files already provide an image of the relationship between him and his mother. Faced with the necessity of revealing his attitudes and emotions, Meursault suspects that these are expected to accord with established norms of propriety. By having to reveal them to others, he learns at least to recognize his attitudes even if he cannot always account for them. His basic attitude is partly an apologetic reluctance to accept as binding those concerns he feels are expected of him (for example, the

---

[1] All page references are to Albert Camus, *L'Etranger* (Paris: Gallimard, 1963 edition).

care of his mother), and partly it is a refusal to comply with formalities (as, for instance, seeing his mother's body when exhorted to do so, or refraining from smoking during the wake).

The physical setup of the wake reflects the contrast between the states of mind on each side of death. The coffin is in the center of the room; Meursault is on one side, the caretaker and the old boarders on the other side facing him, and the glaring light of the bulbs and of the white walls is focused on this confrontation. Meursault ignores the coffin. His attention is directed toward the old people whose eyes are riveted on the coffin or some other object, and whose minds are steeped in gloom with single-minded rigid concentration. Before the boarders enter, Meursault's concerns are governed by considerations for his emotional peace and physical comfort. He refuses to see his mother's body, drinks café au lait, smokes after a little hesitation caused by doubts about propriety, complains of the bright lights that tire his eyes, yields to the mildness of the air and the fragrance of the flowers, and falls asleep. The old people enter, arouse him from his sleep, and the wake which is "the custom" begins. The dreamlike quality of his vision endows the boarders with a fascination of unreality. Their gloomy concentration, the stiffness with which they seem to follow an habitual ritual, isolate Meursault on his side of the coffin and give him "the ridiculous impression" of being judged, no doubt in the sense of being in the limelight and on trial to see whether, in face of their common bereavement, his own emotions match theirs. The weeping of one of the women makes him feel uneasy. He would like to stop her from crying, but does not dare. The caretaker tries in vain to intervene, but after some hesitation he explains "without looking at him" that her ceaseless lamentation is due to her pain at having lost a friend in Meursault's mother, with whom she felt very close ties. Meursault, who does not shed a tear, who is increasingly aware of his backache and discomfort, cannot believe—though he does afterward change his mind—that his dead mother could mean anything to the others. It is obvious that in this confrontation of consciences Meursault's uneasiness arises from a feeling of being separated and excluded from the community of mourners, and a feeling of being at fault, though not guilty, is instilled into his mind because of his inability to experience sorrow or at least to emulate an exemplary expression of it. When he wakes up for a moment he finds everybody asleep except one man who stares at him, waiting for nothing but his awakening; but this challenge to his conscience does not elicit a response. In fact Meursault falls asleep again and wakes up only because his back hurts him even more than before. But Meursault's later recorded reflection "on est toujours un peu fautif" sounds like a delayed echo of suppressed impressions of finding himself on trial and at fault for not experiencing the emotions which others do.

In order to show how superficially Meursault has actually grasped the depth of the old people's emotions, how he has failed to comprehend the bond of a sorrow they believed themselves to have shared with him, how meaningless the meaningful formality of their final expression of sympathy really was to him, Camus shows Meursault's astonishment at seeing them come and shake his hand. Meursault cannot understand why the wake, during which not a single word was exchanged, should have brought them closer to one another.

Meursault's incomprehension of visible manifestations of emotions is made even more obvious during the funeral. During the wake, Meursault's awareness encompassed chiefly his physical discomfort and the bare surface of form in which the emotions of others presented themselves. During the funeral Meursault responds again only to the same kind of manifestations. As the day begins, he is tired, washes, and enjoys his café au lait. He watches the sunrise and breathes in the salty air the wind brings. Longingly he reflects on how he might enjoy a walk in the country were it not for his mother. The smell of the fresh soil dispels his drowsiness. From this moment on, during the long walk to the cemetery, we watch with his eyes the sun rising in the sky and the heat melting the tar on the road as it releases and diffuses the smell of mud, leather, varnish, and incense. We find him bewildered and lost between the monotony of the blue and white in the sky and the black of the hearse, the road, and the clothes. We watch with him the perspiration that trickles down the faces and we feel his hot blood beating against his temples. In the cemetery he sees red geraniums on the graves, the bloodred color of the earth rolling down onto the coffin, and the white flesh of the roots in the ground. But the only emotion he betrays is his joy as his bus finally returns into the nest of lights of Algiers, and as he envisages "lying down and sleeping for twelve hours."

In contrast to his own feelings, we watch with Meursault's eyes the feelings and emotions of others. We see them either as mere records of surface appearances, or as amusing or even ridiculous expressions of stiff formality or of sentimentality. But we also discover through Meursault's descriptions humane concerns ranging from simple curiosity to persistent and exhausting devotion; for us, however, his descriptions of humane concerns are not mere records of bare sensory impressions as they are for him, but apperceptions of meaningful behavior which Meursault fails to understand. From Meursault's point of view it seems as though the director's striped trousers and black coat, and the manner in which he is seated behind his desk with his little legs crossed, were of the same importance as his concern for the well-being of his boarders. Meursault is slightly amused at Pérez' love and does not really understand Pérez' being deeply affected by old Madame Meursault's death. He notes that the priest bends down toward one of the altar boys to adjust the length of the silver chain on the censer, and he notes the priest addressing him as "my son," but he does not even mention what the "few words" were that the priest did say to him, although one may assume that they were words of consolation. Even the simple inquiry by one of the undertaker's employees whether it was his mother Meursault was burying, and especially his curiosity about her age, leave only the record of Meursault's ignorance of how old his mother really was and the ensuing—by no means meaningless—silence of the employee. We know he must have been shocked by Meursault's ignorance of his mother's age, for the director's testimony at the trial reveals that clearly enough. But the most obvious instance of Meursault's incomprehension of emotions is revealed through the manner in which he describes Pérez. He notes the latter's embarrassment, his sagging trousers, his ugly, funny features. In contrast to the director, "who walked with great dignity and without making a useless gesture," and who did not even wipe away the perspiration from his forehead, Meursault sees Pérez, who was unable to keep up with the pace of the hearse, cutting across the fields several times. Instead of an appreciative comment on the old man's determination to make up for his slow and limping pace, to overcome the heat and the strain, Meursault remarks with some emphasis that he himself felt his blood beat against his temples. But among the confused images Meursault remembers there is nevertheless Pérez finally catching up with them at the village, and he does note the tears of exasperation and grief on the sad old face. But here again it is the ugliness of the face, in the wrinkles of which Pérez' tears get caught, that is emphasized: "Mais, à cause des rides, elles ne s'écoulaient pas. Elles s'étalaient, se rejoignaient et formaient un vernis d'eau sur ce visage détruit" (p. 29). Finally, in the most cursory fashion, he notes that Pérez fainted in the cemetery. Instead of reflecting on what his mother's death must have meant to the old man, Meursault merely mentions the ridiculous and slightly amusing aspect of Pérez' sudden breakdown: "Il y a eu encore l'église et les villageois sur les trottoirs, les géraniums rouges sur les tombes du cimetière, l'évanouissement de Pérez (on eût dit un pantin disloqué) . . ." (p. 29).

It is the order of events connected with attending the wake and the funeral that constitutes the linear sequence so far. The main events that follow are related to the preceding ones only in time. Nevertheless, there are some motifs, introduced with a seemingly incidental intent, which do constitute at least a certain thematic transition: (*a*) Meursault's reflections on the reasons for which his employer was apparently displeased with his absence; (*b*) Marie's being taken aback when she finds out that Meursault's mother has just died; (*c*) Meursault's reluctance to go for lunch at Céleste's and to be asked questions about the funeral; (*d*) Meursault's brief comment about the size of his apartment, which has been too large for him since his mother had moved to Marengo; and (*e*) finally, as the Sunday is drawing to a close, Meursault's conclusion that his mother is now buried, that he is going to resume his work, and that the interruption of his routine for two days has not made any change in his life.

Thus these few motifs that do relate to the preceding ones all pertain to his mother and the funeral. But the main incidents deal with occurrences that take place on the two days following the burial. Thematically they stand, in some respects, in sharp contrast to some of the preceding themes. The harassment, the haste, the formal solemnity we have noted give way either to a leisurely, pleasurable activity, or to a calm detached observation and inactivity.

Meursault's record of his day on the beach with Marie shows a singular lack of any reported conversation. We do note her remark that her body is more tanned than his, that she wishes to see a Fernandel movie, and we are told that on noticing Meursault's black tie, she wants to know whether he is in mourning. Finally she explains to Meursault her reason for not staying with him on Sunday. Except for these trivial comments and her silent shock at hearing of his mother's death, we know only that Meursault touches her body, hears her frequent laughter, and enjoys the sun and water with her. Though we are told that the movie was on the whole rather bad, we are really made far more aware of the fact that they touched, that they kissed—though Meursault did not think they kissed well—and that they went to his apartment after the show. The day is devoted to sensuous and sensual pleasures and remains almost undisturbed except for his uneasiness caused by intimated or assumed expectations of his having to conform to established rules or consecrated customs. With this exception of his feeling somewhat at fault when he realizes Marie's shock, Meursault's day passes in joyful self-indulgence, in freedom from any social or spiritual constraining consciousness. Twice on that day we hear him reflect on his not feeling responsible for occurrences that place him sufficiently in the wrong to feel prompted to justify himself, as he perceives himself in the light in which others see him. He can understand his employer, in whose eyes he gained four days away from work when in the normal order of things he should have had only the weekend. But Meursault rightly thinks that he cannot be blamed that his mother was buried before the weekend, and therefore he does not feel personally responsible for gaining two extra days. We know that the employer himself had not remarked on this trivial matter and that it was Meursault's own interpretation of his employer's mood which prompted his self-justification. Regardless of the triviality and the illusory nature of the matter that prompts self-justification, it is Meursault's feeling of being at fault that matters, for it reveals his attitude. It is the notion that there is a right and a wrong, and that one may be considered to be in the wrong while feeling he is in the right, that seems to make Meursault feel uneasy. The second time Meursault almost tries to justify himself is at the moment he realizes Marie's shock. But this time he does not do so, remembering the meaninglessness and foolishness of claiming not to be at fault when he spoke to his employer. This suggests that it is useless to claim innocence on grounds of not having caused a wrong. One is still at fault, he feels, and the most plausible conclusion one may draw is that one's fault lies either in having to choose between two unavoidably conflicting obligatory courses (he can please his employer by not going to the funeral, or may go to the funeral and presumably displease his employer); or of choosing between what appears as a conventional obligation, and one's own pleasure. Since renouncing one's pleasure would be futile in view of the conventional nature of the obligation, one gives preference to one's pleasure but at the same time one places oneself in the wrong from the standpoint of conventional notions of right and wrong. Meursault does choose his pleasure just as he did when he chose to smoke during the wake. From his choice we may deduce his appraisal and conclude that conventions are of no significance to him because they do not imply reflection before an act, because they reduce man to the status of an automaton. When faced with a conventional obligation, Meursault asks himself wherein the importance of the convention lies. When he did decide to smoke, he did so upon reflection: "J'ai réfléchi, cela n'avait aucune importance."

On the following day Meursault, as a bored and apathetic observer, watches from his balcony the typical patterns of Sunday occurrences in the street. At first the emptiness of the street, then the appearance of bourgeois respectability on display, then young people in their Sunday suits crowding the trolleys and laughing loud on their way to the movies or to a soccer game. Then the lazy silence of the street, accentuated by the tobacconist sitting and staring in front of his store and by the waiter sweeping the floor of the empty café. Finally the gradual return of the strollers and of the young people filling the streets until darkness. Thus ends the day of conventional rest, of planned and arranged pleasures and excitements, the Sunday ritual which Meursault can observe from his balcony as a spectacle of regulated customs seen from a height and from a perspective that make the spectacle appear engulfed in form and in time within which gestures and sounds emerge as ephemeral affectations of prestige or as equally ephemeral spurts of exultation and playfulness. All, including the tobacconist and the waiter, follow the patterns in which Sunday has drawn its presence and has reduced the people, whose actions trace the imposed patterns, to marionettes on what becomes a mimic stage when seen from the distance of Meursault's balcony.

Upon his return to the office, Meursault is pleased to find that his employer shows a kindly concern and that in his eyes the death of Meursault's mother is finished business. There are two additional references to the death of Meursault's mother on the Monday after his return: one in Céleste's kindly welcome, the other in Raymond's concern and encouragement. What is more interesting, however, from the point of view of Meursault's attitude is the revealing context in which these references occur. The first, brought up in the conversation with his employer, is embedded in the following manner: "Le patron a été aimable. Il m'a demandé si je n'étais pas trop fatigué et il a voulu savoir aussi l'âge de maman. J'ai dit 'une soixantaine d'années', pour ne pas me tromper et je ne sais pas pourquoi il a eu l'air d'être soulagé et de considérer que c'était une affaire terminée" (p. 40). Meursault, we have noted, is concerned about his employer's attitude toward him, and he likes to please him. In fact we have found him identifying himself with his employer to such an extent that he felt even his unexpressed emotions or guessed his thoughts. Here we see Meursault recognizing simply through an impression that his employer felt "relieved" and that he considered the matter closed. But we know that Meursault has previously guessed his employer's thoughts largely by projecting his own thoughts onto the mind of his employer, who, after all, did not utter any of the thoughts with which Meursault has credited him. We also know that Meursault himself had already considered the matter of his mother's death as closed: "J'ai pensé que c'était toujours un dimanche de tiré, que maman était maintenant enterrée, que j'allais reprendre mon travail et que, somme toute, il n'y avait rien de changé" (p. 39).

That the matter was indeed closed to him becomes even more evident in the course of the second reference, in his brief conversation with Céleste: "Nous sommes arrivés en nage chez Céleste. Il était toujours là, avec son gros ventre, son tablier et ses moustaches blanches. Il m'a demandé si 'ça allait quand même'. Je lui a dit que oui et que j'avais faim" (p. 42). He does not react to Céleste's remark in any way other than by acknowledging that all goes well "quand même," and in the same breath he confirms this by announcing that he is hungry—to all appearances, his only concern.

The third reference at first hides his unconcern, for it is presented against a background of his misunderstanding of Raymond's allusion: "J'ai dû avoir l'air fatigué parce que Raymond m'a dit qu'il ne fallait pas se laisser aller. D'abord, je n'ai pas compris. Il m'a expliqué alors qu'il avait appris la mort de maman mais que c'était une chose qui devait arriver un jour ou l'autre. C'était aussi mon avis" (p. 51). Meursault's last remark confirms his indifference, and it is due only to Raymond's assumption and phrasing that Meursault's indifference appears as the result of his having reconciled himself to an unavoidable reality.

Apart from these instances that refer to materially relatable antecedent motifs, we are introduced to new and different sets of motifs pertaining to Meursault's pleasures and exhilarations, and to others which reveal his attitudes when he is faced with human relationships, attitudes some of which show already familiar features.

We see Meursault enjoying wiping his washed hands on a clean towel before leaving the office for lunch. We hear him complain about the towel's being wet when the office closes at night. To his employer all that is merely regrettable, but in contrast to Meursault's opinion, of no importance. We see him, on the spur of the moment, run after a truck and let himself be submerged in the noise, the dust, and in his view of the blurred horizon along the pier. We see him dripping with perspiration arrive at Céleste's restaurant. He is hungry, eats hurriedly, drinks much wine, takes coffee, returns home for a nap, wakes up, has a desire to smoke, and returns in a hurry to his office. All these details pertaining to his physical needs or desires are mentioned, but about his work very little is revealed, though we are told that he worked all afternoon and that it was hot in the office. On his return from his office in the evening, however, we do learn what makes him happy and contented, and what he was going to fix for supper: "Il faisait très chaud dans le bureau et le soir, en sortant, j'ai été heureux de revenir en marchant lentement le long des quais. Le ciel était vert, je me sentais content. Tout de même, je suis rentré directement chez moi parce que je voulais me préparer des pommes de terre bouillies" (p. 42).

Then we meet Salamano and his dog. Three times we are told that this peculiar relationship has lasted for eight years. What makes Salamano so angry with his dog is the enervating immutability of their unvarying relationship. When Meursault wants to know what the dog had done to make Salamano angry, the old man answers with suppressed rage: "Il est toujours là." While Céleste considers Salamano's relationship to his dog unfortunate, and Raymond thinks that it is disgusting, to Meursault it is not so, and his "au fond, personne ne peut savoir" simply suggests that in his mind a relationship, however irritating, may yet have its compensations. From Meursault's description one may even conclude that such compensations are the effects of a strange accord, an irritating accord, but a sustaining one.

The other incident pertains to Raymond. First Mersault accepts his invitation to supper because that saves him the trouble of having to cook his own. Though Raymond is disliked in the neighborhood, Meursault feels that, as far as he himself is concerned, he has no reason not to speak to him. Evidently, Meursault does not judge Raymond. He listens very carefully to Raymond's account of his mistress' betrayal; when asked for his opinion, he simply acknowledges the story to be interesting, but offers no opinion. Although it seems to him that Raymond was betrayed, he does not know what he himself would do in the same situation. He can understand Raymond's wanting to punish his mistress, but he does not know whether he himself would punish the woman. When Raymond unfolds his crude and cruel plan for a punishment, Meursault merely agrees that she would indeed be punished in that manner. When asked whether he would write the letter, Meursault does not answer, but when asked "si cela m'ennuierait de le faire toute de suite," he does not object. It appears that he does not write the letter because he wants to write it—in fact he seems indifferent—but he does write it to please Raymond: ". . . je me suis appliqué à contenter Raymond parce que je n'avais pas de raison de ne pas le contenter" (pp. 50–51). He has no positive reason to please Raymond, but he wishes to please him, for he has no reason not to do so. We may conclude that Meursault's action is not based on an evaluation of its particular merits, but that he chooses to please by his action if he sees no reason not to please and if his indifference to the action itself precludes a negative stand. When, finally, Raymond, who is pleased with the letter, assumes a familiar tone and declares Meursault to have become his friend, the latter merely acknowledges this by saying "yes." Once again we find the same attitude: "Cela m'était égal d'être son copain et il avait vraiment l'air d'en avoir envie" (p. 51).

So far, Meursault's accounts have permitted the incidents to be placed on individual dates. Then we are given a mere glimpse of the uneventful yet pleasant banality of his experiences which in retrospect reduce a week to a few fleeting moments of quiet satisfaction and mild amusements: "J'ai bien travaillé toute la semaine, Raymond est venu et m'a dit qu'il avait envoyé la lettre. Je suis allé au cinéma deux fois avec Emmanuel qui ne comprend pas toujours ce qui se passe sur l'écran. Il faut alors lui donner des explications" (p. 53). Thereupon the weekend's events are related. First Meursault's and Marie's day on the beach. Then, on Sunday morning, their witnessing of Raymond's altercation with his mistress, Meursault's and Raymond's afternoon, and finally their encounter with Salamano who has lost his dog.

As before, we see Meursault's sensuous and sensual pleasures, and more significantly, his awareness and not merely his experience thereof. Marie excites Meursault's desires and he seeks their gratification. His sensitivity is sensuous, not emotional. When asked whether he loves Marie, he tells her "que cela ne voulait rien dire, mais qu'il me semblait que non." When they hear Raymond beat his mistress, Marie asks Meursault to call the police. Instead of showing any emotion or even concern, Meursault explains his unwillingness to intervene by saying that he does not like policemen. He hears the woman's screaming, he observes and records every detail of Raymond's brutality and of his subsequent humiliation and embarrassment, yet he remains entirely unaffected. After the scene in front of Raymond's apartment, Marie does not eat her lunch—we are told only that she was not hungry—but Meursault does eat almost the entire meal, and later he takes a nap. It does not occur to him to go and see Raymond. When the latter comes to him in the afternoon, Meursault remains stretched out on his bed and listens to his neighbor's account. Thereupon he remarks without any reference to what he has heard or witnessed: "Je lui ai dit qu'il me semblait que maintenant elle était punie et qu'il devait être content" (p. 58). When Raymond, whose pride was hurt when he was struck by the policeman, asks Meursault for his reaction, Meursault reveals a complete lack of empathy: not only did he not put himself in Raymond's place to see whether he would have expected him to strike back, he actually states "je n'attendais rien du tout" and that, besides, he did not like policemen. He does note, however, that this remark pleased Raymond very much.

Completely unaware of his part in serving as Raymond's witness, Meursault agrees to be a witness when told that he would merely have to state that Raymond was let down by the woman. When the two men walk home later in the evening, and Raymond, pleased with his vengeance, shows kindness to his new friend, Meursault notes: "Je le trouvais très gentil avec moi et j'ai pensé que c'était un bon moment" (p. 59). It seems as if he had this feeling of contentment because of the accord between himself and Raymond, not a harmony based on a similarity of dispositions, but one based on contrasting yet complementary attitudes: Raymond involved through vanity and vindictiveness, and Meursault, a willing but completely indifferent accomplice, enjoy their union to which the latter brings impassible understanding, and the former the kindness nurtured by gratification. We are reminded of Meursault's vaguely conceived assumption of a possible accord between Salamano and his dog. From the point of view of thematic coherence it is then not surprising for us to see suddenly Meursault and Raymond approaching their home and finding at the doorstep Salamano looking in vain for his dog. Although the old man does not stop cursing his mangy lost companion, he is visibly distressed over the loss, for he does not know what will become of him if he should be left alone. Before he goes to sleep, Meursault hears through the thin walls the old man crying, and this makes him think of his mother. Thematically we understand this association of ideas when we relate it to her crying at Marengo after she has left her accustomed, though hardly happy, life with her son.

We have seen that it is a matter of some concern to Meursault whether his employer is pleased with him or not. He is in fact, at least to a certain extent, sensitive to the approval of others. He is willing to gain approval if his action supposed to elicit approval is in itself of no importance to him —if he can act with indifference. But he does risk the displeasure of others when he is supposed to act, or refrain from acting, and if his customary mode of existence is thereby affected. He is worried lest Raymond's telephone call irritate his employer, and he expects a reprimand; on the other hand when he is offered a better position in Paris, he refuses: "J'aurais préféré ne pas le mécontenter, mais je ne voyais pas de raison pour changer ma vie." His stated reasons for refusing the offer shed some light on his indifference. To him one life is as good as another. We are told that as a young student he had ambitions, but when he had to give up his studies he very soon understood "que tout cela était sans importance réelle." What he seems to have sought were the simple pleasures which man can find as he passes through life, and not the causes and undertakings which promise success and exultation. Seen from this point of view, what man may be able to change in his life is the cause, the frequency, the degree of exultation. What Meursault calls his life can neither be changed nor made better or worse by changing the nature of one's work. The simple pleasures in life may be found everywhere if one knows how to recognize them and if one has the ability to savor them.

It is in the light of his desire to bring contentment and to please—but without becoming emotionally committed—that Meursault's attitude to marriage needs to be understood. When asked by Marie, he does not mind marrying her. He is glad to please her just as he is glad to please his employer or Raymond. In his eyes, marriage is not a serious matter. He reiterates his admission that he does not love her, and he also assures her that he would "naturally" marry any girl with whom he may find himself in a similar relationship. There is no doubt that it is his affection without commitment that Marie considers odd ("bizarre"). She knows that she loves him for that reason, but she fears that for the same reason she may some day find him repulsive. What seems to Marie particularly odd is Meursault's emotional indifference and his lack of empathic concern. He feels her reproach and tries to justify himself by maintaining that he does feel empathic concern, but that he does not think of it. Since empathic concern is manifest only when thought of, we must conclude that Meursault claims to have the capacity for it but fails to project himself. This lack of projection simply implies a disregard for motivations or purposes of other people; it also implies a disregard for the consequences of decisions and actions. His perception of life is bounded by the here and now, and such limitations exclude imagination and the conception of the present from the point of view of its future effects. They therefore preclude forethought, ambitions, and any commitments with long range effects. Hence such ties as friendship, love, or marriage have little if any significance for him, and prospects pertaining to his career as such do not interest him.

While these characteristics appear odd to Marie, the opposite characteristics appear odd to him. The description of the automaton woman who joins him at his table at Céleste's restaurant is intended to point out among other things the contrast between spontaneity born of indifference to foresight and the systematically and meticulously premeditated plans and actions that preclude the slightest deviation from an unwaveringly chosen course.

Without any obvious transition we are once again, as if by chance, facing Salamano, whose dog is now irretrievably lost. In vain does Meursault suggest that Salamano get himself another dog: ". . . il a eu raison de me faire remarquer qu'il était habitué à celui-là" (p. 68). It seems implied that Meursault recognizes habit—not affection—as the basis of loyalty. Salamano got his dog after his wife's death, and what we know of his relationship to his dog is echoed by the following reference to his marriage: "Il n'avait pas été heureux avec sa femme, mais dans l'ensemble il s'était bien habitué à elle. Quand elle était morte, il s'était senti très seul" (pp. 68–69). When they happen to speak of Meursault's mother, Salamano expresses the assumption that Meursault must feel unhappy since his mother's death, for he knows that Meursault loved his mother very much. In the light of Salamano's experiences we may judge that Meursault did not even have to break the habit of living with his mother: "D'ailleurs, ai-je ajouté, il y avait longtemps qu'elle n'avait rien à me dire et qu'elle s'ennuyait toute seule" (p. 70). It seemed to him natural to send his mother to Marengo since he could not afford to keep a nurse for her. In his loneliness Salamano agrees: "Oui, m'a-t-il dit, et à l'asile, du moins, on se fait des camarades" (p. 70). Seen with Salamano's eyes, Meursault's separation from his mother is not only approved, it is actually to be preferred to the silent loneliness in which she spent her days with her son.

On the fateful Sunday on which Meursault destroys "the equilibrium of the day" and kills "on the beach on which he was happy" a man for no apparent reason, he wakes up with a slight headache, is hit by the glare of the sun as he steps with Marie into the street, and does not eat because they plan to swim as soon as they reach the water. The sea is smooth and bursting with light. Seeing the cheerful happiness of the Masson couple in their beach cottage, Meursault is for the first time really thinking of getting married. The sunlight is making him feel better, but in spite of his eagerness to plunge into the water, he yields to its attraction with calculated restraint. He enjoys the cool water and consciously delights in the perfect accord of his and Marie's mood and movements as they swim away from the shore. When he gets tired, he swims back to the beach and again consciously indulges in the pleasure of his regular strokes and deep breathing. He stretches out on the sand, buries his face in it, and is filled with sensuous enjoyment. When Marie stretches out next to him, he yields to the warmth of her body and of the sun and falls asleep. Before they go to lunch, Marie reminds him that they have not kissed since the morning. Meursault notes: "C'était vrai et pourtant j'en avais envie." Although he has shown complete indifference to any emotional commitments, and no desire for any emotional involvement beyond the point in time in which it holds out the promise of a pleasurable fulfillment, he has not shown himself oblivious to the prospect of such a fulfillment. That this was mere oblivion is shown by the pleasure he feels when they embrace in the shallow water on the shore. While one may not be able to ascribe his oblivion to any particular cause, it is still possible to perceive the circumstances under which it has occurred. The distractions of their visit to Masson's cottage, the earlier headache, the encounter with the Arabs before boarding the bus, the glare of the water, the heat of the sun, the relief in the cool waves, the pleasurable exertion of good swimming, and finally the sand's soothing warmth penetrating his exhausted body, first absorb and then dull the senses by an abundance of impressions to which mind and body yield without allowing latent desires to reach the consciousness of the mind.

After their copious early lunch, Masson and Meursault take a walk at noon on the deserted beach. Again, circumstances assume significance where causes either fail to appear or remain concealed in barely suggested emotional dispositions. Most of the intensely felt circumstances, to which Meursault makes reference from this point on, pertain to the heat and glare, the sounds and the silence on the beach, for example:

> Le soleil tombait presque d'aplomb sur le sable et son éclat sur la mer était insoutenable (pp. 78–79).

> On respirait à peine dans la chaleur de pierre qui montait du sol (p. 79).

> Quelquefois, une petite vague plus longue que l'autre venait mouiller nos souliers de toile. Je ne pensais à rien parce que j'étais à moitié endormi par ce soleil sur ma tête nue (p. 79).

When they meet the Arabs, and just before Raymond and Masson engage in a fight with them, Meursault notes: "Le sable surchauffé me semblait rouge maintenant" (p. 80). After inflicting several wounds on Raymond, the Arabs run away "pendant que nous restions cloués sous le soleil et que Raymond tenait serré son bras dégouttant de sang" (p. 81).

It is Meursault who has to explain to Mrs. Masson and Marie what has happened. In view of the tears of the former and of Marie's having turned pale, he states: "Moi, cela m'ennuyait de leur expliquer. J'ai fini par me taire et j'ai fumé en regardant la mer" (pp. 81–82). No cause is given for Meursault's feeling upset although it is conceivable that the emotional re-action of the women presents him with so obvious a display of empathic involvement that he is silenced and made to turn his eyes away toward the sea, in whose impassible nature, we may assume, he perceives a sympathetic and harmonious counterpart to his own.

When Raymond returns gloomily from the doctor, he insists on going alone down to the beach. Meursault follows Raymond in spite of Masson's advice. The depiction of circumstances stands out again: "Nous avons marché longtemps sur la plage. Le soleil était maintenant écrasant. Il se brisait en morceaux sur le sable et sur la mer. . . . Tout au bout de la plage, nous sommes arrivés enfin à une petite source qui coulait dans le sable, derrière un gros rocher (p. 82)." There they find the two Arabs peacefully stretched out in the sand. One of them "soufflait dans un petit roseau et répétait sans cesse, en nous regardant du coin de l'oeil, les trois notes qu'il obtenait de son instrument" (p. 83). On three other occasions we find references to the notes the Arab is playing amidst the heat of the sun, the silence, and the murmuring sound of the brook: "Pendant tout ce temps, il n'y a plus eu que le soleil et ce silence, avec le petit bruit de la source et les trois notes" (p. 83).

Upon careful reflection and with a display of unusual intervention, Meursault restrains Raymond and prevents him from killing the Arab. Then the description of the encounter is interrupted in the following manner: "On a encore entendu le petit bruit d'eau et de flûte au cœur du silence et de la chaleur" (p. 83). After a new and successful intervention Meursault prevents Raymond from shooting and takes his gun from him:

> Quand Raymond m'a donné son revolver, le soeil a glissé dessus. Pourtant, nous sommes restés encore immobiles comme si tout s'était refermé autour de nous. Nous nous regardions sans baisser les yeux et tout s'arrêtait ici entre la mer, le sable et le soleil, le double silence de la flûte et de l'eau. J'ai pensé à ce moment qu'on pouvait tirer ou ne pas tirer (p. 84).

Even the flute and the water are silenced, and in this silence between the sea, the sand, and the sun, time seems suspended and thus any action as well. In this momentary standstill, the harmony of unbroken suspense is saved—the Arabs withdraw and Raymond and Meursault return to the cottage. Having reached it, Raymond climbs up the wooden steps, but Meursault feels unable to follow him. Although he mentions both the physical and the emotional effort, and although both seem to him sufficiently discouraging at the moment of facing them, it still remains a question which of the two is the more forbidding. To Meursault at least the physical effort of staying in the sun is about the same as that of climbing the steps:

> Je l'ai accompagné jusqu'au cabanon et, pendant qu'il gravissait l'escalier de bois, je suis resté devant la première marche, la tête retentissante de soleil, découragé devant l'effort qu'il fallait faire pour monter l'étage de bois et aborder encore les femmes. Mais la chaleur était telle qu'il m'était pénible aussi de rester immobile sous la pluie aveuglante qui tombait du ciel. Rester ici ou partir, cela revenait au même. Au bout d'un moment, je suis retourné vers la plage et je me suis mis à marcher (p. 84).

But his decision, despite the assumed equality of efforts, clearly points toward a preference. We may conclude that, at the moment of his decision, it is the additional effort of confronting the feminine sensitivity that determines the choice. The unendurable heat on the beach would obviously appear the greater obstacle to physical comfort if the efforts of either climbing the steps leading to the sheltering cottage or of staying out in the sun were solely to be considered. Even if the emotional effort is the obvious immediate determinant, it does not seem to be the only one, for Meursault braves the heat and walks toward the rocks and the brook:

> C'était le même éclatement rouge. Sur le sable, la mer haletait de toute la respiration rapide et étouffée de ses petites vagues. Je marchais lentement vers les rochers et je sentais mon front se gonfler sous le soleil. Toute cette chaleur s'appuyait sur moi et s'opposait à mon avance. Et chaque fois que je sentais son grand souffle chaud sur mon visage, je serrais les dents, je fermais les poings dans les poches de mon pantalon, je me tendais tout entier pour triompher du soleil et de cette ivresse opaque qu'il me déversait. A chaque épée de lumière jaillie du sable, d'un coquillage blanchi ou d'un débris de verre, mes mâchoires se crispaient. J'ai marché longtemps (p. 85).

That he hoped to find relief, rest, solitude, and refuge by the brook from which the two Arabs had fled is clearly shown in the following passage:

> Je voyais de loin la petite masse sombre du rocher entourée d'un halo aveuglant par la lumière et la poussière de mer. Je pensais à la source fraîche derrière le rocher. J'avais envie de retrouver le murmure de son eau, envie de fuir le soleil, l'effort et les pleurs de femme, envie enfin de retrouver l'ombre et son repos (p. 85).

The presence of Raymond's enemy there is surprising and disappointing to Meursault, who came to the brook without a thought of the incident. This encounter, which ends in the killing of the Arab, cannot be explained in terms of premeditation or motivation, nor can a cause be readily determined; but the circumstances can.

While the Arab holds his knife and Meursault his revolver, both are ready to defend themselves, but neither seems to consider provoking the other. Furthermore, the distance between them is sufficient to preclude a clash and to enable both to keep a constantly watchful eye on each other. This is an important circumstance, for it permits a stalemate; but the oppressive heat is beginning to make itself felt in the balance of the silent suspense:

> Je devinais son regard par instants, entre ses paupières mi-closes. Mais le plus souvent, son image dansait devant mes yeux, dans l'air enflammé.

Le bruit des vagues était encore plus paresseux, plus étale qu'à midi. C'était le même soleil, la même lumière sur le même sable qui se prolongeait ici. Il y avait déjà deux heures que la journée n'avançait plus, deux heures qu'elle avait jeté l'ancre dans un océan de métal bouillant. A l'horizon, un petit vapeur est passé et j'en ai deviné la tache noire au bord de mon regard, parce que je n'avais pas cessé de regarder l'Arabe (p. 86).

As before, when Meursault stood in the same place with Raymond and realized that either a fatal course or a silent withdrawal was still possible, now again a simple turning away of his body could eliminate the threat. But he feels, just as then, hemmed in and pushed by the heat: "Mais toute une plage vibrante de soleil se pressait derrière moi. J'ai fait quelques pas vers la source. L'Arabe n'a pas bougé. Malgré tout, il était encore assez loin" (pp. 86–87). It is interesting to note the wording "vers la source" (instead of, for example, "toward the man"), a wording that lends added emphasis to the pressure of the heat and thus to his search for the relief he hopes to find at the brook, rather than to a provocative step which he did not even consider. He was, in fact, thinking of turning away.

Under the impact of the burning heat, Meursault—helpless yet fully aware—makes another move forward. He thus reduces the margin of safe distance, and the danger of a clash becomes imminent.

La brûlure du soleil gagnait mes joues et j'ai senti des gouttes de sueur s'amasser dans mes sourcils. C'était le même soleil que le jour où j'avais enterré maman et, comme alors, le front surtout me faisait mal et toutes ses veines battaient ensemble sous la peau. A cause de cette brûlure que je ne pouvais plus supporter, j'ai fait un mouvement en avant. Je savais que c'était stupide, que je ne me débarrasserais pas du soleil en me déplaçant d'un pas. Mais j'ai fait un pas, un seul pas en avant. Et cette fois, sans se soulever, l'Arabe a tiré son couteau qu'il m'a présenté dans le soleil (p. 87).

With the sun's rays still pouring fire on him, and with cautious distance reduced to explosive proximity, hurt to the point of feeling wounded by the light reflected by the knife's blade, blinded by the sweat that covers his eyes, the last safeguard—watchfulness—is lost. The whole body stiffens with pain, and the pressure of the tightly held gun releases the trigger. The fatal shot is the sound of the body's contraction under pain, proximity is the spatial circumstance that favors reaching the aim, and momentary blindness is a break in the saving watchfulness. The dry and deafening sound of the shot awakens the mind to a grasp of the reality with which it finds itself confronted: "J'ai compris que j'avais détruit l'équilibre du jour, le silence exceptionnel d'une plage où j'avais été heureux" (p. 88).

Having understood what he has destroyed, and no longer under the sole impact of pain and tension, he shoots four more times "sur un corps inerte où les balles s'enfonçaient sans qu'il y parût" (p. 88). It is the "alors" in "Alors, j'ai tiré encore quatre fois" (p. 88) that may contain an explanation of the question raised repeatedly during the later investigation and to which Meursault can find no answer. The "corps inerte" offers sufficient evidence that Meursault knew his victim was already dead. The apparent absurdity of the act, for which he naturally cannot give a reason, becomes less meaningless when seen in its context. It becomes an act of rage and despair—senseless as most such acts are—but conceivable. Seeing what he has done, he knows that he is doomed to unhappiness: "Et c'était comme quatre coups brefs que je frappais sur la porte du malheur" (p. 88). It seems he was seeking to relieve his wretchedness by taking vengeance on the inert body of his victim, the body which now blocked the road leading back to happiness.

Once in prison, Meursault is faced with the necessity of recognizing his identity during his meetings with the examining magistrate and with the lawyer the court has appointed for him. One is tempted to see in his "il s'agissait d'interrogatoires d'identité qui n'ont pas duré longtemps" an intended emphasis on his unawareness of what the trial means—a necessary emphasis, since most of the second part of the work is devoted to an examination of his identity by raising his attitudes to the level of awareness. The initial stage of the investigation elicits an admission of the spontaneity of his past reactions. Hence his surprise when asked to explain the emotions that accompanied them:

Il m'a demandé si j'avais eu de la peine ce jour-là [i.e., on the day of his mother's funeral]. Cette question m'a beaucoup étonné et il me semblait que j'aurais été très gêné si j'avais eu à la poser. J'ai répondu cependant que j'avais un peu perdu l'habitude de m'interroger et qu'il m'était difficile de le renseigner (pp. 93–94).

Just as at Marengo, he is again confronted with strange conventions and with expectations of attitudes and beliefs he cannot recognize as his own. After the first meeting with the magistrate, he wants to shake the latter's hand, but remembers just in time that one does not shake hands with a killer. In the beginning he does not take the magistrate seriously—as if the investigation were a mere ritual without importance. He does not see why he needs a lawyer and seems slightly amused to find that the court should appoint one for his defense. The magistrate smiles when Meursault declares his case to be simple, but he does not seem to perceive the humor in Meursault's last remark because he takes the law

69

seriously: "J'ai trouvé qu'il était très commode que la justice se chargeât de ces détails. Je le lui ai dit. Il m'a approuvé et a conclu que la loi était bien faite" (p. 92). Meursault seems to find his lawyer dressed according to some prescribed uncomfortable fashion "in spite of the heat" just as he found the director at Marengo to be.

Far more significant than these external conventions are the emotions and attitudes approved and expected by convention which Meursault is expected to have felt and displayed. While the lawyer actually subjects Meursault to the realization of the differences between what he did feel and what he should properly have felt, Meursault is given to understand that he is not being judged for a single deed alone. For his deed to be judged justly, it must be considered in the light of revelations about his personality. When he fails to perceive the relationship between his deed and his personality, it is pointed out to him that he does not understand the ways of the law. He is told that he showed callousness on the day of the funeral, and he is warned that he will have to be able to give good reasons for that attitude at the trial. Obviously, one is not supposed to be insensitive on such occasions. The helpful lawyer suggests that Meursault might have been stricken with grief which could account for his behavior. However, Meursault, who has lost the habit of self-inquiry, cannot confirm having felt such an approved emotion. In an apparent effort to show himself cooperative, he states: "Sans doute, j'aimais bien maman" but finds the statement rather meaningless. We may assume that this is due to his failure to recognize the need of being stricken with grief merely because the person for whom one feels affection is inevitably no longer alive. His statement of affection does not satisfy the lawyer, who becomes even more disturbed by Meursault's subsequent comment: "Tous les êtres sains avaient plus ou moins souhaité la mort de ceux qu'ils aimaient" (p. 94). None of Meursault's final explanations appears acceptable: in vain does he claim that his feelings were generally affected by his physical needs, that he had been tired, sleepy, and unaware of what was going on, but that he was able to state with certainty that he would have preferred it had his mother not died.

In view of Meursault's inadequacy in measuring up to his lawyer's expectations of what proper and respectable attitudes are, the lawyer himself offers once more an estimable explanation: "Il m'a demandé s'il pouvait dire que ce jour-là j'avais dominé mes sentiments naturels" (p. 94). Meursault refuses the explanation "parce que c'est faux." It would seem as if he were intent on emotional and intellectual honesty. While it is true that he happens to be sincere, it is also likely that his sincerity is the result of spontaneity rather than of a considered adherence to principles. (No principle was detectable as governing his decision to write the letter for Raymond; he wrote it simply to please Raymond and saw no reason not to please him.) He would like to be understood and appreciated as he is and not for any principles he might adhere to: "Surtout, je voyais que je le mettais mal à l'aise. Il ne me comprenait pas et il m'en voulait un peu. J'avais le désir de lui affirmer que j'étais comme tout le monde, absolument comme tout le monde" (p. 95). This statement suggests what we may believe to be Meursault's assumption that to be everyman means to be natural, that is, whatever one happens to be spontaneously and without regard for particular principles to which one is known to subscribe.

What the examining magistrate wants Meursault to be is exactly what everyman is not, namely, committed in a particular manner. The magistrate's reasoning seems to imply that *every man* has a commitment that lends meaning to his actions and to his life, and that "everyman" has no reality. Why, he insists on knowing, did Meursault pause between the first and the following shots? For him an action can be only the visible expression of an attitude or of an intention—actual or virtual. What possible reason, he seems to wonder, other than vicious cruelty could have motivated such a useless show of brutality? Meursault can only feel that there was no cause and is therefore unable to offer a satisfactory answer. The heat, the pain, the tension were circumstances, not causes. It appears that for the magistrate there can hardly exist any other reason for the deed than sinful cruelty, and therefore he expects Meursault—if he is a Christian—to feel remorseful and repentant. That is why he pulls out the crucifix and demands to know if Meursault knows its meaning and whether he is aware that a repentant sinner may earn forgiveness. Meursault does not understand the magistrate's action or his reasoning, for he can see only the surface of phenomena, not their source, and their surface is for him on the same level of perception as the heat in the room or the flies that come to rest on his face.

For the magistrate, life has meaning only because it has a spiritual foundation. To him it is therefore inconceivable for man to detach the surface from its foundation, to see life without a faith in God. For Meursault, the meaning of life is in the momentary experience of perception and feeling. On the magistrate's insistence, he agrees that Christ has suffered for him, but he agrees only because it is hot and because he hopes to rid himself thereby of the man he does not understand. That Meursault's concurrence was without conviction, in fact without much

71

understanding, can be seen in his denial of faith and of any expectation of solace just when the triumphant magistrate hopes to have at last convinced him to recognize that the meaning of life is rooted in its spiritual foundation.

Although Meursault has not been able to grasp or to accept such a meaning of life, he does, without fully realizing all the implications of his reflections, explain at least to himself his reason for rejecting the magistrate's belief. The latter reproaches him for his "âme endurcie" and tries to show him that every criminal he has ever known shed tears upon beholding "the image of pain" on the crucifix. Meursault certainly does not feel like a criminal because he does not feel guilty: "J'allais répondre que c'était justement parce qu'il s'agissait de criminels. Mais j'ai pensé que moi aussi j'étais comme eux. C'était une idé à quoi je ne pouvais pas me faire" (pp. 100–101). Technically he is a criminal because he did kill, but he cannot accept the notion of being a criminal because his act, as he experienced it, was not only free of criminal intent; it actually occurred against his intention. Since he does not feel guilty, he does not feel any real remorse and, therefore, no urge for repentance: ". . . plutôt que du regret véritable, j'éprouvais un certain ennui" (p. 101). Judging by the description of his experience during the shooting, all that he can feel is to have been an instrument—hence his distinction between real remorse and vexation.

Meursault was thus forced to take a stand against the searching questions raised by the magistrate and by his lawyer. To some he had no answer, and he rejected suggested answers to others. During the eleven months of investigation he became aware of the proceedings not only as being a strange ritual one could observe dispassionately but also as serving to awaken his awareness of himself. If they did not reveal to him his identity for what it was, at least he was given an opportunity to recognize what it was not.

The isolation in prison probes his identity further by removing him from experiences in which he was used to sensing pleasure or in which he moved on the surface of indifferent observation. When he hears that Marie, who was allowed to visit him once, is not permitted to come again, Meursault suddenly feels his isolation: ". . . de ce jour-là, j'ai senti que j'étais chez moi dans ma cellule et que ma vie s'y arrêtait" (p. 104). It is through not being able to have what he is missing and through the manner in which he finds compensations that Meursault learns the meaning of freedom and the value of purposeful reminiscence and reflection as means to overcome the restriction of being reduced exclusively to his own resources. In the beginning he misses the beach and the sea in which he used to feel a deliverance from the sensation of the burden of his body. He is troubled by his desire for a woman or for a cigarette. After a few months, however, the effort he has to make in allowing time to pass helps him acquire the habit of filling every moment with sleep, with memories, with the prison routine, and with rereading the story of the Czechoslovak. To some extent he loses the sense of time, but only of time in the past or in the future, not that of the yesterday and the tomorrow and especially not that of the today. The immediacy of each present moment oppresses him with the same massive concreteness and density as the walls of his cell or as the heat on the beach did when it blocked his movements. Physically confined in space and mentally restricted in time, he remembers a comment the nurse made during the funeral: "Non, il n'y avait pas d'issue." Cut off from the fulfillment of desires or from the pursuit of spontaneous inclinations, he is reduced to reliving in his memory past pleasures, past observations of things that surrounded his existence, and to rereading the same piece of miscellaneous news about a man who jestingly, yet with fatal results, concealed his identity. Meursault recaptures his self, his past identity, in his memories, in his desires, in his former pleasures, and in the things among which he moved. The memory of his life in freedom fills his life in captivity. When he feels that there is no way out, he seems to mean that there is no way out from enforced monotony in space and time: "Lorsqu'un jour, le gardien m'a dit que j'étais là depuis cinq mois, je l'ai cru, mais je ne l'ai pas compris. Pour moi, c'était sans cesse le même jour qui déferlait dans ma cellule et la même tâche que je poursuivais" (p. 115). It is not his former way of life—that which constitutes his identity—that Meursault would think of changing; in fact, the memory of it consoles him, and the lack of freedom to live it again oppresses him. What seems to fascinate him in the story he finds in the old newspaper is not so much the fate of the man who denied his identity as the image that reflects the opposite of his self which he would not change nor conceal—not even in a jest— for he seems to have recognized it in the mirror of alternatives as unalterably his own.

When the trial begins, Meursault does not feel scared. He knows that it is he who stands trial, but he does not quite understand what is involved, just as he did not understand what was involved in the preliminary investigation. He is again an outsider and an observer at yet another strange ritual. He feels as if he were exposed to the curious gaze of people who seek to discover his peculiarity:

Tous me regardaient: j'ai compris que c'étaient les jurés. Mais je ne peux pas dire ce qui les distinguait les uns des autres. Je n'ai eu qu'une impression: j'étais devant une banquette de tramway et tous ces voyageurs anonymes épiaient le nouvel arrivant pour en apercevoir les ridicules (p. 119).

At first he does not even realize that it is because of his case that the crowd is assembled in the courtroom:

Je crois bien que d'abord je ne m'étais pas rendu compte que tout ce monde se pressait pour me voir. D'habitude, les gens ne s'occupaient pas de ma personne. Il m'a fallu un effort pour comprendre que j'étais la cause de toute cette agitation (p. 119).

Not only does he not feel that he himself is involved, he even considers himself as an "intruder" as he watches everybody greeting everybody else in a closed world in which he feels out of place. When he is greeted by one of the journalists, he almost shows the embarrassment one feels when, in spite of one's inferior status, one hears a kind word in a gathering to which one really does not belong.

If Meursault was troubled by the rituals at Marengo, at least he managed to grasp them and even to free himself from succumbing to them when upon reflection they seemed to be senselessly exacting. But now the procedures at court are so strange to him that he cannot even quite grasp them "parce que je ne connaissais pas les usages du lieu . . . je n'ai pas très bien compris tout ce qui s'est passé ensuite" (p. 122). Initially he shows an interest in the court proceedings, but his bewilderment forces him into the role of a passive observer.

In addition to the witnesses, whom he knows and who take the stand one after another, he also notices two other individuals in the courtroom. Their presence, it seems, places the testimony of the witnesses and the declarations of the prosecutor and of his lawyer into a special perspective. One is a journalist who gives Meursault the odd impression of being watched by himself. The other is the little automaton, the woman who impressed him by her punctiliousness at the restaurant. Unlike the journalist, she is the very opposite of himself. These silent witnesses of the trial represent, it seems, Meursault's own purposeless spontaneity in action and unawareness of the consequences for which he is tried on the one hand, and on the other the calculated purposefulness in the name of which he is to be condemned. The court seeks motivations and purposes, but not in the spirit of the previous preliminary investigations, the aim of which was benevolent understanding. Motivations and purposes are now being sought with a self-righteous certainty of their existence, with the aim of uncovering them and of revealing the depravity and guilt of the man who failed to perceive them in the light of a prevailing morality. Meursault is finally presented with an image of his identity. This time, however, he is not merely made to grasp what he is not; by probing each reason for each act, he is made to understand what he really seems to be when judged from the point of view of principles and conventions to which his fellow men subscribe. In that view, each act is explicable on ethical grounds and is related to every other act because they are determined by one basic attitude. In that view, there is no chance, there are no random occurrences, and there is no freedom to appraise an act on its own merits without reference to its presumed essential worth.

Meursault feels at first only as an intruder, but during the proceedings he is actually largely excluded from participation. He becomes a case and has no chance of intervening or of affecting the course of events. This circumstance has a twofold effect. First it isolates the case of the prosecution and allows it to stand out against the guilt-laden, apologetic, and therefore unsuccessful, defense. Secondly, and as a consequence of the first effect, Meursault is forced to remain an observer. This time again, just as during the investigation, he does not witness merely a strange ritual toward which he can feel indifferent; he is made to see himself.

He is credited with intelligence and consciousness. He is assumed to be the master of his will, fully aware of his reasons for action. Therefore, he is made to bear complete responsibility, especially since his general attitude and the logical sequence of events preclude any extenuating circumstances. At one point he is even made to admit to himself that the prosecutor's "façon de voir les événements ne manquait pas de clarté. Ce qu'il disait était plausible" (p. 141).

He is made to recognize that he has shown no contrition and not even remorse. In his earlier talks with the magistrate he expressed annoyance rather than remorse because he felt no real guilt. Now that the prosecutor seems to have established his guilt before the court, Meursault no longer attributes his lack of remorse to a feeling of innocence but to a simple human disposition to be completely absorbed in the present and in the immediate future without looking back with searching reflections upon past attitudes, feelings, and actions. It is equally interesting to note that he no longer feels that he has the right to be without remorse, for under the impact of the prosecution he is made to grasp that spontaneity may not be a valid justification where premeditation is presumed to govern human behavior. Furthermore, Meursault is shown that guilt in action and unrepentance have roots in the "soul." He hears the prosecutor accusing him of not having a soul, of not having any principles to guard him against crime and thereby to move his heart by a sense of guilt. He is depicted as a callous monster, as a menace to society whose most essential rules he has flouted.

Meursault shows no direct appraisal of the point of view that led to this judgment and verdict. When given an opportunity to comment on the verdict, he limits his statement, after reflection, to a mere "no." This may simply mean that he feels unable to comment in accordance with the trend of thought that has led to the verdict, but it may also mean that the particular point of view from which his identity as a guilty and unrepentant monster has been revealed to him and to others has left him with such a sense of repugnant distortions that all he can do is to reject it. We may conclude that such is indeed his indirect appraisal of the proceedings and of the judgment, for while his lawyer rambles on, Meursault's reflection reveals his nostalgia for the simple life that is no longer his, and it further reveals the nauseating futility of the trial.

A la fin, je me souviens seulement que, de la rue et à travers tout l'espace des salles et des prétoires, pendant que mon avocat continuait à parler, la trompette d'un marchand de glace a résonné jusqu'à moi. J'ai été assailli des souvenirs d'une vie qui ne m'appartenait plus, mais où j'avais trouvé les plus pauvres et les plus tenaces de mes joies: des odeurs d'été, le quartier que j'aimais, un certain ciel du soir, le rire et les robes de Marie. Tout ce que je faisais d'inutile en ce lieu m'est alors remonté à la gorge et je n'ai eu qu'une hâte, c'est qu'on en finisse et que je retrouve ma cellule avec le sommeil (p. 148).

He also questions the finality of the verdict which was arrived at by mere people whose unerring judgment can hardly be taken for granted since they are subject to habits and influences which by themselves affect the thought that leads to decisions. Furthermore, the verdict is pronounced in the name of a nebulous notion of the French people rather than in the name of a lucid and incontrovertible concept of justice.

Thus while logic may render a judgment plausible, the facts on which the logic rests may be simply assumed without their truly reflecting the reality from which they are supposedly drawn. Secondly, the decision based on a logical judgment is itself precarious, and in view of its questionable basis it is doubly unreliable. Yet despite the elusiveness of facts and the questionableness of judgment, the earthly destiny of man pronounced guilty in the light of such a judgment follows an "imperturbable" course.

Meursault discovers at last the "disproportion ridicule" between untenable verdicts and the rigid irresistible rituals enforced by them. One complies or one is crushed. If one cannot comply nor evade the consequences of non-compliance, there is no escape in space and none in time. There is no room to move—just as in Meursault's tiny cell, where his gaze can free itself from the constraining walls only by a view of the sky which, as it changes from morning to morning, becomes a visible measure of time in which the ritual runs its undeviating course. The end of this course is marked by the cutting edge of the guillotine, by death. The priest's opinion according to which all men are condemned to death lends a special meaning to the verdict based on false assumptions and precarious judgments. Death remains inevitable, but here, because of human intervention, it is hastened and is the direct effect of the "rite implacable" and thus the effect of Meursault's failure to comply with the constraining conventions and rituals which determined his guilt as much as or more than the murder. Meursault's wish for at least the slightest chance of eluding his premature and contrived death becomes by implication also a wish to elude the rituals he was guilty of ignoring. His wish is also a desire for at least a brief extension of his span of life just long enough to relive the exhilaration of freedom he knew and in the enjoyment of which he was free to neglect the thought of death.

This realization, this joyful awareness of being alive and free, can only become intensely experienced at the sight of an execution and while one's joy of living is poisoned: the brutal contrast between life and death, between joyful freedom and the nauseating trap of ritualized life and murder is, it seems, for Meursault the most immediate road by which his heart approves the spontaneous love of his earthly life and resolutely rejects the conventional principles or institutionalized mores. This seems to be the meaning of his exclamation:

> Comment n'avais-je vu que rien n'était plus important qu'une exécution capitale et que, en somme, c'était la seule chose vraiment intéressante pour un homme! Si jamais je sortais de cette prison, j'irais voir toutes les exécutions capitales. J'avais tort, je crois, de penser à cette possibilité. Car à l'idée de me voir libre par un petit matin derrière un cordon d'agents, de l'autre côté en quelque sorte, à l'idée d'être le spectateur qui vient voir et qui pourra vomir après, un flot de joie empoisonnée me montait au cœur (p. 155).

The priest, who senses this attitude but cannot comprehend it, asks him therefore in a reproachful tone: "Aimez-vous donc cette terre à ce point?" (p. 167).

At the height of his awareness, Meursault finally, and yet for the first time, fully grasps both the indifference and the tenderness of the universe. In these qualities he recognizes the reflection of his own attitudes that gave him his happiness in the freedom of living the life of tender indifference and that still give him happiness in the knowledge of finding at least in his mind self-justification through the harmony between the world and himself: ". . . vidé d'espoir, devant cette nuit chargée de signes et d'étoiles, je m'ouvrais pour la première fois à la tendre indifférence du monde. De l'éprouver si pareil à moi, si fraternel enfin, j'ai senti qui j'avais été heureux, et que je l'étais encore" (pp. 171–72).

Throughout the story and with steadily increasing clarity and intensity, Meursault learns to appreciate his way of life, his love of life, for he learns to distinguish it from the life he rejects because of the striking contrast the two modes of living present, and because of the hateful contempt with which men reject and condemn him. In their furious rejection and murderous condemnation Meursault finds the proof of the meaning and value of life he has assigned to it—intuitively at first and consciously at last. For the sake of that proof, and in order to feel less lonely among men by being made to feel tenderly united with his world, his last wish is a call for a resoundingly imposed alienation: "Pour que tout soit consommé, pour que je me sente moins seul, il me restait à souhaiter qu'il y ait beaucoup de spectateurs le jour de mon exécution et qu'ils m'accueillent avec des cris de haine" (p. 172). With that justification he can meet death convinced that he had a good life, that he like everyone else was among the privileged, the ones privileged to live it simply, freely, and tenderly. This is why he tells the priest that if he were granted to live beyond the grave, he would like his life to be "une vie où je pourrais me souvenir de celle-ci." If he could, he would like to begin the same life all over again, a wish that evokes the final remembrance of his mother:

Pour la première fois depuis bien longtemps, j'ai pensé à maman. Il m'a semblé que je comprenais pourquoi à la fin d'une vie elle avait pris un "fiancé", pourquoi elle avait joué à recommencer. Là-bas, là-bas aussi, autour de cet asile où des vies s'éteignaient, le soir était comme une trêve mélancolique. Si près de la mort, maman devait s'y sentir libérée et prête à tout revivre. Personne, personne n'avait le droit de pleurer sur elle (p. 171).

The privilege of life is so great that those who have found its earthly promise fulfilled may well be envied but never mourned. Thus even his seeming insensitiveness, which was at the base of his condemnation, appears to him justified. Meursault rises as judge of his judges, and he condemns them for their false assumptions and for their spurious emotions.

Meursault is almost to the end an unmotivated character encountering more or less motivated representatives of a system of principles which he can hardly grasp, representatives whose purpose it is to insure man's adherence to their principles. This encounter, as well as others, is due to a number of contingent incidents. Among these there are two which Camus introduces to make the encounter possible. One is the death of Meursault's mother, the other the presence of the Arab at the brook. Meursault finds himself in what Heidegger calls *"Dasein,"* an existing situation in which he becomes aware of the conditions within an order he not only has not created but finds so alien that he cannot accept it when it has entered his consciousness. The contingency of the incidents serves to manifest the basic concept of this "plot" in which the main character is not endowed with a "nature," except that of "tendre indifférence," and is therefore lacking in motivation and purpose and consequently does not generate incidents. Instead, his nature evolves in reaction to contingencies, to existence. The narrative presentation of these and other contingencies endows the incidents with the semblance of chance occurrences, and Meursault's reactions with the spontaneity of intuitive responses to contingent incidents.

From the point of view which assumes human nature a priori, and therefore premeditative awareness, purpose, motivation, a clear chain of intended events linked in the order of cause and effect, chance occurrences and spontaneous reactions are suspect:

> Raymond a dit que ma présence à la plage était *le résultat d'un hasard.*[2] Le procureur lui a demandé alors comment il se faisait que la lettre qui était à l'origine du drame avait été écrite par moi. Raymond a répondu *que c'était un hasard.* Le procureur a rétorqué *que le hasard* avait déjà beaucoup de méfaits sur la conscience dans cette histoire. Il a voulu savoir si c'était *par hasard* que je n'étais pas intervenu quand Raymond avait giflé sa maîtresse, *par hasard* que j'avais servi de témoin au commissariat, *par hasard* encore que mes déclarations lors de ce témoignage s'étaient révélées de pure complaisance (p. 135).

Thus we see that the story presents Meursault in a chain of spontaneous reactions to contingent situations but with a gradual and finally clearly evolving purposeful stand toward them. As far as Meursault is concerned, the story presents him in the existentialist perspective of existence preceding essence. By contrast it reveals his antagonists with an already set nature, with

---

[2] Italics are mine unless otherwise indicated.

consciousness of intention and purpose. They are endowed not only with conscious intention; they are and expect others to be intentionally conscious. Without consciously intentional or subconsciously intended purposes a plot structure is hardly conceivable, for causal coherence rests on the impression of plausible necessity by which purposes or motivations engender consequences. Furthermore, since the purposes of some characters elicit in other characters either agreement or opposition, we must assume that manifestations of agreement or opposition are to be expected. Instead of a manifest agreement with the purposes of others Meursault shows at best acquiescence, and instead of showing manifest opposition we find him, for example, during the investigation and during his trial, either agreeing to differ or withdrawing into passive resistance except in his encounter with the priest. His mere acquiescence appears clearly in his contingent encounter with Raymond where an actual agreement with the latter's purposes would stamp Meursault as an accomplice, or else his opposition would make him a character whose principles would not permit even the mildest indifference. The text has shown Camus' utmost concern with the presentation of Meursault's acquiescence both in writing the letter and in serving as a witness. Meursault does not agree with Raymond's purpose, he merely understands his neighbor's intention; he does not act for himself, he acts for Raymond whom he has no reason not to please (". . . parce que je n'avais pas de raison de ne pas le contenter"). He does believe Raymond that the girl had let him down and that is all he is asked to declare as a witness.

His acquiescence and his passive resistance divest the work to a considerable extent of its plot structure, but it is worth reminding ourselves that this structural feature is the necessary consequence of Camus' presentation of Meursault's gradually evolving awareness in a series of encounters in life. Meursault cannot be accused of callous indifference in the particular encounter with Raymond because he is shown not to have acquired as yet an awareness that might induce him to take a resolutely opposing stand. In fact, this encounter seems intended to demonstrate, at this point in time, the degree of Meursault's worldly unawareness of the life he is facing, and his inability to envisage consequences by transcending his present and by projecting himself into the future. Meursault must act in the manner in which he does in order to permit us to see his evolving personality. Camus had to divest this adult of the maturity we could expect from a man in real life in order to be able, with the help of this device, to lead Meursault, the adult, from an at least minimally plausible unawareness to a relatively hastened awakening of consciousness within the short span of the accountable time in the story.

Agreement or opposition is recognizable by some manifestation of word or action. Meursault barely acts and only grudgingly communicates. These characteristics are among the visible manifestations of his acquiescence and of his passive resistance. His communicativeness, even eloquence, in his encounter with the priest stands in sharp contrast to any previous form of self-expression by which he reveals himself to others.

There is a significant linking image depicting the visitors' room in prison. The description of the room itself suggests Meursault's difficulty in communicating in a situation established for the purpose of communication by word of mouth. The prisoners are separated from their visitors by a wide corridor formed by two high iron grilles. The spatial and material obstacles of this separation suffice to represent the intellectual and emotional obstacles a message encounters in its efforts to bridge the gap between one mind and another. The shouting voices of those around Meursault create a commotion and a confusion defeating the purpose of the meeting of minds. But the silent presence of a watchful guard at one end of the corridor between the grilles reduces even further the liberty of expression already limited by the mere presence of other people, however unconcerned. The loud disconnected chatter of the fat woman who is laughing and yelling with her strident voice, who brings a basket to her husband and tells him to check its contents, seems to represent the assertiveness of banality and petty concerns which dispel anxiety and overcome fear. On the other hand the little old woman with her tight-set lips and the young son she is visiting impart their feelings to each other without uttering a word by fixing their eyes on each other with a mournful passionate gaze. They transmit to the reader their anxiety, their solitude, their longing, as well as their tacit submission to a condition against which they seem helpless. Two sets of motifs carrying contrasting correlative themes are thus juxtaposed: the world of active, aggressive, self-centered, self-assured, loud, and optimistic triviality in which the pettiest concerns assume an inordinate importance and absorb existence to the point where the absence of freedom to live goes unnoticed; the other in which the anxiety of living deprived of freedom and the fear of the rule of an implacable order reduce men to the realization of the futility of any self-assertion, of the vanity of opposition, and of the compelling force that constrains its victim to yield to surrender. Although one cannot equate the purpose of the former with the purposes of the court, one can detect parallels between Meursault's reactions, in so far as they are devoid of conceptual assumptions, to the gesticulating, yelling, and self-confident couple on the one hand, and to the strikingly similar aspects of the lawyers in court on the other. Hence that world foreshadows the court and its purposes as perceived by Meursault before conceptual assumptions enter his consciousness.

Meursault stands physically between those two worlds in the visitors' room. Here, as in life, he feels attracted to those who acquiesce and submit in silence, although he himself does not do so without some "tendre indifférence," without some mental reservations, without some compulsion during physical discomfort, and without increasing and finally rebellious opposition to the insistent admonition that he consent to what he feels would amount to his intellectual disfigurement. The world of self-assured gestures and vociferous self-righteousness causes at first only uneasiness, but his uneasiness gradually turns to aversion, repugnance, and rejection. Seen with Meursault's eyes, which perceive the court and its purposes at first only through its perceptible outward manifestations, the court is identified with the world of the screaming couple. Just as this couple is juxtaposed in the image to the silent mother and son, in the plot, too, the world of the court is juxtaposed to the world of Meursault. These worlds exist side by side without affecting each other until the order of the courts is violated, until living infringes on purposes held inviolable. The life which has no other purpose than living may take its purposeless course until some contingency proves that it is lacking in purposes consecrated by tradition. Then the court judges life and seeks to uncover the cause of the violation in the firm belief that any life has purposes which the court is bound to safeguard. Purposelessness is seen as a threat to life, for life must rest on the direction purposes prescribe, and it derives its worth from achieving them.

Surveying the incidents with a distanciated vision we recognize their contingent nature as their most striking characteristic in the first part of the work. The events and circumstances confronting Meursault are contingent, and their sequence gives the appearance of having been chosen at random except for the two main contingent events at the beginning and at the end of the first part. Even Meursault's reactions, especially his negative reactions, give in most cases at least the impression of being contingent partly because they seem devoid of any manifest purpose (as for instance when he refuses his employer's offer, or when he cannot attach any importance to marriage). Partly it is the contingency of the stimulus which endows his reactions with a sort of reflected contingency, although a closer analysis does reveal in Meursault at least faint predispositions. In the second part the stimuli to Meursault's reactions follow a set course; they are predetermined by procedure and Meursault's reactions are gradually forced into a clearer pattern within which, as we have noted, his initial uneasiness turns to aversion and ultimately to a resolute rejection motivated by a recognition of his own purposes. Thus the central theme of the story is Meursault's transition from an intuitive acquiescing tender indifference or passive resistance in face of contingencies to a conscious acceptance and approval of his emotional non-commitment, of his ever-renewable spontaneous joy of free living in face of an order that demands emotional commitments, regardless of their authenticity and in face of a ritualistic predetermined course of life, the final rewards of which are to be sought in the faith in an immortal soul. And the central theme of the plot is first the challenge of contingencies to instinctive or intuitive predispositions and then the challenge of a purposeful order to a mind that discovers the gratuitous nature of purposes that seek fulfillment beyond earthly life. If we were to express this confrontation in terms established in existentialist nomenclature, we could say that Meursault, the *être pour-soi*, the man reflecting upon himself and recognizing in the rigid and unchangeable system of principles facing him an immutably arrested *être en-soi*, makes his conscious and free choice in favor of a Gidean disponibility and rejects the force bent on fixing his identity by imposing upon it arbitrary assumptions and a prescribed course of attitude and action.

The Generic Coherence of Themes

In *La Symphonie pastorale* the sequential progression of incidents can be reconstructed in spite of frequent time-shifts, and the segmental themes derived from that progression reveal definite linear thematic developments, particularly Gertrude's intellectual ascent and the pastor's gradual transition from charity to hedonic love. The progression of incidents in *L'Etranger* follows without time-shift a straight linear sequence with often clearly marked points in time, but in the first part of the work segments of incidents are materially frequently disconnected. Consequently the themes carried by these segments show no linear coherence. The segments, however, do achieve coherence—generic coherence. The impression of a mere contiguity of themes is primarily the result of the material difference of the segments of incidents, and it is reinforced by the already mentioned device of chance occurrence. This characteristic pertains to the death of Meursault's mother; to his first meeting with Marie ("J'ai retrouvé dans l'eau Marie Cardona" [p. 32]); to Salamano ("En montant, dans l'escalier noir, j'ai heurté le vieux Salamano" [p. 42]); or later in chapter IV ("De loin, j'ai aperçu sur le pas de la porte le vieux Salamano" [p. 59]); to Raymond

("Juste à ce moment est entré mon deuxième voisin de palier" [p. 44]). Meursault's visit with Raymond, during which the former becomes his neighbor's acquiescing tool, is also presented as a chance occurrence ("Nous sommes montés et j'allais le quitter quand il m'a dit" [p. 45]). The same applies to Meursault's encounter with the Arab on the beach before the shooting ("J'avais envie de retrouver le murmure de son eau, envie de fuir le soleil, l'effort et les pleurs de femme, envie enfin de retrouver l'ombre et son repos. Mais quand j'ai été plus près, j'ai vu que le type de Raymond était revenu" [p. 85]). When asked at the trial why he had returned to the place where he found the Arab, Meursault answers: "c'était le hasard" (p. 125). Raymond, too, states at the trial that the occurrence at the beach was a matter of chance.

In the second part there is a core of sequentially and materially coherent segments. The trial and the anticipated execution constitute in scope and importance the major segments of motifs, and by virtue of their regulated prescriptive nature they eliminate any impression of chance occurrences. Thus in comparing the segments of the first part with one another we note that all incidents, except those in chapter I, occur either by chance or appear to be brought about by spontaneous inclinations. In contrast with that, almost all incidents within chapter I are imposed and regulated by exigencies of convention, custom, and ritual. This chapter and most of the second part have this feature in common.

In formulating the central themes of story and plot, we noted Meursault's initial uneasiness in face of a ritualistic adherence to principles and convention, and his final rejection of mandatory attitudes and forms of conduct. This theme is complemented and contrasted by that of his initially intuitive love of life turning to a conscious belief in the value of life itself —of living regardless of rigid principles one's adherence to which is claimed to endow life with meaning and value. These two themes are brought into an interrelationship by the *thematic development of Meursault's gradual rise toward self-discovery,* a clear perception of his identity, and finally to a conscious and resolute self-assertion. This is a *development* in the sense that we can establish a change from Meursault's early uncertainty and awkwardness, due to his ignorance of conventional proprieties; a change from his feelings of guilt and from his apologies when first confronted with principled or at least conventional attitudes and conduct, to his rejection of these principles, conventions, and conduct. Finally, his development culminates in a conscious acceptance of the "tendre indifférence" of nature as *the* natural and human attitude worth taking in view of death's being the great equalizer, the force without compassion that renders each life of the same supreme worth and offers man at each moment a chance and encouragement to renew his life. It is this equalizing force which bids man to remain instinctively and intuitively attached to the experience of living rather than intellectually or spiritually attached to some particular form of life in which the mode of living takes precedence over living itself.

The theme of ritualistic adherence to principles, convention, and custom has its own development, and we find it in the first part primarily in chapter I and then in the whole of the second part, where it is treated with increasing intensity at the highest point of which it is supported by the complementary *theme of inevitable rigidity* with which ritualistic adherence is inforced. The theme of ritualistic adherence to principles, conventions, and custom is particularly reinforced by the *theme of the worth of life being dependent on a commitment to certain beliefs* which alone endow life with meaning, and in the absence of which living becomes not only worthless but criminal, since human relations rest on a commitment to beliefs and to the form in which they achieve an assured manifestation.

Camus draws a clear distinction between habit and custom. Habit is a pattern into which man falls by dint of sheer repetition of actions or by simple perseverance in certain modes of existence. In *L'Etranger* custom and rite are manifestations of an actual procedural order derived from a conscious commitment to that order or at least from a subliminally accepted validity of it. Before we proceed with the presentation of the textual development of the theme of ritualistic adherence to principles, convention, and custom, the distinction between habit and ritualistic custom may be usefully demonstrated. We shall note that a few linking phrases provide revealing indications; they will appear in brackets whereas other pertinent passages will be in italics in the subsequent quotations.

The following quotation depicts habit as the result of a mechanical and even comforting expectation of the known which does not necessitate an active search and therefore does not elicit a creative urge to discover the new: "J'ai pris l'autobus à deux heures. Il faisait très chaud. J'ai mangé au restaurant, chez Céleste, [comme d'habitude]" (p. 10). In the following passage Camus shows the power habit has of creating attachments, of substituting itself for an emotion, of leading to a confusion between itself and an affection.

> Quand elle était à la maison, maman passait son temps à me suivre des yeux en silence. Dans les premiers jours où elle était à l'asile, elle pleurait souvent. Mais [c'était à cause de l'habitude]. *Au bout de quelques mois, elle aurait pleuré si on l'avait retirée de l'asile.* [Toujours à cause de

l'habitude.] C'est un peu pour cela que dans la dernière année je n'y suis presque plus allé (p. 12).

This is an instance in which Camus points to an effect of habit which Meursault is able to escape largely because of his disposition to resist emotional involvements and attachments. The pathos in the situation of Meursault's mother is that she identifies habit with love, be that emotion genuine or a mere substitute.

Meursault is aware of the grotesque features of habitual and unchanging appearances: "Nous sommes arrivés en nage chez Céleste. [Il était toujours là,] avec son gros ventre, son tablier et ses moustaches blanches" (p. 42). It is interesting to note that the phrase "Il était toujours là" recurs in a reference Salamano makes to his dog. One can hardly escape the impression that Meursault is feeling resentful of the emotional commitment and loyalty to which habit impels its victims. The grotesque nature of sentimentality by habit is clearly depicted by Salamano's routine that enslaves him. A set of linking phrases, referring to recurrence and duration in time, has the effect of underscoring in an apparently purposely exaggerated manner Salamano's enslavement by sentimentality sustained by habit alone:

Salamano était en train d'insulter son chien. Il lui disait: "Salaud! Charogne!" et le chien gémissait. J'ai dit: "Bonsoir", mais le vieux insultait toujours. Alors je lui ai demandé ce que le chien lui avait fait. Il ne m'a pas répondu. Il disait seulement: "Salaud! Charogne!" Je le devinais, penché sur son chien, en train d'arranger quelque chose sur le collier. J'ai parlé plus fort. Alors sans se retourner, il m'a répondu avec une sorte de rage rentrée: ["Il est toujours là."] (pp. 43–44).

En montant, dans l'escalier noir, j'ai heurté le vieux Salamano, mon voisin de palier. Il était avec son chien. [Il y a huit ans qu'on les voit ensemble.] (p. 42).

Ils ont l'air de même race et pourtant ils se détestent. Deux fois par jour, à onze heures et à six heures, le vieux mène son chien promener. [Depuis huit ans,] ils n'ont pas changé leur itinéraire (p. 43).

Le chien rampe de frayeur et se laisse traîner. A ce moment, c'est au vieux de le tirer. Quand le chien a oublié, il entraîne de nouveau son maître et il est de nouveau battu et insulté. Alors, ils restent tous les deux sur le trottoir et ils se regardent, le chien avec terreur, l'homme avec haine. *C'est ainsi tous les jours.* Quand le chien veut uriner, le vieux ne lui en laisse pas le temps et il le tire, l'épagneul semant derrière lui une traînée de petites gouttes. Si par hasard le chien fait dans la chambre, alors il est encore battu. [Il y a huit ans] que cela dure. Céleste dit toujours que "c'est malheureux," mais au fond, personne ne peut savoir (p. 43).

But when habit turns into a compulsive or even rigid ceremonial performance, a tone of irony pervades the description, as in the depiction of the
Sunday performance Meursault watches from his balcony:

> Ma chambre donne sur la rue principale du faubourg. L'après-midi était
> beau. Cependant, le pavé était gras, les gens rares et pressés encore.
> C'étaient d'abord des familles allant en promenade, deux petits garçons
> en costume marin, la culotte au-dessous du genou, un peu empêtrés dans
> leurs vêtements raides, et une petite fille avec un gros nœud rose et des
> souliers noirs vernis. Derrière eux, une mère énorme, en robe de soie
> marron, et le père, un petit homme assez frêle que je connais de vue. Il
> avait un canotier, un nœud papillon et une canne à la main. En le voyant
> avec sa femme, j'ai compris pourquoi dans le quartier on disait de lui qu'il
> était distingué. Un peu plus tard passèrent les jeunes gens du faubourg,
> cheveux laqués et cravate rouge, le veston très cintré, avec une pochette
> brodée et des souliers à bouts carrés. J'ai pensé qu'ils allaient aux cinémas
> du centre. C'était pourquoi ils partaient si tôt et se dépêchaient vers le tram
> en riant très fort (p. 35).

The irony is even more pronounced in his depiction of the automaton
woman:

> J'ai dîné chez Céleste. J'avais déjà commencé à manger lorsqu'il est
> entré une bizarre petite femme qui m'a demandé si elle pouvait s'asseoir
> à ma table. Naturellement, elle le pouvait. Elle avait des gestes saccadés
> et des yeux brillants dans une petite figure de pomme. Elle s'est débarrassée
> de sa jaquette, s'est assise et a consulté fiévreusement la carte. Elle a appelé
> Céleste et a commandé immédiatement tous ses plats d'une voix à la fois
> précise et précipitée. En attendant les hors-d'œuvre, elle a ouvert son sac,
> en a sorti un petit carré de papier et un crayon, a fait d'avance l'addition,
> puis a tiré d'un gousset, augmentée du pourboire, la somme exacte qu'elle
> a placée devant elle. A ce moment, on lui a apporté des hors-d'œuvre qu'elle
> a engloutis à toute vitesse. En attendant le plat suivant, elle a encore sorti
> de son sac un crayon bleu et un magazine qui donnait les programmes
> radiophoniques de la semaine. Avec beaucoup de soin, elle a coché une à
> une presque toutes les émissions. Comme le magazine avait une douzaine
> de pages, elle a continué ce travail méticuleusement pendant tout le repas.
> J'avais déjà fini qu'elle cochait encore avec la même application. Puis elle
> s'est levée, a remis sa jaquette avec les mêmes gestes précis d'automate et
> elle est partie. Comme je n'avais rien à faire, je suis sorti aussi et je l'ai
> suivie un moment. Elle s'était placée sur la bordure du trottoir et avec une
> vitesse et une sûreté incroyables, elle suivait son chemin sans dévier et sans
> se retourner. J'ai fini par la perdre de vue et par revenir sur mes pas. J'ai
> pensé qu'elle était bizarre, mais je l'ai oubliée assez vite (pp. 66–67).

Where habit does not force upon one any emotional commitment to any person, where it is primarily an acquired particular pattern of attitude and conduct, its cessation may indeed be painful, but its replacement by another habit, unfailingly adopted in the course of time, does bring comfort:

> Il y a eu aussi les cigarettes. Quand je suis entré en prison, on m'a pris ma ceinture, mes cordons de souliers, ma cravate et tout ce que je portais dans mes poches, mes cigarettes en particulier. Une fois en cellule, j'ai demandé qu'on me les rende. Mais on m'a dit que c'était défendu. Les premiers jours ont été très durs. C'est peut-être cela qui m'a le plus abattu. Je suçais des morceaux de bois que j'arrachais de la planche de mon lit. Je promenais toute la journée une nausée perpétuelle. Je ne comprenais pas pourquoi on me privait de cela qui ne faisait de mal à personne. Plus tard, j'ai compris que cela faisait partie aussi de la punition. Mais à ce moment-là, [je m'étais habitué] à ne plus fumer et cette punition n'en était plus une pour moi (pp. 111–12).

But the fact that a new habit provides some comfort does not make habit as such therefore desirable. Its possibly undesirable effects and its potential for the grotesque have already been pointed out. Yet in spite of Camus' relative disapproval of habit, he does nevertheless seem to show that by virtue of men's natural tendency to seek in habit a respite from the pace of living and even a consolation, habit is relatively more endurable and at times even more acceptable than its social manifestation: custom.

How clearly and how insistently Camus has treated the theme of habit in order to place later special emphasis on the partly similar, partly contrasting correlative theme of ritualistic custom, how he has wished to minimize the pain endured through the termination of one habit and the consolation brought by a new one, in contrast to the "coutume" and the "rite" to which one is made to submit, can be appreciated in the following passage:

> C'est peu après qu'elle m'a écrit. Et c'est à partir de ce moment qu'ont commencé les choses dont je n'ai jamais aimé parler. De toute façon, il ne faut rien exagérer et cela m'a été plus facile qu'à d'autres. Au début de ma détention, pourtant, ce qui a été le plus dur, c'est que j'avais des pensées d'homme libre. Par exemple, l'envie me prenait d'être sur une plage et de descendre vers la mer. A imaginer le bruit des premières vagues sous la plante de mes pieds, l'entrée du corps dans l'eau et la délivrance que j'y trouvais, je sentais tout d'un coup combien les murs de ma prison étaient rapprochés. Mais cela dura quelques mois. Ensuite, je n'avais que des pensées de prisonnier. J'attendais la promenade quotidienne que je faisais dans la cour ou la visite de mon avocat. Je m'arrangeais très bien avec le

reste de mon temps. *J'ai souvent pensé alors que si l'on m'avait fait vivre dans un tronc d'arbre sec, sans autre occupation que de regarder la fleur du ciel au-dessus de ma tête, [je m'y serais peu à peu habitué.]* J'aurais attendu des passages d'oiseaux ou des rencontres de nuages comme j'attendais ici les curieuses cravates de mon avocat et comme, dans un autre monde, je patientais jusqu'au samedi pour étreindre le corps de Marie. Or, à bien réfléchir, je n'étais pas dans un arbre sec. Il y avait plus malheureux que moi. C'était d'ailleurs une idée de maman, *et elle le répétait souvent, [qu'on finissait par s'habituer à tout.]* (pp. 109–10).

It is carefully structured: first we are told that the pain must not be over-emphasized ("il ne faut rien exagérer"), then the two parallel presentations of his thoughts as a free man and then those of a prisoner; these are followed by a depiction of the worst privation which could still have become a matter of habit ("je m'y serais peu à peu habitué") and would still have had its soothing effect; finally, the linking phrase alludes once more to Meursault's mother and evokes the significant point at which the theme of habit began to unfold.

The development of the theme of ritualistic customs begins with barely perceptible suggestions. At first, Meursault is merely confused, bewildered, and exhausted. However, the ritualistic procedures, the underlying order of which escapes him, become gradually and increasingly repugnant to him. He does not quite understand why his employer does not express his sympathy to him, but he assumes that there is probably a certain order to be followed, an order which his employer undoubtedly knows but which Meursault himself can only guess:

Mais il le fera sans doute après-demain, quand il me verra en deuil. Pour le moment, c'est un peu comme si maman n'était pas morte. Après l'enterrement, au contraire, ce sera une affaire classée et tout aura revêtu une allure plus officielle (p. 10).

Meursault does know, however, that he is expected to display the visible signs of mourning in order to conform with custom:

J'étais un peu étourdi parce qu'*il a fallu que je monte* chez Emmanuel pour lui emprunter une cravate noire et un brassard. Il a perdu son oncle, il y a quelques mois (p. 10).

At Marengo, he is obliged to see the director before seeing his mother, and he is expected to want to see her at the proper time:

J'ai voulu voir maman tout de suite. Mais le concierge m'a dit qu'*il fallait que je rencontre le directeur* (p. 11).

> Le directeur m'a encore parlé. Mais je ne l'écoutais presque plus. Puis il m'a dit: *"Je suppose que vous voulez voir votre mère."* Je me suis levé sans rien dire et il m'a précédé vers la porte (p. 12).

Much to his surprise, he finds out that his mother fell into the ritualistic pattern of her environment to the point of wishing to be buried with Church rites:

> "Un dernier mot: votre mère a, paraît-il, exprimé souvent à ses compagnons le désir d'être enterrée religieusement. J'ai pris sur moi de faire le nécessaire. Mais je voulais vous en informer." Je l'ai remercié. Maman, sans être athée, n'avait jamais pensé de son vivant à la religion (p. 13).

Even a handshake assumes a ceremonious function in this environment laden with rituals. Meursault does not grasp its meaning after the wake, but later, during the investigation, he is more sensitive to it, and refrains from shaking the magistrate's hand:

> En sortant, et à mon grand étonnement, ils m'ont tous serré la main— comme si cette nuit où nous n'avions pas échangé un mot avait accru notre intimité (p. 21).

> En sortant, j'allais même lui tendre la main, mais je me suis souvenu à temps que j'avais tué un homme (p. 92).

The procedure in the director's office is regulated to the point where even official signatures are timed. The director's formal attire before the funeral, his last offer to let Meursault see the body, and finally his order to seal the coffin all create the impression of carefully planned ceremonious arrangements:

> Le concierge a traversé la cour et m'a dit que le directeur me demandait. Je suis allé dans son bureau. Il m'a fait signer un certain nombre de pièces. J'ai vu qu'il était habillé de noir avec un pantalon rayé. Il a pris le téléphone en main et il m'a interpellé: "Les employés des pompes funèbres sont là depuis un moment. Je vais leur demander de venir fermer la bière. Voulez-vous auparavant voir votre mère une dernière fois?" (p. 22).

Meursault is embarrassed at the realization of his having objected to expected conduct in refusing to see his mother's body when the concierge offered to open the coffin:

> A ce moment, le concierge est entré derrière mon dos. Il avait dû courir. Il a bégayé un peu: "On l'a couverte, mais je dois dévisser la bière pour que vous puissiez la voir." Il s'approchait de la bière quand je l'ai arrêté. Il m'a dit: "Vous ne voulez pas?" J'ai répondu: "Non." Il s'est interrompu et j'étais gêné parce que je sentais que je n'aurais pas dû dire cela (p. 14).

90

On the other hand he feels at ease when he can recognize the reasonableness of a prescriptive custom; in fact he finds it interesting and right:

> Il m'avait dit qu'il fallait l'enterrer très vite, parce que dans la plaine il faisait chaud, surtout dans ce pays. C'est alors qu'il m'avait appris qu'il avait vécu à Paris et qu'il avait du mal à l'oublier. A Paris, on reste avec le mort trois, quatre jours quelquefois. Ici on n'a pas le temps, on ne s'est pas fait à l'idée que déjà il faut courir derrière le corbillard. Sa femme lui avait dit alors: "Tais-toi, ce ne sont pas des choses à raconter à Monsieur." Le vieux avait rougi et s'était excusé. *J'étais intervenu pour dire: "Mais non. Mais non." Je trouvais ce qu'il racontait juste et intéressant* (pp. 15–16).

But when he does not recognize the reason for obeying an assumed custom, he hesitates and, when he does not conceive of any reasonable objection and is not forewarned that there may indeed be one, he acts according to his own judgment.

> J'ai bu. J'ai eu alors envie de fumer. *Mais j'ai hésité parce que je ne savais pas si je pouvais le faire devant maman.* J'ai réfléchi, cela n'avait aucune importance. J'ai offert une cigarette au concierge et nous avons fumé (p. 17).

The concierge, who seems aware of Meursault's ignorance of what is expected, politely suggests at an appropriate moment that they do have their customs:

> A un moment, il m'a dit: "Vous savez, les amis de Madame votre mère vont venir la veiller aussi. *C'est la coutume.* Il faut que j'aille chercher des chaises et du café noir" (p. 17).

The phrase: "C'est la coutume" has its component motifs later in the second part where convention is presented not only as formalized but reasonably legalized as well. The examining magistrate not only points out that "la loi est là," he also remarks that "la loi était bien faite":

> Puis il a voulu savoir si j'avais choisi un avocat. J'ai reconnu que non et je l'ai questionné pour savoir s'il était *absolument nécessaire d'en avoir un.* "Pourquoi?" a-t-il dit. J'ai répondu que je trouvais mon affaire très simple. Il a souri en disant: "C'est un avis. Pourtant, *la loi est là. Si vous ne choisissez pas d'avocat, nous en désignerons un d'office.*" J'ai trouvé qu'il était très commode que la justice se chargeât de ces détails. Je le lui ai dit. *Il m'a approuvé et a conclu que la loi était bien faite* (pp. 91–92).

Similarly, during the trial, the judge reminds the director of the home at Marengo that he has to comply with legal procedure:

> . . . le président lui a demandé si c'était bien de moi qu'il avait parlé. Comme le directeur ne comprenait pas la question, il lui a dit: "C'est la loi" (p. 127).

How bewildering the procedure of the trial itself seemed to Meursault, can be judged not only from the confusion he shows before the hearings, but also from his own admission: "... *parce que je ne connaissais pas les usages du lieu,* que je n'ai pas très bien compris tout ce qui s'est passé ensuite" (p. 122).

Meursault's meeting with his lawyer can hardly fail to recall for us his meeting with the director at Marengo: the formal attire, despite the heat, the preparatory studies of the respective dossiers, even the studied informality of their behavior, clearly indicate the component quality of the motifs and Camus' apparent endeavor to point to the thematic correlation of the textually widely separated settings in which these materially similar motifs occur:

> Le lendemain, un avocat est venu me voir à la prison. Il était petit et rond, assez jeune, les cheveux soigneusement collés. Malgré la chaleur (j'étais en manches de chemise), il avait un costume sombre, un col cassé et une cravate bizarre à grosses raies noires et blanches. Il a posé sur mon lit la serviette qu'il portait sous le bras, s'est présenté et m'a dit qu'il avait étudié mon dossier (p. 93).

In one respect at least it would be justified to point to the component quality of one particular aspect of the settings themselves. During the wake, the bright lights and Meursault's solitary chair on one side of the coffin clearly place him in the limelight and under the observing gaze of those sitting on the other side, facing him. While that setting was simply annoying, the one in the magistrate's office, by virtue of its obviously yet incredibly ceremonious nature, is to Meursault actually amusing:

> *Au début, je ne l'ai pas pris au sérieux.* Il m'a reçu dans une pièce tendue de rideaux, il avait sur son bureau une seule lampe qui éclairait le fauteuil où il m'a fait asseoir pendant que lui-même restait dans l'ombre. *J'avais déjà lu une description semblable dans des livres et tout cela m'a paru un jeu* (p. 92).

And whereas at the wake the old man was silently watching the sleeping Meursault's indifference and even indolence, we find during the second session with the magistrate a more obviously procedural means of recording his views which cause the magistrate to exclaim: "Je n'ai jamais vu d'âme aussi endurcie que la vôtre."

> Peu de temps après, j'étais conduit de nouveau devant le juge d'instruction. Il était deux heures de l'après-midi et cette fois, son bureau était plein d'une lumière à peine tamisée par un rideau de voile. Il faisait très chaud. Il m'a fait asseoir et avec beaucoup de courtoisie m'a déclaré que mon

avocat, "par suite d'un contretemps", n'avait pu venir. Mais j'avais le droit de ne pas répondre à ses questions et d'attendre que mon avocat pût m'assister. J'ai dit que je pouvais répondre seul. Il a touché du doigt un bouton sur la table. Un jeune greffier est venu s'installer presque dans mon dos.

Nous nous sommes tous les deux carrés dans nos fauteuils. L'interrogatoire a commencé (pp. 95–96).

On the one hand, Meursault's inability to take ritualistic procedures seriously leads to his amusement, but on the other one must never forget that it also suggests the tragic irony with which Camus treats the fate of his somewhat Rousseauesque victim of a coercive order and of its formalized procedures. While Meursault puts himself into the role of the observer, he is at the same time in a favorable position to describe in a mildly mocking tone the scene, as its sounds evoke at first the merry vision of one of "ces fêtes de quartier."

A sept heures et demie du matin, on est venu me chercher et la voiture cellulaire m'a conduit au Palais de justice. Les deux gendarmes m'ont fait entrer dans une petite pièce qui sentait l'ombre. Nous avons attendu, assis près d'une porte derrière laquelle on entendait des voix, des appels, des bruits de chaises et tout un remue-ménage qui m'a fait penser à ces fêtes de quartier où, après le concert, on range la salle pour pouvoir danser. Les gendarmes m'ont dit qu'il fallait attendre la cour et l'un d'eux m'a offert une cigarette que j'ai refusée. Il m'a demandé peu après "si j'avais le trac". J'ai répondu que non. Et même, dans un sens, cela m'intéressait de voir un procès. Je n'en avais jamais eu l'occasion dans ma vie: "Oui, a dit le second gendarme, mais cela finit par fatiguer" (p. 118).

The component motif of the balcony scene in which he observed the Sunday parade is immediately recalled. In a parallel manner he perceives himself as the observed, as a particular specimen of man, different from the others, and who by virtue of this difference feels at first to be only incidentally amongst them, but who gradually finds out that he is actually excluded from their midst, and exposed to be seen in all his shocking aberrations from what is expected:

Après un peu de temps, une petite sonnerie a résonné dans la pièce. Ils m'ont alors ôté les menottes. Ils ont ouvert la porte et m'ont fait entrer dans le box des accusés. La salle était pleine à craquer. Malgré les stores, le soleil s'infiltrait per endroits et l'air était déjà étouffant. On avait laissé les vitres closes. Je me suis assis et les gendarmes m'ont encadré. C'est à ce moment que j'ai aperçu une rangée de visages devant moi. *Tous me regardaient: j'ai compris que c'étaient les jurés. Mais je ne peux pas dire ce qui les distinguait les uns des autres. Je n'ai eu qu'une impression: j'étais devant une [banquette de tramway] et tous ces voyageurs anonymes épiaient le nouvel arrivant pour en apercevoir les ridicules. Je sais bien que c'était une idée niaise puisque ici ce n'était pas le ridicule qu'ils cherchaient, mais le crime.* Cependant la différence n'est pas grande et c'est en tout cas l'idée qui m'est venue.

J'étais un peu étourdi aussi par tout ce monde dans cette salle close. J'ai regardé encore le prétoire et je n'ai distingué aucun visage. *Je crois bien que d'abord je ne m'étais pas rendu compte que tout ce monde se pressait pour me voir.* D'habitude, les gens ne s'occupaient pas de ma personne. *Il m'a fallu un effort pour comprendre que j'étais la cause de toute cette agitation* (pp. 118–19).

He discovers that in the ritual in which he is examined to be judged either worthy of remaining in the circle of imposed conformity, or unfit and excluded, he himself has almost no say because he does not know by what rules the ritual is acted out:

Une chose pourtant me gênait vaguement. Malgré mes préoccupations, j'étais parfois tenté d'intervenir et mon avocat me disait alors: "Taisez-vous, cela vaut mieux pour votre affaire." En quelque sorte, on avait l'air de traiter cette affaire en dehors de moi. Tout se déroulait sans mon intervention. Mon sort se réglait sans qu'on prenne mon avis. De temps en temps, j'avais envie d'interrompre tout le monde et de dire: "Mais tout de même, qui est l'accusé? C'est important d'être l'accusé. Et j'ai quelque chose à dire!" Mais réflexion faite, je n'avais rien à dire (pp. 139–40).

The linking image of the "banquette de tramway" is of course clearly a component motif alluding to that early one used in describing Meursault's impression at the wake:

C'est à ce moment que je me suis aperçu qu'ils étaient tous assis en face de moi à dodeliner de la tête, autour du concierge. J'ai eu un moment l'impression ridicule qu'ils étaient là pour me juger (p. 19).

These two linking images reflect Meursault's crucial confrontations with his judges of ritualistic propriety: with the old people around the polite but slightly pompous concierge who does not prove to be beyond reproach himself, and with the jury and the judges who prove in the end to be only human, subject to perspiration and erroneous judgments like any other humans. These images of custodians of ritualistic procedure are complemented by three images of silent and almost motionless witnesses: the man in the gray suit, Meursault's objectified self; the old man at the wake, and the automaton woman at the trial. At the wake

Meursault is merely opposed by the ritual while still part of it. At the trial, he is surrounded by it and no longer a participant but an object upon whom the ritual centers as it might center upon a sacrificial animal. The two linking images thus also reflect two different stages of Meursault's confrontation with order and ritual: at the wake Meursault reveals himself to others; at the trial, the others reveal him to himself as they see him: ridiculous for being different, and criminal for neglecting the appearances of dedicated compliance and conformity. We have already stated the part of the old man at the wake; he was the witness of Meursault's self-revelation. He does not reappear at the trial and is not even noted by the director of the home who does report observations made by others. Only Meursault himself is aware of the old man's gaze:

> La nuit a passé. Je me souviens qu'à un moment j'ai ouvert les yeux et j'ai vu que les vieillards dormaient tassés sur eux-mêmes, à l'exception d'un seul qui, le menton sur le dos de ses mains agrippées à la canne, me regardait fixement comme s'il n'attendait que mon réveil. Puis j'ai encore dormi. Je me suis réveillé parce que j'avais de plus en plus mal aux reins (pp. 20–21).

But Meursault does not respond to what he only intuitively feels may be a call to awaken to what is expected, because he is not aware of what the expectations are. The old man is a witness of Meursault's indolence and ignorance. Meursault fails to perceive his own image in the old man's intentionally serious gaze, just as much later in his cell he does not detect his own intentional smile in the reflection of his unintentionally serious features:

> Ce jour-là, après le départ du gardien, je me suis regardé dans ma gamelle de fer. Il m'a semblé que mon image restait sérieuse alors même que j'essayais de lui sourire. Je l'ai agitée devant moi. J'ai souri et elle a gardé le même air sévère et triste (p. 115).

These two linking images reflect Meursault's initial carefree blindness that prevented him from seeing himself at all with the seriousness with which others saw him, and finally his vain attempt to smile at his own seriousness with which he has come to see himself.

The automaton woman reappears at the trial but once again she is seen only by Meursault. She represents an exaggerated and therefore distorted manifestation of human compliance with order and blind obedience to rigid procedures. Meursault does not see her specifically as such a type, but Camus has placed her, together with the journalist who is Meursault's alter ego, for purposes of contrast and irony at the very points of his story where she can fulfill that function most effectively, namely at the moment the witnesses are called (p. 123), during the entire initial interrogation in the course of which the case is reviewed by the judge, and finally just before the verdict is pronounced. Significantly, after the verdict only the journalist is shown, and Meursault is alone with himself.

It is worth noting that Meursault, who is not familiar with the customs of the court and shows great interest in watching his own trial, does not reveal only his ignorance, naïveté, and bewilderment. Meursault's declared unfamiliarity allows Camus to remain to all appearances on the level of mere surface descriptions of happenings as seen by the uninitiated Meursault; descriptions which, to the reader, do suggest ritualistic patterns of gestures and of conduct in the court:

> Mon avocat est arrivé, en robe, entouré de beaucoup d'autres confrères. Il est allé vers les journalistes, a serré des mains. Ils ont plaisanté, ri et avaient l'air tout à fait à leur aise, jusqu'au moment où la sonnerie a retenti dans le prétoire. Tout le monde a regagné sa place. Mon avocat est venu vers moi, m'a serré la main et m'a conseillé de répondre brièvement aux questions qu'on me poserait, de ne pas prendre d'initiatives et de me reposer sur lui pour le reste.
>
> A ma gauche, j'ai entendu le bruit d'une chaise qu'on reculait et j'ai vu un grand homme mince, vêtu de rouge, portant lorgnon, qui s'asseyait en pliant sa robe avec soin. C'était le procureur. Un huissier a annoncé la cour. Au même moment, deux gros ventilateurs ont commencé de vrombir. Trois juges, deux en noir, le troisième en rouge, sont entrés avec des dossiers et ont marché très vite vers la tribune qui dominait la salle. L'homme en robe rouge s'est assis sur le fauteuil du milieu, a posé sa toque devant lui, essuyé son petit crâne chauve avec un mouchoir et déclaré que l'audience était ouverte (pp. 121–22).

The same holds true of the description of actual procedure, the rigid ritualistic pattern of which is for the reader obvious while Meursault's own mind apparently merely records impressions of verbal formulae to which he is expected to respond with a repetitious "Oui, monsieur le Président"—as if it were versicle and response.

> Mon interrogatoire a commencé aussitôt. Le président m'a questionné avec calme et même, m'a-t-il semblé, avec une nuance de cordialité. On m'a encore fait décliner mon identité et malgré mon agacement, j'ai pensé qu'au fond c'était assez naturel, parce qu'il serait trop grave de juger un homme pour un autre. *Puis le président a recommencé le récit de ce que j'avais fait, en s'adressant à moi toutes les trois phrases pour me demander: "Est-ce*

bien cela?" A chaque fois, j'ai répondu: "Oui, monsieur le Président", selon
les instructions de mon avocat. Cela a été long parce que le président appor-
tait beaucoup de minutie dans son récit. Pendant tout ce temps, les jour-
nalistes écrivaient. Je sentais les regards du plus jeune d'entre eux et de
la petite automate. *La banquette de tramway était tout entière tournée vers*
le président. Celui-ci a toussé, feuilleté son dossier et il s'est tourné vers moi
en s'éventant (p. 124).

That Meursault remains somewhat confused by the proceedings, without,
however, missing any of the gestures or declarations in which the ritual
is manifested, is evident from the description of the prosecutor's appearance and his use of formulae:

> *Celui-ci me tournait à demi le dos et, sans me regarder, il a déclaré*
> *qu'avec l'autorisation du président,* il aimerait savoir si j'étais retourné vers
> la source tout seul avec l'intention de tuer l'Arabe. "Non", ai-je dit. "Alors,
> pourquoi était-il armé et pourquoi revenir vers cet endroit précisément?"
> J'ai dit que c'était le hasard. Et le procureur a noté avec un accent mauvais:
> "Ce sera tout pour le moment." *Tout ensuite a été un peu confus, du moins*
> *pour moi. Mais après quelques conciliabules, le président a déclaré que*
> *l'audience était levée et renvoyée à l'après-midi pour l'audition des témoins*
> (pp. 125–26).

By the time the lawyers conclude their performances, however, Meursault does become aware of more than just the visible manifestations of
the ritual he is witnessing and enduring. He begins to see the emptiness
of the gestures with which both lawyers accompany their respective
formulae:

> Etaient-elles si différentes, d'ailleurs, ces plaidoiries? L'avocat levait les bras
> et plaidait coupable, mais avec excuses. Le procureur tendait ses mains et
> dénonçait la culpabilité, mais sans excuses (p. 139).

With a touch of sarcasm, he describes them leaning over his soul, perhaps
not too differently from ancient priests who leaned over the bowels of the
animal they have sacrificed in a ritual:

> Et j'ai essayé d'écouter encore parce que le procureur s'est mis à *parler de*
> *mon âme.*
>
> [Il disait qu'il s'était penché sur elle et qu'il n'avait rien trouvé, Mes-
> sieurs les jurés.] (p. 143).
>
> ["Moi aussi, a-t-il dit (his lawyer), je me suis penché sur cette âme, mais,
> contrairement à l'éminent représentant du ministère public, j'ai trouvé quel-
> que chose et je puis dire que j'y ai lu à livre ouvert."] (p. 147).

These parallel component motifs carry again the theme of a ritual akin to a responsive reading.

Finally, at the conclusion of his lawyer's defense, which Meursault finds inferior to the prosecution, the congratulatory gestures and remarks of the lawyer's colleagues underline the ritualistic nature of the performance which in the eyes of the initiated participants deserves high praise:

> La cour a suspendu l'audience et l'avocat s'est assis d'un air épuisé. Mais ses collègues sont venus vers lui pour lui serrer la main. J'ai entendu: "Magnifique, mon cher." L'un d'eux m'a même pris à témoin: "Hein?" m'a-t-il dit. J'ai acquiescé, mais mon compliment n'était pas sincère, parce que j'étais trop fatigué (p. 149).

Camus' intention of criticizing rituals and ritualism does not limit itself to mere touches of sarcasm. In following the patterns of certain component motifs, we discover a subtle critique that emerges from their contextual disposition; and another critique, far more expressive, which emerges from recurring motifs pertaining to Meursault's personal attitudes and experiences.

The first of these reveal the effects of a ritualistic formal setting on the testimony of witnesses. We find that their statements become stilted when they are no longer expressions within an experience, but answers to questions which impose a form upon the response and distort the intention that engenders it. Most of the testimony of the witnesses shows these effects, and we may here limit ourselves to a few examples. Let us consider the changes occurring in the significance of a theme because of a change in its contextual setting. At Marengo, where Meursault thought that one of the director's remarks might be interpreted as a reproach, it became clear that the director had no such intention:

> J'ai cru qu'il me reprochait quelque chose et j'ai commencé à lui expliquer. Mais il m'a interrompu: "Vous n'avez pas à vous justifier, mon cher enfant. J'ai lu le dossier de votre mère. Vous ne pouviez subvenir à ses besoins. Il lui fallait une garde. Vos salaires sont modestes. Et tout compte fait, elle était plus heureuse ici." J'ai dit: "Oui, monsieur le Directeur." Il a ajouté: "Vous savez, elle avait des amis, des gens de son âge. Elle pouvait partager avec eux des intérêts qui sont d'un autre temps. Vous êtes jeune et elle devait s'ennuyer avec vous" (pp. 11–12).

At the trial, the director reveals upon request that Meursault's mother did complain, but he adds a weak explanation:

> ... j'ai entendu appeler le directeur de l'asile. *On lui a demandé* si maman se plaignait de moi *et il a dit que oui* mais que c'était un peu la manie de ses

pensionnaires de se plaindre de leurs proches. *Le président lui a fait préciser si elle me reprochait de l'avoir mise à l'asile et le directeur a dit encore oui. Mais cette fois, il n'a rien ajouté* (pp. 126–27).

It is true that further questioning reveals the director's knowledge of some of Meursault's attitudes shown at Marengo, but this knowledge has no bearing on the change in thematic significance we have just considered. The following passage reveals that the director does not offer his declarations until asked to do so: "A une autre question, il a répondu" or: "On lui a demandé." What the passage possibly also suggests is that the director may not have found any pleasure in making his revelations, and that he was merely complying with court procedures:

A une autre question, il a répondu qu'il avait été surpris de mon calme le jour de l'enterrement. *On lui a demandé ce qu'il entendait par calme.* Le directeur a regardé alors le bout de ses souliers et il a dit que je n'avais pas voulu voir maman, je n'avais pas pleuré une seule fois et j'étais parti aussitôt après l'enterrement sans me recueillir sur sa tombe. Une chose encore l'avait surpris: un employé des pompes funèbres lui avait dit que je ne savais pas l'âge de maman (p. 127).

Céleste comes prepared to make a statement, but the stage and the form make him tongue-tied. It must also be noted that Céleste appeared in his most proper attire at this ceremonious occasion:

Céleste jetait de temps en temps des regards de mon côté et roulait un panama entre ses mains. *Il portait le costume neuf* qu'il mettait pour venir avec moi, certains dimanches, aux courses de chevaux. *Mais je crois qu'il n'avait pas pu mettre son col parce qu'il portait seulement un bouton de cuivre pour tenir sa chemise fermée.* On lui a demandé si j'étais son client et il a dit: "Oui, mais c'était aussi un ami"; *ce qu'il pensait de moi* et il a répondu que j'étais un homme; *ce qu'il entendait par là* et il a déclaré que tout le monde savait ce que cela voulait dire; *s'il avait remarqué que j'étais renfermé* et il a reconnu seulement que je ne parlais pas pour ne rien dire. *L'avocat général lui a demandé* si je payais régulièrement ma pension. Céleste a ri et il a déclaré: "C'étaient des détails entre nous." *On lui a demandé encore ce qu'il pensait de mon crime.* Il a mis alors ses mains sur la barre et l'on voyait qu'il avait préparé quelque chose. Il a dit: "Pour moi, c'est un malheur. Un malheur, tout le monde sait ce que c'est. Ça vous laisse sans défense. Eh bien! pour moi c'est un malheur." Il allait continuer, mais *le président lui a dit que c'était bien et qu'on le remerciait.* Alors Céleste est resté un peu interdit. Mais il a déclaré qu'il voulait encore parler. *On lui a demandé d'être bref.* Il a enore répété que c'était un malheur. *Et le président lui a dit: "Oui, c'est entendu. Mais nous sommes là pour juger les malheurs de ce genre. Nous vous remercions."* Comme s'il était arrivé au bout de sa science et de sa bonne volonté, Céleste s'est alors retourné vers moi. Il m'a semblé que ses yeux brillaient et que ses lèvres tremblaient. Il avait l'air de me demander ce qu'il pouvait encore faire (pp. 130–32).

Marie's desperate exclamation at the end of her testimony and the reaction to it are ample evidence that Camus did indeed carefully devise a critique of ceremonious pronouncements by showing the distortions and limitations procedure is capable of forcing upon intended statements:

Puis il a dit avec quelque ironie qu'il ne voudrait pas insister sur une situation délicate, qu'il comprenait bien les scrupules de Marie, mais (et ici son accent s'est fait plus dur) que son *devoir* lui commandait de s'élever *au-dessus des convenances. Il a donc demandé à Marie de résumer cette journée* où je l'avais connue. *Marie ne voulait pas parler, mais devant l'insistance* du procureur, elle a dit notre bain, notre sortie au cinéma et notre rentrée chez moi. L'avocat général a dit qu'à la suite des déclarations de Marie à l'instruction, il avait consulté les programmes de cette date. Il a ajouté que Marie elle-même dirait quel film on passait alors. D'une voix presque blanche, en effet, elle a indiqué que c'était un film de Fernandel. *Le silence était complet dans la salle quand elle a eu fini.* Le procureur s'est alors levé, très grave et d'une voix que j'ai trouvée vraiment émue, le doigt tendu vers moi, il a articulé lentement: "Messieurs les jurés, le lendemain de la mort de sa mère, cet homme prenait des bains, commençait une liaison irrégulière, et allait rire devant un film comique. Je n'ai rien de plus à vous dire." Il s'est assis, toujours dans le silence. *Mais, tout d'un coup, Marie a éclaté en sanglots, a dit que ce n'était pas cela, qu'il y avait autre chose, qu'on la forçait à dire le contraire de ce qu'elle pensait, qu'elle me connaissait bien* et que je n'avais rien fait de mal (pp. 133–34).

Even Camus' vocabulary indicates his awareness of the ceremonious, ritualistic nature of the questioning. His careful repetition of indications where questions end and answers begin points equally clearly to his purposeful examination of the modifications brought about by the contextual constellation, determined by an inescapable ritualistic conclusion: the verdict.

Après avoir demandé au jury et à mon avocat s'ils avaient des questions à poser, le président a entendu le *concierge*. Pour lui comme pour tous les autres, *le même cérémonial s'est répété. En arrivant, le concierge m'a regardé et il a détourné les yeux. Il a répondu aux questions qu'on lui posait.* Il a dit que je *n'avais pas voulu voir maman, que j'avais fumé, que j'avais dormi* et que *j'avais pris du café au lait.* J'ai senti alors quelque chose qui

100

soulevait toute la salle et, *pour la première fois, j'ai compris que j'étais coupable.* On a fait répéter au concierge l'histoire du café au lait et celle de la cigarette. L'avocat général m'a regardé avec une lueur ironique dans les yeux (p. 128).

"Oui, MM. les jurés apprécieront. Et ils concluront qu'un étranger pouvait proposer du café, mais qu'un fils *devait le refuser* devant le corps de celle qui lui avait donné le jour." Le concierge a regagné son banc (p. 129).

The other critique of rituals and of ritualism is carried by a theme that pervades the story as a whole. Its motifs consist of various materially different linking phrases all of which carry essentially the same theme, that of rigidity, narrowness, unavoidability, and slavery to which man is subjected by situations, arrangements, or procedures that preclude true alternatives. In view of the material differences between the motifs, it is natural to expect that the theme will reveal variations, but these do not conceal their basic thematic unity.

At the wake Meursault suffers from the bright lights in the glare of which his attitudes are on trial. In vain does he request to have the light reduced. If the glare does indeed represent the limelight, then the concierge's answer carries also the meaning that in rigidly prescriptive situations there is no room for flexibility and man is bound to be seen as he appears in the light of such prescriptions. "Je lui ai demandé si on pouvait éteindre une des lampes. L'éclat de la lumière sur les murs blancs me fatiguait. Il m'a dit que ce n'était pas possible. *L'installation était ainsi faite: c'était tout ou rien*" (p. 17). Similarly, in the glaring sun during the funeral, while Meursault was fanning himself with his hand-kerchief and was almost constantly aware of the heat that made his blood beat against his temples, the director "marchait avec beaucoup de dignité, sans un geste inutile." Pérez, in particular, was performing feats of devotion despite his emotional and physical suffering. Even the employee of the funeral home has a thought for Meursault's mother in spite of the heat of which he is keenly aware. The trial has shown that the funeral also provided a ritualistic stage on which Meursault's sensitivity was on trial. It is against this background and ceremony where everything is foreseen and where everything seems to Meursault to happen "avec tant de précipitation, de certitude et de naturel," that we must read the nurse's remark, but far more significantly Meursault's comment that it was the only thing he could remember and that he agreed. His conscious agreement pertains to the actual motif, but his intuitive agreement pertains to the theme, the scope of which extends far beyond the single situation to which the nurse's statement applies:

101

> Tout s'est passé ensuite avec *tant de précipitation, de certitude et de naturel,* que je ne me souviens plus de rien. Une chose seulement: à l'entrée du village, l'infirmière déléguée m'a parlé. Elle avait une voix singulière qui n'allait pas avec son visage, une voix mélodieuse et tremblante. Elle m'a dit: "Si on va doucement, on risque une insolation. Mais si on va trop vite, on est en transpiration et dans l'église on attrape un chaud et froid." *Elle avait raison. Il n'y avait pas d'issue* (p. 29).

The previous statement, "c'était tout ou rien," is a parallel statement to "Il n'y avait pas d'issue." The first seems to suggest that there is an alternative to the glare, but it is only an apparent alternative, for Meursault does not want darkness, which is the only possible alternative, but less light, and that is not possible. Therefore "Il n'y avait pas d'issue" carries essentially the same theme, though with greater and clearer emphasis, as its component motif "c'était tout ou rien."

"Il n'y avait pas d'issue" is a linking phrase and we find it again, in a sequentially considerably removed context. It occurs in connection with Meursault's experience of feeling restricted in his movements, hemmed in by the walls of his tiny cell, and exposed to the only voice that keeps him company: his own.

> Mais en même temps et pour la première fois depuis des mois, j'ai entendu distinctement le son de ma voix. Je l'ai reconnue pour celle qui résonnait déjà depuis de longs jours à mes oreilles et j'ai compris que pendant tout ce temps j'avais parlé seul. *Je me suis souvenu alors de ce que disait l'infirmière à l'enterrement de maman. Non,* [*il n'y avait pas d'issue*] *et personne ne peut imaginer ce que sont les soirs dans les prisons* (pp. 115–16).

So far this linking phrase (or its component motif "c'était tout ou rien"), has occurred in situations of physical restrictions affecting Meursault's bodily freedom and comfort. In the above quotation, however, we find the first hint of yet another constraint which expands the notion of merely physical constraint into the more poignant one of implacable restrictions placed upon his emotional life as well: "personne ne peut imaginer ce que sont les soirs dans les prisons."

Before following the recurrence of that linking phrase, we should first note how the theme of spatial confinement is developed with the aid of motifs that are component with the linking phrase, but materially different from it. The most obvious instance of spatial confinement and its effects on Meursault's emotional freedom can be found in a description of the initial period of his imprisonment:

> Au début de ma détention, pourtant, ce qui a été le plus dur, c'est que j'avais des pensées d'homme libre. Par exemple, l'envie me prenait d'être

sur une plage et de descendre vers la mer. A imaginer le bruit des premières vagues sous la plante de mes pieds, l'entrée du corps dans l'eau et la délivrance que j'y trouvais, *je sentais tout d'un coup combien les murs de ma prison étaient rapprochés* (p. 109).

Later, after the trial, Meursault is removed to a different and very small cell. It is significant to note the emphasis of Meursault's growing feeling of constraint expressed through a shrinking of space. In the above quotation only the walls of the prison restrict his movements; in the next quotation he feels hemmed in by the cell itself. But it is even more interesting to see the context within which this increased restriction is mentioned:

> Pour la troisième fois, j'ai refusé de recevoir l'aumônier. Je n'ai rien à lui dire, je n'ai pas envie de parler, je le verrai bien assez tôt. *Ce qui m'intéresse en ce moment, c'est d'échapper à la mécanique, de savoir si l'inévitable* [*peut avoir une issue*]. On m'a changé de *cellule. De celle-ci, lorsque je suis allongé, je vois le ciel et je ne vois que lui.* Toutes mes journées se passent à regarder sur son visage le déclin des couleurs qui conduit le jour à la nuit. Couché, je passe les mains sous ma tête et j'attends. Je ne sais combien de fois je me suis *demandé s'il y avait des exemples de condamnés à mort qui eussent échappé au* [*mécanisme implacable,*] *disparu* avant l'exécution, rompu les cordons d'agents. Je me reprochais alors de n'avoir pas prêté assez d'attention aux récits d'exécution (pp. 152–53).

Here Meursault is faced with the inevitable annihilation of his life. To give this heightened feeling the fullest expression, Camus not only uses the spatial motif, but reinforces it with the previously used linking phrase. Thus we find in the same passage a reference to his new cell, and the concern whether "l'inévitable peut avoir une issue." In conjunction with these motifs a new motif, "mécanisme implacable," is introduced. We readily recognize, in spite of material differences, that the earlier lack of choice, the all or nothing, the no escape, the shrinking space, and the implacable mechanism are all component motifs. They carry with growing intensity the variations on the theme of Meursault's repugnance with regard to any restrictions, and particularly those that become inevitable because of human contrivances, based on the precariousness of judgment.

The last quoted passage begins with a reference to the chaplain whom Meursault has refused to receive. It is the chaplain who ostensibly appears with the intention of offering to Meursault an alternative, a freedom from the walls of the cell, a freedom of the spirit to surmount spatial restrictions. However, Meursault is not interested in spiritual leaps. Later when he stands face to face with the chaplain, he makes a revealing distinction between guilt and sin, and with it the notion of physical limitations is reintroduced. It is within physical limitations, limitations of space, human proximity, prescriptive procedures, that freedom is circumscribed and guilt defined. In Meursault's mind the chaplain is within that world with him; and from that world the chaplain's notions of spiritual freedom and spiritual obligations are excluded, and so are therefore innocence and sin, bliss and contrition:

> Je lui ai dit que je ne savais pas ce qu'était un péché. On m'avait seulement appris que j'étais un coupable. J'étais coupable, je payais, on ne pouvait rien me demander de plus. *A ce moment, il s'est levé à noveau et j'ai pensé que dans cette cellule si étroite, s'il voulait remuer, il n'avait pas le choix. Il fallait s'asseoir ou se lever* (p. 166).

It is worth mentioning that among the motifs carrying the theme of an implacable spatial restriction, there is one that occurs at the very point of Meursault's committing the fatal mistake that leads to the shooting: "J'ai pensé que je n'avais qu'un demi-tour à faire et ce serait fini. *Mais toute une plage vibrante de soleil se pressait derrière moi*" (pp. 86–87). We may attribute the use of this motif within this context to Camus' desire to show what sort of acts man is likely to commit, how much he may act against his spontaneous inclinations or even his judgment if the freedom of alternatives is removed. In this sense, the use of the motif here permits us to see a connection between the critique of the testimony under restrictive conditions of inquiry and the critique of the implacability of ritualistic procedures, both of which lead to the same aberrations as implacable physical restrictions do.

Thus the motif of the "mécanisme implacable," occurring as it does in natural and in carefully devised situations, carries within the pervasive theme of ritualism also a critique of its procedures. Just as Camus made a distinction between natural habit and a more or less cultivated ceremonial custom, he also makes a distinction between restrictions and compulsions over which man has no control, and with a clearly intended emphasis, those which man has imposed upon himself. By these he may not be able to abide in spirit, but as long as he can prove that he is abiding by them at least in form, he may do so with impunity.

The theme carried by the motif of the "mécanisme implacable" is already found in an earlier passage in which the examining magistrate is depicted as having abandoned any effort to elicit an approved and therefore desirable response from Meursault. The motifs carrying the theme, however, are materially different. One of these suggests that in the mind of the magistrate Meursault's case is now classifiable and classified, and the other motif carries the theme of foreseeable and expected procedural rigidity:

> Par la suite j'ai souvent revu le juge d'instruction. Seulement, j'étais accompagné de mon avocat à chaque fois. On se bornait à me faire préciser certains points de mes déclarations précédentes. Ou bien encore le juge discutait les charges avec mon avocat. Mais en vérité ils ne s'occupaient jamais de moi à ces moments-là. Peu à peu en tout cas, le ton des interrogatoires a changé. *Il semblait que le juge ne s'intéressât plus à moi et [qu'il eût classé mon cas en quelque sorte].* Il ne m'a plus parlé de Dieu et je ne l'ai jamais revu dans l'excitation de ce premier jour. Le résultat, c'est que nos entretiens sont devenus plus cordiaux. *Quelques questions, un peu de conversation avec mon avocat, les interrogatoires étaient finis.* [*Mon affaire suivait son cours,*] *selon l'expression même du juge* (pp. 101–2).

That the motif of classification is indeed a linking phrase and that its theme is correlative with that of the motif "mécanisme implacable" becomes quite clear from its later recurrence in connection with the implacability of the verdict and the inevitability of its execution under the unfailing guillotine:

> Car en réfléchissant bien, en considérant les choses avec calme, je constatais que *ce qui était défectueux avec le couperet, [c'est qu'il n'y avait aucune chance,] absolument aucune.* Une fois pour toutes, en somme, la mort du patient avait été décidée. [*C'était une affaire classée,*] *une combinaison bien arrêtée, un accord entendu et sur lequel il n'était pas question de revenir.* Si le coup ratait, par extraordinaire, on recommençait. Par suite, ce qu'il y avait d'ennuyeux, c'est qu'il fallait que le condamné souhaitât le bon fonctionnement de la machine. Je dis que c'est le côté défectueux. Cela. est vrai, dans un sens. Mais, dans un autre sens, j'étais obligé de reconnaître que tout le secret d'une bonne organisation était là. En somme, le condamné était obligé de collaborer moralement. C'était son intérêt que tout marchât sans accroc (pp. 156–57).

Camus' critique of the "mécanisme implacable" is both explicit and tinged with irony, but there are passages, underscored by materially different but clearly component motifs, which in addition to the critique also carry his rejection of mechanical rigidity. In the first two quotations the linking phrases "rite implacable" and "préméditation irrésistible" cause us to pause and consider Meursault's yearning for at least a chance of freedom:

> Là, peut-être, j'aurais trouvé des récits d'évasion. J'aurais appris que dans un cas au moins la roue s'était arrêtée, que dans cette [*préméditation*

irrésistible,] *le hasard et la chance, une fois seulement, avaient changé quelque chose. Une fois!* ...

Ce qui comptait, c'était une possibilité d'évasion, *un saut hors du* [*rite implacable,*] une course à la folie qui offrît toutes les chances de l'espoir (p. 153).

In the following passage "la mécanique," "certitude insolente," and "déroulement imperturbable" are slight modifications of the linking phrases we have seen so far, and their function here is to restate with emphasis not only the rejection of ritualistic bonds but the reason (the precariousness of judgment) for the rejection as well:

... *la mécanique me reprenait.*

Malgré ma bonne volonté, je ne pouvais pas accepter cette [*certitude insolente*]. Car enfin, il y avait une disproportion ridicule entre *le jugement* qui l'avait fondée *et son* [*déroulement imperturbable*] à partir du moment où ce jugement avait été prononcé (p. 154).

In considering the above passage as well as the following, we note that Camus seems to have intended to question even the notion of glory a person might have in paying his debt to society, in obeying with dignity and penitence the law under which society lives and under which it condemns the guilty in the name of justice. He questions that notion because he questions man's right to determine what justice is. In facing the guillotine, Meursault seems to have no thought of death that awaits him under the blade, the death to which, as the priest told him, we were all condemned. The implacability of natural death does not disturb Meursault as he imagines his execution; only his regret of life does. He has no quarrel with death, in fact he believes that nobody has any right to bewail the death of men who have had the privilege of living. His quarrel is with man's presumption of belief in the justification of shortening human life "discrètement, avec un peu de honte et beaucoup de précision":

J'étais obligé de constater aussi que jusqu'ici j'avais eu sur ces questions des idées qui n'étaient pas justes. J'ai cru longtemps—et je ne sais pas pourquoi—*que pour aller à la guillotine, il fallait monter sur un échafaud, gravir des marches.* Je crois que c'était à cause de la Révolution de 1789, je veux dire à cause de tout ce qu'on m'avait appris ou fait voir sur ces questions. Mais un matin, je me suis souvenu d'une photographie publiée par les journaux à l'occasion d'une exécution retentissante. *En réalité, la machine était posée à même le sol, le plus simplement du monde.* Elle était beaucoup plus étroite que je ne le pensais. C'était assez drôle que je ne m'en fusse pas avisé plus tôt. Cette machine sur le cliché m'avait frappé par son aspect d'ouvrage de précision, fini et étincelant. *On se fait toujours des idées exagérées de ce qu'on ne connaît pas. Je devais constater au contraire que tout était simple: la machine est au même niveau que l'homme qui marche vers elle. Il la rejoint comme on marche à la rencontre d'une personne.* Cela aussi était ennuyeux. *La montée vers l'échafaud, l'ascension en plein ciel, l'imagination pouvait s'y raccrocher.* Tandis que, là encore, *la mécanique écrasait tout:* on était tué discrètement, avec un peu de honte et beaucoup de précision (pp. 157–58).

As we try to establish the major principles which underlie the conventions and the rituals, we must first determine what attitudes and conduct the conventions and rituals presuppose. One basic assumption of the point of view from which Meursault's conduct is judged, which governs the investigation, the charge, the condemnation, and even the defense, is that man acts with awareness, that his conduct may therefore be considered an expression of principles to which he consciously adheres, or to which he may at least refer, after moments of regrettable unawareness, in order to recognize his aberration, to feel remorse, and to repent. The second assumption, derived from the former, is that a particular action or attitude is not only premeditated and willed, but also relatable to any other known action or attitude of the same person, for all acts are supposed to reflect the principles to which one adheres or to which one fails to adhere.

Where such assumptions are considered valid, the role of unconsciousness and the likelihood of chance in human behavior are largely discounted. What does matter is the motivation discernible in an act and the purpose that act is supposed to serve, for motivation and purpose reflect through the act the source and the efficaciousness of the inspiration.

The main justification of principles is that they maintain the order and the procedures in which a society finds the safeguard for its preservation. A formal adherence to order and procedures is then considered the most obvious proof of one's adherence to principles. Hence, it is assumed that he who adheres most consistently and most obviously to procedures, order, and principles is also beyond suspicion and beyond reproach, and his acts are bound to be considered and considerate.

The director at Marengo shows regard not only for Meursault but also for the old people in the home. His dispositions are taken with great consideration for the sensitivity of those intrusted to his care, and even his sense of humor is devoid of malice:

En principe, les pensionnaires ne devaient pas assister aux enterrements. Il les laissait seulement veiller: "C'est une question d'humanité", a-t-il

107

remarqué. Mais en l'espèce, il avait accordé l'autorisation de suivre le convoi à un vieil ami de maman: "Thomas Pérez." Ici, le directeur a souri. Il m'a dit: "Vous comprenez, c'est un sentiment un peu puéril. Mais lui et votre mère ne se quittaient guère. A l'asile, on les plaisantait, on disait à Pérez: "C'est votre fiancée." Lui riait. Ça lui faisait plaisir. Et le fait est que la mort de Mme Meursault l'a beaucoup affecté. Je n'ai pas cru devoir lui refuser l'autorisation. Mais sur le conseil du médecin visiteur, je lui ai interdit la veillée d'hier" (p. 23).

There is, however, a touch of irony in Camus' presentation of the director's ability to make consideration and self-interest compatible:

"Nous l'avons transportée dans notre petite morgue. Pour ne pas impressionner les autres. Chaque fois qu'un pensionnaire meurt, les autres sont nerveux pendant deux ou trois jours. Et ça rend le service difficile" (p. 12).

The significance and importance attached to the visible manifestations of one's beliefs or feelings may be judged from several passages. The defense lawyer points out to Meursault that a preliminary inquiry has shown a lack of feelings that were expected:

On avait alors fait une enquête à Marengo. Les instructeurs avaient appris que "j'avais fait preuve d'insensibilité" le jour de l'enterrement de maman. "Vous comprenez, m'a dit mon avocat, cela me gêne un peu de vous demander cela. Mais c'est très important. Et ce sera un gros argument pour l'accusation, si je ne trouve rien à répondre." Il voulait que je l'aide. Il m'a demandé si j'avais eu de la peine ce jour-là (p. 93).

Il a réfléchi. Il m'a demandé s'il pouvait dire que ce jour-là j'avais dominé mes sentiments naturels. Je lui ai dit: "Non, parce que c'est faux." Il m'a regardé d'une façon bizarre, comme si je lui inspirais un peu de dégoût. Il m'a dit presque méchamment que dans tous les cas le directeur et le personnel de l'asile seraient entendus comme témoins et que "cela pouvait me jouer un très sale tour" (pp. 94–95).

At the trial, the director is embarrassed to report that Meursault did not wish to see his dead mother, that he did not shed any tears, and that without remaining at the grave he left immediately after the burial. It appears that to the director these were visible signs of a lack of filial love and of a particular insensitivity to the mystery of death. The prosecutor does not even need to ask any further questions, for it is clear to him that Meursault has already revealed a predisposition to sin and crime which he cannot prevent because of his lack of humane compassion and because of his inability to feel the pain of loss which love alone can induce. The audience, too, seems to draw the same conclusion:

Puis le président a demandé à l'avocat général s'il n'avait pas de question à poser au témoin et le procureur s'est écrié: "Oh! non, cela suffit", avec un tel éclat et un tel regard triomphant dans ma direction que, pour le première fois depuis bien des années, j'ai eu une envie stupide de pleurer parce que j'ai senti combien j'étais détesté par tous ces gens-là (p. 127).

The judge, too, is concerned about the lack of filial responsibility: "Il m'a demandé pourquoi j'avais mis maman à l'asile."

The concierge's testimony that Meursault did not wish to see his mother, that he slept, smoked, and drank café au lait is sufficient for condemnation to rise from the courtroom:

J'ai senti alors quelque chose qui soulevait toute la salle et, pour la première fois, j'ai compris que j'étais coupable. On a fait répéter au concierge l'histoire du café au lait et celle de la cigarette (p. 128).

Finally, the prosecutor, enlarging on the themes of filial insensitivity and irresponsibility which the above motifs are seen to carry, concludes that if the soul, laid bare by testimony, is seen as the main witness, then the guilt of murder is established, for the same principles from which sensitivity and responsibility are derived would also assure innocence—if not in deed at least in intention:

"Le même homme qui au lendmain de la mort de sa mère se livrait à la débauche la plus honteuse a tué pour des raisons futiles et pour liquider une affaire de mœurs inqualifiable."

Il s'est assis alors. Mais mon avocat, à bout de patience, s'est écrié en levant les bras, de sorte que ses manches en retombant ont découvert les plis d'une chemise amidonnée: "Enfin, est-il accusé d'avoir enterré sa mère ou d'avoir tué un homme?" Le public a ri. Mais le procureur s'est redressé encore, s'est drapé dans sa robe et a déclaré qu'il fallait avoir l'ingénuité de l'honorable défenseur pour ne pas sentir qu'il y avait entre ces deux ordres de faits une relation profonde, pathétique, essentielle. *"Oui, s'est-il écrié avec force, j'accuse cet homme d'avoir enterré un mère avec un cœur de criminel."* Cette déclaration a paru faire un effet considérable sur le public. Mon avocat a haussé les épaules et essuyé la sueur qui couvrait son front. Mais lui-même paraissait ébranlé et j'ai compris que les choses n'allaient pas bien pour moi (pp. 136–37).

Since there is no evidence to assume Meursault's innocence in intention, his guilt appears incontrovertibly proven.

But the themes of insensitivity and irresponsibility, which are due to his lack of adherence to the principles of sensitivity, compassion, loyalty, and devotion, are not carried only by motifs of direct revelation. The old woman crying at the wake, and who does not appear at the trial, is Camus' image of sensitivity and sentimentality before that imaginary court at Marengo in the limelight of which Meursault is judged. The context in which the old woman's crying is introduced seems to support this interpretation of her role, for she is mentioned as having begun crying at the very moment Meursault had the impression of being judged:

> C'est à ce moment que je me suis aperçu qu'ils étaient tous assis en face de moi à dodeliner de la tête, autour du concierge. J'ai eu un moment l'impression ridicule qu'ils étaient là pour me juger.
>
> Peu après, une des femmes s'est mise à pleurer. Elle était au second rang, cachée par une de ses compagnes, et je la voyais mal. Elle pleurait à petits cris, régulièrement: il me semblait qu'elle ne s'arrêterait jamais (p. 19).

We know that Meursault's final discovery of his identity includes the resolute condemnation of the old woman's sentimentality and tears. Nevertheless, it was important for Meursault's insensitivity to be seen and judged for a case to be made against him on those grounds and in order to point out in face of a general condemnation why, in the end, Meursault, in spite of all opinions to the contrary, did feel justified in maintaining his tender indifference. Among others, the old woman greatly strengthens the theme of reprehensible indifference, but Pérez makes an even stronger case. His silent suffering at the funeral is an eloquent repudiation of Meursault's insensitivity as it appears in the eyes of the court. Pérez is made to appear as a model of socially approved compliance with principles and conduct. His grief and his tears attest to his sensitivity and to the spirit of the principles the court is supposed to uphold:

> On lui a demandé ce que j'avais fait ce jour-là et il a répondu: "Vous comprenez, moi-même j'avais trop de *peine*. Alors, je n'ai rien vu. C'était la *peine* qui m'empêchait de voir. Parce que c'était pour moi une très *grosse peine*. Et même, je *me suis évanoui*. Alors, je n'ai pas pu voir Monsieur." L'avocat général lui a demandé si, du moins, *il m'avait vu pleurer*. Pérez a répondu que non (pp. 129–30).

Camus does not present compassion, loyalty, and devotion without a spiritual base, and as arbitrarily selected principles serving social functions alone. They are shown to be derived from a belief in human fellowship in Christ, from the belief in Christ's suffering for man, from the faith in divine mercy. Such is the theme of the investigating magistrate's admonitions and exhortations.

Before promising to intervene on Meursault's behalf "avec l'aide de

110

Dieu," he asks "sans transition"—and as far as Meursault is concerned "toujours sans logique apparente"—whether Meursault loved his mother and why he waited between the first and the second shot. By the measure of love and compassion he seeks to detect in Meursault, the magistrate also hopes to detect Meursault's depth of commitment to a faith in God and divine mercy. He would like Meursault to find in faith the strength for repentance in a state of humble submission. The magistrate's insistence that everybody believes in God, that it is impossible not to believe in God, is the cry of a man for whom the entire meaning of life depends upon the recognition and conviction that without a divine source of in-spiration human life is worthless, and principles, by implication, gratuitous:

> Mais il m'a coupé et m'a exhorté une dernière fois, dressé de toute sa hauteur, en me demandant si je croyais en Dieu. J'ai répondu que non. Il s'est assis avec indignation. Il m'a dit que c'était impossible, que tous les hommes croyaient en Dieu, même ceux qui se détournaient de son visage. C'était là sa conviction et, s'il devait jamais en douter, sa vie n'aurait plus de sens. "Voulez-vous, s'est-il exclamé, que ma vie n'ait plus de sens?" A mon avis, cela ne me regardait pas et je le lui ai dit. Mais à travers la table, il avançait déjà le Christ sous mes yeux et s'écriait d'une façon déraisonnable: "Moi, je suis chrétien. Je demande pardon de tes fautes à celui-là. Comment peux-tu ne pas croire qu'il a souffert pour toi?" J'ai bien remarqué qu'il me tutoyait, mais j'en avais assez. La chaleur se faisait de plus en plus grande. Comme toujours, quand j'ai envie de me débarrasser de quelqu'un que j'écoute à peine, j'ai eu l'air d'approuver. A ma surprise, il a triomphé: "Tu vois, tu vois, disait-il. N'est-ce pas que tu crois et que tu vas te confier à lui?" Evidemment, j'ai dit non une fois de plus. Il est retombé sur son fauteuil (pp. 99–100).

Meursault's simple and reiterated denial of sharing the magistrate's faith evokes the latter's sad remark of a man whose verdict is not that of a judge but of a human being who has failed in his supreme effort to save a soul and thereby also a life:

> Ensuite, il m'a regardé attentivement et avec un peu de tristesse. Il a murmuré: "Je n'ai jamais vu d'âme aussi endurcie que la vôtre" (p. 100).

Based on faith in God, principles are also shown to be derived from a belief in the human soul, for it is the soul wherein faith is anchored, awareness kept awake, and responsibility rendered effective. It is there-fore over Meursault's soul that we see the prosecutor bent, and it is its emptiness, its spiritual void, which makes him recoil in horror and demand the death penalty just as one discards in a ritualistic fashion the impure—without reproach but also without pity:

> Et j'ai essayé d'écouter encore parce que le procureur s'est mis à parler de mon *âme*.
>
> Il disait qu'il s'était penché sur elle et qu'il n'avait rien trouvé, Messieurs les jurés. Il disait qu'à la vérité, je n'en avais *point, d'âme*, et que *rien d'humain, et pas un des principes moraux qui gardent le cœur des hommes ne m'était accessible.* "San doute, ajoutait-il, nous ne saurions le lui reprocher. Ce qu'il ne saurait acquérir, nous ne pouvons nous plaindre qu'il en manque. Mais quand il s'agit de cette cour, la vertu toute négative de la tolérance doit se muer en celle, moins facile, mais plus élevée, de la justice. Surtout lorsque le vide du cœur tel qu'on le découvre chez cet homme devient un gouffre où la société peut succomber" (p. 143).
>
> Il a dit enfin que son devoir était douloureux, mais qu'il l'accomplirait fermement. Il a déclaré *que je n'avais rien à faire avec une société dont je méconnaissais les règles les plus essentielles* et que je ne pouvais pas en appeler à ce cœur humain dont j'ignorais les réactions élémentaires. "Je vous demande la tête de cet homme, a-t-il dit, et c'est le cœur léger que je vous la demande" (p. 145).

The basic themes of the belief in God and in the human soul are complemented by the belief in eternal life propounded by the priest. In his person Meursault faces the living representation of faith, of concern over the human soul, and of the belief in its indestructibility. Significantly, it seems, the character was chosen to permit faith, principles, and ritual to stand out in their culminating fusion. Meursault refused repeatedly to meet with the priest, but during one unavoidable confrontration he succeeded in repudiating in an outburst of defiance the entire complex of suppositions, assertions, and norms to which he was expected to submit his thoughts, his hopes, his feelings and his conduct. It is against this fusion of faith, principles, and ritual that Meursault's self-recognition and defiance are now counterpoised, but their varied manifestations in the form of initial uncertainties, mild opposition, and later of self-assertion did become apparent earlier. The linking phrase "Ce n'est pas de ma faute" and "je n'aurais pas dû lui dire cela" relate, with minor variations, several early motifs in which Meursault is seen groping in the maze of unfamiliar norms governing attitude and conduct:

> J'ai demandé deux jours de congé à mon patron et il ne pouvait pas me les refuser avec une excuse pareille. Mais il n'avait pas l'air content. Je lui ai même dit: "*Ce n'est pas de ma faute.*" Il n'a pas répondu. J'ai pensé alors que *je n'aurais pas dû lui dire cela.* En somme, je n'avais pas à m'excuser. C'était plutôt à lui de me présenter ses condoléances (pp. 9–10).

112

A ce moment, le concierge est entré derrière mon dos. Il avait dû courir. Il a bégayé un peu: "On l'a couverte, mais je dois dévisser la bière pour que vous puissiez la voir." Il s'approchait de la bière quand je l'ai arrêté. Il m'a dit: "Vous ne voulez pas?" J'ai répondu: "Non." Il s'est interrompu et j'étais gêné parce que *je sentais que je n'aurais pas dû lui dire cela* (p. 14).

En me réveillant, j'ai compris pourquoi mon patron avait l'air mécontent quand je lui ai demandé mes deux jours de congé: c'est aujourd'hui samedi. Je l'avais pour ainsi dire oublié, mais en me levant, cette idée m'est venue. Mon patron, tout naturellement, a pensé que j'aurais ainsi quatre jours de vacances avec mon dimanche et cela ne pouvait pas lui faire plaisir. Mais d'une part, *ce n'est pas ma faute si on a* enterré maman hier au lieu d'aujourd'hui et d'autre part, j'aurais eu mon samedi et mon dimanche de toute façon (p. 31).

And again, when speaking to Marie:

Je lui ai dit que maman était morte. Comme elle voulait savoir depuis quand, j'ai répondu: "Depuis hier." Elle a eu un petit recul, mais n'a fait aucune remarque. *J'ai eu envie de lui dire que ce n'était pas ma faute,* mais je me suis arrêté parce que j'ai pensé que je l'avais déjà dit à mon patron. *Cela ne signifiait rien. De toute façon, on est toujours un peu fautif* (p. 33).

Either because he fails to reconcile conflicting obligations, or because he does not understand the principles and their manifestations in human conduct, he feels out of place and vaguely at fault for not being able to live in that natural harmony with men which he intuitively feels with the world of nature that places no demands on his emotions and therefore elicits his natural and spontaneous yielding without anxiety of disapproval. This is why he at first suspects the authenticity of an emotional reaction of others: "J'avais même l'impression que cette morte, couchée au milieu d'eux, ne signifiait rien à leurs yeux. Mais je crois maintenant que c'était une impression fausse" (p. 20). Not being able to show it himself, he cannot quite understand if others do, and when he is unable to doubt their authenticity, he turns away toward the "tendre indifférence" of the sea in search of the emotional harmony he himself needs as a relief from an unendurable otherness of feelings. Although merely uninvolved and uncommitted, tenderly indifferent, he feels suspected. Later he finds himself condemned for his lack of humane responses for which his indolence is believed to be the plausible reason.

Not until the "interrogatoires d'identité" have begun, and only during his last encounter with the priest, is his own identity fully revealed to himself.

113

Comme si cette grande colère m'avait purgé du mal, vidé d'espoir, devant cette nuit chargée de signes et d'étoiles, je m'ouvrais pour la première fois à la tendre indifférence du monde. De l'éprouver si pareil à moi, si fraternel enfin, j'ai senti que j'avais été heureux, et que je l'étais encore (pp. 171–72).

Intuitively he acted in accord with himself when he showed indifference to Raymond's plea for friendship or to Marie's wish for marriage. His indifference was underscored by the linking phrase "cela m'était égal." What mattered to him was the instinctively felt equilibrium between himself and the natural world in which emotional commitments play no part. This is the world he knew he had destroyed on the beach by unavoidably arousing an organized emotional response of men to his act which they were bound to judge as an outburst of his uncontrolled emotions and not as an accident due to circumstances. What mattered to him was the life where he found the simple joys, "les plus pauvres et les plus tenaces de mes joies: des odeurs d'été . . . un certain ciel du soir, le rire et les robes de Marie"; where he could enjoy the thrill of a mad chase after a truck in a spontaneous burst of exhilaration; where he could live with simple habits and intensely felt pleasures without self-scrutiny, without concern for appearance, without care for right or wrong; where he could be what he was without pretense and without the fear of not recognizing his face distorted by the pain of longing for freedom and by the sorrow of the awareness of deprivation.

The work began with the theme of death, and its ending deals with the same theme. In the early treatment of the theme, death is surrounded by rituals, but from Meursault's point of view, death is of little concern; it is dismissed. He lives his earthly life fully in the present, without thought of time, without forethought, and hence without the thought of death. Life is lived and enjoyed in the bright sun and in freedom. The rituals surrounding death are extraneous to his life; they are brief, disruptive, but endurable interventions which leave him unaffected. In the final treatment of the theme, rituals not merely surround death, death becomes part of a ritualistic procedure. It is the *procedure* that elicits first his repudiation, not death itself. In the end, however, Meursault's thoughts do turn to death. Be it the will of men or a mere conclusion to life, he has to face it in any case and experience life as it is lived in the shadow of death. There is an interesting linking phrase which relates two passages, one at the beginning, the other at the end of the work:

Je m'étais un peu tourné de son côté, et je le regardais lorsque le directeur m'a parlé de lui. Il m'a dit que souvent ma mère et M. Pérez allaient se

114

promener le soir jusqu'au village, accompagnés d'une infirmière. Je regardais la campagne autour de moi. A travers les lignes de cyprès qui menaient aux collines près du ciel, cette terre rousse et verte, ces maisons rares et bien dessinées, je comprenais maman. *Le soir, dans ce pays, devait être comme une trêve mélancolique* (p. 26).

Pour la première fois depuis bien longtemps, j'ai pensé à maman. Il m'a semblé que je comprenais pourquoi à la fin d'une vie elle avait pris un "fiancé", pourquoi elle avait joué à recommencer. *Là-bas, là-bas aussi, autour de cet asile où des vies s'éteignaient, le soir était comme une trêve mélancolique.* Si près de la mort, maman devait s'y sentir libérée et prête à tout revivre (p. 171).

Just as the day yields to the night, life yields when death approaches, and the "trêve mélancolique" is that period when the end of life is close. The certainty of death removes one's fears, and because death is certain and near, the thought of it can be dismissed and life renewed awhile. Potentially death being always near, life is constantly at that point where it may be lived fully anew. Because of death life may be a constant renewal in the present, in the here and now of the living experience. That is the life he loved and lived instinctively, the life which at each moment holds out the promise of immediate fulfillment, the life made precious by ever present death.

Yet this is the life for the love of which he is reproached. This is the life he is asked to deny for the sake of another, called eternity. He had cherished intuitively every moment of life because each moment was equally precious and equal to any cherished moment in the life of anybody else. Yet now he is asked to accept what to him seems an illusory notion of the soul's eternal life, and with it principles which deny spontaneity, which force men into a pattern of attitudes and conduct that repress the exultation of living, the enchantment and thrill of the privilege to live freely and newly each moment before death, the great equalizer, puts its inevitable end to it. This is his faith which he has discovered as his own through all his confrontations with the artifice of conventionalized, coercive human norms which he cannot accord with living because he cannot bring them into harmony with the "tendre indifférence" of nature:

Alors, je ne sais pas pourquoi, il y a quelque chose qui a crevé en moi. Je me suis mis à crier à plein gosier et je l'ai insulté et je lui ai dit de ne pas prier. Je l'avais pris par le collet de sa soutane. Je déversais sur lui tout le fond de mon cœur avec des bondissements mêlés de joie et de colère. Il avait l'air si certain, n'est-ce pas? Pourtant, aucune de ses certitudes ne valait un cheveu de femme. Il n'était même pas sûr d'être en vie puisqu'il vivait comme un mort. Moi, j'avais l'air d'avoir les mains vides. Mais j'étais sûr de moi, sûr de tout, plus sûr que lui, sûr de ma vie et de cette mort qui allait venir. Oui, je n'avais que cela. Mais du moins, je tenais cette vérité autant qu'elle me tenait. J'avais eu raison, j'avais encore raison, j'avais toujours raison. J'avais vécu de telle façon et j'aurais pu vivre de telle autre. J'avais fait ceci et je n'avais pas fait cela. Je n'avais pas fait telle chose alors que j'avais fait cette autre. Et après? C'était comme si j'avais attendu pendant tout le temps cette minute et cette petite aube où je serais justifié. Rien, rien n'avait d'importance et je savais bien pourquoi. Lui aussi savait pourquoi. Du fond de mon avenir, pendant toute cette vie absurde que j'avais menée, un souffle obscur remontait vers moi à travers des années qui n'étaient pas encore venues et ce souffle égalisait sur son passage tout ce qu'on me proposait alors dans les années pas plus réelles que je vivais. Que m'importaient la mort des autres, l'amour d'une mère, que m'importaient son Dieu, les vies qu'on choisit, les destins qu'on élit, puisqu'un seul destin devait m'élire moi-même et avec moi des milliards de privilégiés qui, comme lui, se disaient mes frères. Comprenait-il, comprenait-il donc? Tout le monde était privilégié. Il n'y avait que des privilégiés. Les autres aussi, on les condamnerait un jour. Lui aussi, on le condamnerait. Qu'importait si, accusé de meurtre, il était exécuté pour n'avoir pas pleuré à l'enterrement de sa mère? Le chien de Salamano valait autant que sa femme. La petite femme automatique était aussi coupable que la Parisienne que Masson avait épousée ou que Marie qui avait envie que je l'épouse. Qu'importait que Raymond fût mon copain autant que Céleste qui valait mieux que lui? Qu'importait que Marie donnât aujourd'hui sa bouche à un nouveau Meursault? Comprenait-il donc, ce condamné, et que du fond de mon avenir. . . . J'étouffais en criant tout ceci. Mais, déjà, on m'arrachait l'aumônier des mains et les gardiens me menaçaient. Lui, cependant, les a calmés et m'a regardé un moment en silence. Il avait les yeux pleins de larmes. Il s'est détourné et il a disparu (pp. 168–70).

If this faith and the life he lived by it intuitively have evoked nothing but scorn, detestation, and even horror in men who sat in judgment over him, he himself feels that it was this condemnation, exclusion, and contempt that has awakened him to the realization not only of being a stranger but of wanting to remain one; and that he needed the hatred of others to keep the consolation of his belief in his loneliness among men:

Pour que tout soit consommé, pour que je me sente moins seul, il me restait à souhaiter qu'il y ait beaucoup de spectateurs le jour de mon exécution et qu'ils m'accueillent avec des cris de haine (p. 172).

116

5

La Nausée

The Generic Coherence of Themes

The first entry on the undated pages of *La Nausée*[1] begins with Roquentin's stated project of keeping a diary "to see clearly." His first impression
of the change of which he has become conscious is an impression of altered vision: "Il faut dire comment je vois cette table, la rue, les gens, mon
paquet de tabac, puisque c'est *cela*[2] qui a changé. Il faut déterminer exactement l'étendue et la nature de ce changement" (p. 11). Looking at the
cardboard box on the table, he wants to know the difference between his
seeing it before the change and his present impression, but an exact description of perceptible features does not furnish the insight he is seeking.
Although he is certain that he may regain the impression, he knows that
he must catch it at the very moment it occurs, for it does not leave any
clear traces within him. The description of objects or the memory of the
circumstances in connection with which the impression was experienced
do not suffice to recall it. A feeling of disgust and an attendant feeling of
anxiety caused by the impression do not at first affect his confidence of being perfectly sane, but Roquentin does not dismiss entirely the possibility
of having been the victim of "une petite crise de folie." He is willing to
consider himself in that light as soon as he is able to feel the calm confidence of being "bien bourgeoisement dans le monde." The familiarity with
regularly recurring events—streetcars and trains following a known timetable or accustomed sights—helps to dispel his anxiety and remove the
threat of uneasiness caused by unfathomable impressions.

As in an overture, the initial undated pages of the diary present two major themes, the theme of nausea and the theme of bourgeois stability; of
disgust coupled with anxiety and of confident complacency. The first of
these themes is carried by initially unfathomable incidents that demand
exploration. Its development marks a progression from baffling uncer-

---

[1] All page references are to Jean-Paul Sartre, *La Nausée* (Paris: Gallimard, 1962 edition).

[2] Italics in text.

tainty, through perceptions of disconnectedness to unfolding insights into the realm of coherence, cohesion, consonance. The motifs used to carry the development of this theme do not constitute a linear progression of sequentially coherent incidents, but their individual themes mark the stages of a linear development. In this sense *La Nausée* does have a story. The contrasting correlative theme of secure self-satisfaction, or rather variations on this theme, are carried by various materially different motifs. The variations on this theme are introduced at different stages of the development of the theme of nausea.

The initial sketch clearly presents Roquentin as a character surprised by unexpected and inexplicable impressions accompanied by feelings of anxiety and disgust. Not only is there no suggestion of his vision intentionally divesting phenomena of their habitual and familiar functions and meanings, there is in fact a suggestion whereby a possible passing aberration might account for the strange experience. From the point of view of Roquentin's momentarily regained feelings of security and confidence, plausibility demands that he consider, upon reflection, his previous impressions with suspicion and outside the realm of reasonable reality. This is an important device because it permits the first sentence of the diary itself to emerge as a declaration of reasonable consciousness, as the authentication of an impression that deserves inquiry: "Quelque chose m'est arrivé, je ne peux plus en douter."

By the manner in which the analysis and description of Roquentin's impression is undertaken, two objectives are satisfied: first the need of plausibility, for the reader expects the witness of the phenomenon to recognize it as real; the other, the rational perspective from which the first stage of the thematic development is undertaken. We are told that the impression did not present itself to Roquentin "like an ordinary certainty, like anything evident." Here then is a witness who seeks ordinary certainties and evidence, and who is equipped to recognize both. Here is an historian who is used to seeking in his subject "des sentiments entiers sur lesquels on met des noms génériques comme Ambition, Intérêt." We no longer need to doubt the reasonableness and considerable competence of the man undertaking the inquiry. At the same time, however, we are made to recognize that in spite of these reassuring qualities his intellectual equipment may not be adequate to the task. At least we can follow his inquiry with confidence in his good faith and with suspense, for he has forewarned us that his impressions elude ordinary identification, classification, or familiar nomenclature.

Already on the undated pages we find a reference to the occasion that produced the first impression. In his attempt at describing it, he is reduced to noting outward appearances only, and the description is introduced by the following phrase: "Il n'y a rien eu de ce qu'on appelle à l'ordinaire un événement" (p. 11). Thereupon we learn that he picked up a pebble, was going to throw it into the sea, but dropped it and left. The next occasion that produced a similar impression occurred on the morning on which he was unable to pick up a soiled piece of paper, in spite of the fact that in the past he used to find great pleasure in picking up chestnuts, old rags, and especially the corners of soiled paper. His report is again introduced by a phrase, very similar to the preceding one: "C'est tout et ce n'est même pas un événement" (p. 22). In neither instance was there an *event* that caused the deep impression. The particular emphasis of the linking phrase is obviously intended to remove any notion that his feeling of not being free to act as he pleases is due to some quality of an event. The long description of his predilection for picking up and touching dirty objects lying in the mud also has the purpose of eliminating any assumption that his feeling of disgust might be due to the dirt with which the objects are covered. Having thus eliminated the possibility of false assumptions, Sartre uses a repetitious label to present Roquentin's impressions as they become perceptible to his touch:

> [Dans mes mains,] par example, il y a quelque chose de neuf, une certaine façon de prendre ma pipe ou ma fourchette. Ou bien c'est la fourchette qui a, maintenant, une certaine façon de se faire prendre, je ne sais pas. Tout à l'heure comme j'allais entrer dans ma chambre, je me suis arrêté net, parce que je sentais [dans ma main] un objet froid qui retenait mon attention par une sorte de personnalité. J'ai ouvert la main, j'ai regardé: je tenais tout simplement le loquet de la porte. Ce matin, à la Bibliothèque, quand l'Autodidacte est venu me dire bonjour, j'ai mis dix secondes à le reconnaître. Je voyais un visage inconnu, à peine un visage. Et puis il y avait sa main, comme un gros ver blanc [dans ma main.] Je l'ai lâchée aussitôt et le bras est retombé mollement (pp. 15–16).

These then are among the first impressions that prompt Roquentin to recognize that something has indeed happened to him and that the cause of the change needs to be discovered. Having related his feeling of being unable to pick up the paper lying in the mud, Roquentin is painfully aware of his lost freedom of action, and the recurrence of what is almost a repetitious label shows his inquiry to be still limited to an exploration of sensory perceptions:

> Je suis resté courbé, une seconde, j'ai lu "Dictée: le Hibou blanc", puis je me suis relevé, les mains vides. *Je ne suis plus libre, je ne peux plus faire ce que je veux.*[3]

---

[3] Italics are mine except where otherwise indicated. The word *"toucher"* in the next line is italic in the text.

Les objets, cela ne devrait pas *toucher,* puisque cela ne vit pas. On s'en sert, on les remet en place, on vit au milieu d'eux: ils sont utiles, rien de plus. Et moi, *ils me touchent, c'est insupportable. J'ai peur d'entrer en contact avec eux* tout comme s'ils étaient des bêtes vivantes.

Maintenant, je vois; je me rappelle mieux ce que j'ai senti, l'autre jour, au bord de la mer, quand je tenais ce galet. *C'était une espèce d'écœurement douceâtre.* Que c'était donc désagréable! Et cela venait du galet, j'en suis sûr, *cela passait du galet* [dans mes mains.] Oui, c'est cela, c'est bien cela: *une sorte de nausée* [dans les mains] (p. 23).

Things, he remarks, should be useful and used, but Roquentin feels that they touch him. They seem to confront him, which suggests that he does not confront them with a "certitude ordinaire," with the intention of handling them or using them as he ought to use them, recognizing their function or usefulness.

Two revelations provide a significant background and thus a starting point from which the changes and transitions of his intellectual stand may be traced. In spite of the fact that he begins the first of these revelations about himself with: "Je crois que c'est moi qui ai changé: c'est la solution la plus simple," we find in what he states immediately thereafter that he himself may have changed very little, but that he has become aware of his attitude of not confronting things or events, and that this awareness has led him to assume that it was he who had changed:

Mais enfin je dois reconnaître que je suis sujet à ces transformations soudaines. Ce qu'il y a, c'est que je pense très rarement; alors une foule de petites métamorphoses s'accumulent en moi sans que j'y prenne garde et puis, un beau jour, il se produit une véritable révolution. C'est ce qui a donné à ma vie cet aspect heurté, incohérent. Quand j'ai quitté la France, par example, il s'est trouvé bien des gens pour dire que j'étais parti sur un coup de tête. Et quand j'y suis revenu, brusquement, après six ans de voyage, on eût encore très bien pu parler de coup de tête (p. 16).

As he reflects on the apparently purely intuitive decision that made him suddenly return to France, he can actually remember only the occasion, and of its external manifestations mostly the perfume of Mercier's beard. The impression that accompanied his decision was a vague "insipid idea," which he could not fathom, and a feeling of having been sickened by it. Recalling this old experience, Roquentin is led to feel that his new impressions may be related to a similar unconscious process in the course of which problems not confronted intellectually finally burst to the fore and make him conscious of his state of mind, which he can hardly recognize as his own:

> Si je ne me trompe pas, si tous les signes qui s'amassent sont précurseurs d'un nouveau bouleversement de ma vie, eh bien, j'ai peur. Ce n'est pas qu'elle soit riche, ma vie, ni lourde, ni précieuse. Mais j'ai peur de ce qui va naître, s'emparer de moi—et m'entraîner où? Va-t-il falloir encore que je m'en aille, que je laisse tout en plan, mes recherches, mon livre? Me réveillerai-je dans quelques mois, dans quelques années, éreinté, déçu, au milieu de nouvelles ruines? Je voudrais voir clair en moi avant qu'il ne soit trop tard (p. 17).

Under the impact of his profoundly painful realization of not feeling free any longer, of not being able to pick up a piece of paper in spite of the promise of some pleasure it holds out for him, Roquentin pursues—though not without fear and hesitation of what he may uncover—his own portrait. He states that he continues to live in a frame of mind in which no searching questions are raised, and in which self-awareness is not awakened to the realization and formulation of coherences:

> Autrefois—longtemps même après qu'elle m'ait quitté—j'ai pensé pour Anny. Maintenant, je ne pense plus pour personne; je ne me soucie même pas de chercher des mots. Ça coule en moi, plus ou moins vite, je ne fixe rien, je laisse aller. La plupart du temps, faute de s'attacher à des mots, mes pensées restent des brouillards. Elles dessinent des formes vagues et plaisantes, s'engloutissent: aussitôt, je les oublie (p. 19).

At first he does not even wish to admit to himself his loss of freedom, but in confronting it he recognizes that he is living without retrospect and hence without awareness of coherence which retrospection alone can reveal. Since the recognition of the significance and relative importance of purposes—and hence freedom of action—is possible only in a state of awareness of coherences, he is determined to explore and to confront himself without simply yielding to vague impulses of unfathomable states of mind:

> Pourquoi n'en ai-je pas parlé? Ça doit être par orgueil, et puis, aussi, un peu par maladresse. Je n'ai pas l'habitude de me raconter ce qui m'arrive, alors je ne retrouve pas bien la succession des événements, je ne distingue pas ce qui est important. Mais à présent c'est fini: j'ai relu ce que j'écrivais au café Mably et j'ai eu honte; je ne veux pas de secrets, ni d'états d'âme, ni d'indicible; je ne suis ni vierge ni prêtre, pour jouer à la vie intérieure (p. 22).

Although he does not yet know what that "voluminous and insipid idea" was that sickened him at Hanoi and that seems to threaten him now, he is at least determined to seek safeguards in a conscious exploration of coherences in things and events, and thus in a conscious appraisal of what matters.

The second revelation about himself offers variations on the other main theme, namely, that of complacent and confident security. Roquentin is describing the familiar order on the periphery of which he is moving in solitude. Complacent and confident security is presented as the otherness from which he is gradually distinguishing and detaching himself in the process of perceiving it—an experience which reveals essentially the same process as that we have noted in Meursault. In the library he has devoted his time to a set assignment to which he has brought the orderly perception of the scholar who knows what he is looking for and what he intends to accomplish with a routine familiar to him. At the café Mably he is having a sandwich for lunch. There, too, everything is "always normal" because of its manager, whose manner is decisive and whose appearance is reassuring. Mr. Fasquelle lives in a world where everything is expected to be all right. During lunch he walks among the tables and confidently asks his customers: "C'est bien comme cela, monsieur?" He confronts his tasks with but a single concern, the proper functioning of his establishment. Outside the expected orderly function and expected utility, there is nothing in his mind: "Je souris de le voir si vif: aux heures où son établissement se vide, sa tête se vide aussi." In that familiar and orderly world there are the employees who interrupt their work routine by another: they come regularly after lunch for coffee and a game of poker dice. In their secure world of certainties they are at one with one another, they create a world for one another in which little events form a coherent chain within which man plays his part, and in which he recognizes and remembers the clear stages of his existence. The existence of Roquentin, the historian; of Mr. Fasquelle, the café manager; of the group of employees, is characterized by their confidence of finding at their tasks or among themselves the security of the familiar and of the expected. Mr. Fasquelle does not exist when he is alone; he falls asleep. And as for the employees, their existence, too, depends on the others: "Eux aussi, pour exister, il faut qu'ils se mettent à plusieurs." Roquentin, the historian, is so far secure in the library with his work, with his subject, in the world of Rollebon; but Roquentin, the man, is all alone: "Moi je vis seul, entièrement seul." Even in his intimate relationship with Françoise who runs the "Rendez-vous des Cheminots" he is alone. As far as she is concerned, he is "avant tout un client de son café."

The motif of his solitude recurs as a repetitious label. Roquentin has no share in the confident and familiar world in which men gather to exist together in secure plausibility:

> [Quand on vit seul,] on ne sait même plus ce que c'est que raconter: le vraisemblable disparaît en même temps que les amis. Les événements aussi, on les laisse couler; on voit surgir brusquement des gens qui parlent et qui s'en vont, on plonge dans des histoires sans queue ni tête: on ferait un exécrable témoin (p. 19).

In his loneliness he has no share in the carefree joy of those who see their way in a coherent world that makes sense, who attach great importance to mutual agreement that confirms the justification of their confidence in reasonableness and common sense, and who distrust the solitary man whose views may escape the control and the approval of others:

> [Je suis seul] au milieu de ces voix joyeuses et raisonnables. Tous ces types passent leur temps à s'expliquer, à reconnaître avec bonheur qu'ils sont du même avis. Quelle importance ils attachent, mon Dieu, à penser tous ensemble les mêmes choses. *Il suffit de voir la tête qu'ils font quand passe au milieu d'eux un de ces hommes aux yeux de poisson, qui ont l'air de regarder en dedans et avec lesquels on ne peut plus du tout tomber d'accord* (p. 21).

Although Roquentin seems to have remained in his solitude out of predilection, he is very much aware of being a mere amateur in his practice of solitude, and of his possible need of company and of the refuge it offers: "Mais je restais tout près des gens, [à la surface de la solitude,] bien résolu, en cas d'alerte, à me réfugier au milieu d'eux: au fond j'étais jusqu'ici un amateur" (p. 20). Although his new impressions and anxiety appear to him as danger signals that call for a retreat into sociableness ("Pour la première fois cela m'ennuie d'être seul"), he is, nevertheless, already aware that solitude may be the only condition for the perception of strong, fierce, pure, and beautiful sensations yielded by fleeting, seemingly disconnected, implausible impressions the simultaneous perception of which does reveal special coherence in spite of their improbable contiguity—improbable because it breaks through the cadre of expected familiar notions of coherence:

> Mais tout l'invraisemblable, en compensation, tout ce qui ne pourrait pas être cru dans les cafés, on ne le manque pas. Par example samedi, vers quatre heures de l'après-midi, sur le bout de troittoir en planches du chantier de la gare, une petite femme en bleu ciel courait à reculons, en riant, en agitant un mouchoir. En même temps, un nègre avec un imperméable crême, des chaussures jaunes et un chapeau vert, tournait le coin de la rue et sifflait.

La femme est venue le heurter, toujours à reculons, sous une lanterne qui est suspendue à la palissade et qu'on allume le soir. Il y avait donc là, en même temps, cette palissade qui sent si fort le bois mouillé, cette lanterne, cette petite bonne femme blonde dans les bras d'un nègre, sous un ciel de feu. *A quatre ou cinq,* je suppose que nous aurions remarqué le choc, toutes ces couleurs tendres, le beau manteau bleu qui avait l'air d'un édredon, l'imperméable clair, les carreaux rouges de la lanterne; *nous aurions ri de la stupéfaction qui paraissait sur ces deux visages d'enfants.*

Il est rare qu'un [homme seul] ait envie de rire: l'ensemble s'est animé pour moi d'un sens très fort et même farouche, mais pur. Puis il s'est disloqué, il n'est resté que la lanterne, la palissade et le ciel: c'était encore assez beau. Une heure après, la lanterne était allumée, le vent soufflait, le ciel était noir: il ne restait plus rien du tout.

Tout ça n'est pas bien neuf; ces émotions inoffensives je ne les ai jamais refusées; au contraire. Pour les ressentir [il suffit d'être un tout petit peu seul,] juste assez pour se débarrasser au bon moment de la vraisemblance (pp. 19–20).

At this point the theme of solitude in the coherent world of complacent security and confidence weaves into an emerging new theme of coherence and cohesion. Upon his decision to seek coherence, Roquentin finds it to rest upon utilitarian or simply expedient tasks of living in a world with others. It is the coherence of plausibility which is either *experienced* as a comforting, never questioned order into which life is fitted and from which it receives its pattern; or it is *perceived,* in retrospect, as a chain of little incidents the coherence of which is derived from their sequence in time. Solitude is a circumstance favoring non-confrontation, but when a confrontation does occur, phenomena may nevertheless appear coherent although outside familiar patterns of plausible coherence and common acceptability, outside experientially acquired notions of extrinsic relationships such as accustomed contiguity or sequence, cause-effect necessity, practical applicability or utility. When one is not alone, when one shares one's experiences with others, inconsecutiveness or inconsequence provoke either laughter at what appears incongruous, or repugnance and rejection of what is strikingly inconsonant with collective expectations. But if there is no habitually or purposefully oriented vision, it is possible in solitude, that is, in the absence of and in the freedom from collective expectations, to perceive phenomena in and by themselves. The effect of such a perception can be either nausea or a "strong," "fierce," "pure," and "beautiful" sensation of an *intrinsic consonance* such as described in the scene at the railroad station. Roquentin, however, is as yet only vaguely aware of the possibility of this twofold effect of his perception. The thematic correlation between the scene at the station and the ragtime tune, the emergence of their common theme of intrinsic coherence and cohesion, occurs therefore only in conjunction with the exploration of the predominant effects of Roquentin's perceptions, namely, nausea.

As if to provide both a parallel and a contrast to the theme of Roquentin's solitude, a contiguous entry in the diary is devoted to Lucie, the maid in his hotel. She is not only lonely, but in her loneliness she finds herself confronted with a striking inconsonance. If she were not alone, she could at least turn away from it by resolutely rejecting what is repulsive to her. But since she is alone, she is neither free to reject nor to endure the horror of unrelieved disgust. Therefore she takes precarious refuge in evasion. She tries to overcome her loneliness and the care and sorrow of her condition by seeking to communicate with others—in this case with the proprietress of the hotel. She seeks the comfort of being approved, of being justified, and for that she needs at least the sympathetic understanding of someone else. In her effort to overcome her sorrow, she needs another human being to witness her "taking the upper hand," to witness her self-justification in her proclaimed reasonableness, generosity, and in her concern over her husband. Lucie succeeds at times in suspending her cares when she can find support in the ephemeral sympathy of others. When she is alone, she keeps herself from thinking by singing, but her mutterings start as soon as her singing stops. Lucie cannot rid herself of the predicament confronting her by turning away from it in reasonable indifference, nor by "drowning herself in despair." Sartre describes her as being "bound." She indulges in a pretense of self-mastery and stability.

Since she "keeps herself from thinking" she remains in escapist indecision while clinging to the solace of a self-deceptive superiority: ". . . elle prend le dessus, elle n'est capable ni de se consoler ni de s'abandonner à son mal. Elle y pense un petit peu, un tout petit peu, de-ci de-là, elle l'écornifle" (p. 24). In her inability to cope with the repugnant inconsonance that confronts her, she is condemned to fluctuate between the sorrow of ineffectual commitments and the self-deceptive pretensions of strength to meet them. It is this lack of decisiveness and of freedom that condemns her to evasion and spuriousness. There is no genuine firmness, no cohesion in her behavior. Thematically this marks the transition to the next entry in the diary, although the motifs are materially completely divorced from those pertaining to Lucie.

Here we are faced with M. de Rollebon. Ten years prior to the writing of the diary, a simple chronological account of the life of the marquis, which Roquentin found in a book, endeared the colorful and clever Rolle-bon to him to such an extent that he went to Bouville rather than any other city in order to study the materials he could find in the local library. But now, ten years later, rereading his old notes, he remarks: "La figure du marquis est comme cette encre: elle a bien pâli, depuis que je m'en oc-cupe." What is it, then, that has caused him to feel baffled by Rollebon's behavior, and has turned his attention away from the marquis in spite of the ample documentation at his disposal?

> D'abord, à partir de 1801, je ne comprends plus rien à sa conduite. Ce ne sont pas les documents qui font défaut: lettres, fragments de mémoires, rapports secrets, archives de police. J'en ai presque trop, au contraire. Ce qui manque dans tous ces témoignages, c'est [le fermeté, la consistance]. Ils ne se contredisent pas, non, mais ils ne s'accordent pas non plus; ils n'ont pas l'air de concerner la même personne (p. 26).

Obviously the simple sequential coherence of incidents perceived in retro-spect is no longer of any interest to him. It is the firmness or consistency that Roquentin is seeking but is unable to find. These will be the very qualities he will seek when the diary ends, and he will hope to find them in writing the book the clarity of which might fall over his past:

> Au fond, qu'est-ce que je cherche? Je n'en sais rien. Longtemps l'homme, Rollebon, m'a intéressé plus que le livre à écrire. Mais, maintenant, l'homme ... l'homme commence à m'ennuyer. C'est au livre que je m'attache, je sens un besoin de plus en plus fort de l'écrire—à mesure que je vieillis, dirait-on (p. 26).

But it is important to note that Roquentin is already beginning to be aware of the kind of consistency and order he is seeking. It is not the precon-ceived or pre-established order one imposes on facts; it is not the classifica-tory principle within which phenomena are unified that he is eager to per-ceive; it is the intrinsic coherence and consistency that he wishes to dis-cover:

> Ce sont des hypothèses honnêtes et qui rendent compte des faits: mais je sens si bien qu'elles viennent de moi, qu'elles sont tout simplement une manière d'unifier mes connaissances. Pas une lueur ne vient du côté de Rollebon. Lents, paresseux, maussades, les faits s'accommodent à [la rigueur de l'ordre] que je veux leur donner; *mais il leur reste extérieur.* J'ai l'im-pression de faire un travail de pure imagination. Encore suis-je bien sûr que des personnages de roman auraient l'air plus vrais, seraient, en tout cas, plus plaisants (p. 27).

126

The expressions "la fermeté" and "la consistance" occur in a statement in which their lack is pointed out: "Ce qui manque dans tous ces témoignages, c'est la fermeté, la consistance" (p. 26). The component motif "la rigueur de l'ordre" expresses, in its context, the notion of an unwanted order and thus essentially the same idea of the lacking inner cohesion. Materially different or similar component motifs serving the functions of repetitious labels and linking phrases at the same time underscore and relate those instances of Roquentin's perception in which objects appearing in and by themselves produce his experience of nausea.

In contrast to the density of a "narrow sky, black with rain," Roquentin finds the pale sky "brouillé de blanc" intolerable:

Un soleil froid blanchit la poussière des vitres. Ciel [pâle, brouillé de blanc]. Les ruisseaux étaient gelés ce matin.

Je digère lourdement, près du calorifère, je sais d'avance que la journée est perdue. Je ne ferai rien de bon, sauf, peut-être, à la nuit tombée. C'est à cause du soleil; [il dore vaguement de sales brumes blanches,] suspendues en l'air au-dessus du chantier, il coule dans ma chambre, [tout blond, tout pâle, il étale sur ma table quatre reflets ternes et faux] (p. 27).

The cold light the sun projects is for Roquentin like a "pitiless judgment" that causes one to turn his thoughts back to himself, away from the "grande traînée blafarde" left on everything it happens to fall on. In that case nausea may become a reaction to oneself rather than to things outside oneself: "Un quart d'heure suffirait, j'en suis sûr, pour que je parvienne au suprême dégoût de moi" (p. 28). In vain does he turn to his Rollebon studies; his difficulties in perceiving inner consistency cause him to be utterly bored by his subject. He gets up from his work, moves "dans cette lumière pâle" which disgusts him: "je ne peux pas assez dire comme elle me dégoûte." In vain, too, does he try to combat the light of day by lighting his lamp on the table.

When he looks into the mirror, his face appears to him meaningless. He cannot see anything strikingly expressive in it, primarily because it is lacking in firmness:

C'est le reflet de mon visage. Souvent, dans ces journées perdues, je reste à le contempler. Je n'y comprends rien, à ce visage. Ceux des autres ont un sens. Pas le mien . . . .

Mon regard descend lentement, [avec ennui,] sur ce front, sur ces joues: il ne rencontre [rien de ferme], il s'ensable. Evidemment, il y a là un nez, des yeux, une bouche, mais tout ça n'a pas de sens, ni même d'expression humaine. Pourtant Anny et Vélines me trouvaient l'air vivant; il se peut que je sois trop habitué à mon visage (p. 30).

... je vois de légers tressaillements, je vois [une chair fade] qui s'épanouit et palpite avec abandon. Les yeux surtout, de si près, sont horribles. [C'est vitreux, mou, aveugle], bordé de rouge, on dirait des écailles de poisson.

Je m'appuie de tout mon poids sur le rebord de faïence, j'approche mon visage de la glace jusqu'à la toucher. Les yeux, le nez et la bouche disparaissent: il ne reste plus rien d'humain (p. 31).

By contrast the beautiful red flame of his hair does give him pleasure, and without its *"couleur nette,"* he would feel nauseated:

Il y a quand même une chose qui fait plaisir à voir, au-dessus des molles régions des joues, au-dessus du front: c'est cette belle flamme rouge qui dore mon crâne, ce sont mes cheveux. Ça, c'est agréable à regarder. C'est une [couleur nette] au moins: je suis content d'être roux. C'est là, dans la glace, ça se fait voir, [ça rayonne]. J'ai encore de la chance: si mon front portait une de ces chevelures [ternes] qui n'arrivent pas à se décider entre le châtain et le blond, ma figure se perdrait [dans le vague], elle me donnerait le *vertige* (p. 30).

His boredom with the meaninglessness of his features and his fear of being made to feel dizzy by their vagueness are the immediate effects of seeing his facial details in and by themselves. But he cannot see them with the carefree confidence stemming from known social acceptance. In his solitude he has not learned to see himself with the approving eyes of his friends:

Peut-être est-il impossible de comprendre son propre visage. Ou peut-être est-ce parce que je suis [un homme seul]? Les gens qui vivent en société ont appris à se voir, dans les glaces, tels qu'ils apparaissent à leurs amis. Je n'ai pas d'amis: est-ce pour cela que ma chair est si nue? On dirait—oui, on dirait la nature sans les hommes (p. 32).

Again we see him in search of firmness and the "sensation vive et tranchée" it may procure: "Ce n'est pas ce que je cherchais: rien de fort, [rien de neuf]; du doux, du flou, [du déjà vu]!" Here the "rien de neuf," the "already seen," reveal a new aspect of a thing perceived in and by itself. It is perceived not only outside a pattern of any meaningful relationships, it is not only lacking in firmness and consistency, it is also boring because of its unchanging, predictable, familiar persistent existence. Furthermore, it is so in its wholeness, in its "ensemble," the cohesion of which evades one's perception because its details are lacking the quality of being recognizable constituent parts of an intrinsic and necessarily cohesive unity: "Et, malgré tout, ce monde lunaire m'est familier. Je ne peux pas dire que j'en *recon-*

naisse[4] les détails. Mais l'ensemble me fait une impression de [déjà vu] qui m'engourdit: je glisse doucement dans le sommeil" (p. 31).

In this entire entry of the diary the massed motifs carrying the theme of vagueness, softness, inconsistency, foreshadow the imminence of nausea; and the motifs carrying the theme of yearning for firmness, cohesion, and meaning point to the subsequent relief from it. Nausea, however, is shown to be no longer dependent for its appearance upon such propitious circumstances as solitude or the dull light of the sun seen through the fog:

> Ça ne va pas! ça ne va pas du tout: je l'ai, la saleté, la Nausée. Et cette fois-ci, c'est nouveau: ça m'a pris dans un café. Les cafés étaient jusqu'ici mon seul refuge parce qu'ils sont *pleins de monde et bien éclairés:* il n'y aura même plus ça; quand je serai traqué dans ma chambre, je ne saurai plus où aller (p. 32).

It seems that Roquentin's feeling "surrounded, seized by a slow colored mist, a whirlpool of fog, of lights in the smoke" is now the effect and no longer the circumstance of nausea. Thus nausea is presented isolated from circumstances or basic predispositions in order to be seen as the direct result of a vision of unrelated, inconsistent, persistent existence. But to these aspects of nauseating existence new characteristic features are added. Standing on the doorstep of the café, Roquentin remarks: ". . . je ne voyais ni pourquoi c'était là, ni pourquoi c'était comme ça" (p. 32). Things seen in and by themselves are now not merely stripped of their extrinsic relationships and of their functions; their very existence and their particular manifestation in space and form—"là" and "comme ça"—are questioned, and hence their gratuitousness and fortuitousness are suggested. Roquentin does not recognize the waitress who comes to help him take off his overcoat. He does not "recognize" her because he sees her hair, her earrings, her cheeks, the pink stains under the cheekbones. This view of disconnected details instead of the unity of the whole face yields distortions because such a perception is lacking the sense of proportion with which the cohesion of wholeness is comprehended: "Je regardais ses grandes joues qui n'en finissaient pas de filer vers les oreilles" (p. 33). It is the distortion of that stripped perception, repeated for purposes of emphasis, that is the immediate cause of nausea:

> Les joues filaient, filaient vers les oreilles et Madeleine souriait:
> "Qu'est-ce que vous prenez, monsieur Antoine?"
> Alors la Nausée m'a saisi, je me suis laissé tomber sur la banquette, je ne

---

[4] Italics in text.

savais même plus où j'étais; je voyais tourner lentement les couleurs autour de moi, j'avais envie de vomir. Et voilà: depuis, la Nausée ne m'a pas quitté, elle me tient (p. 33).

In the same manner in which he sees Madeleine, Roquentin also sees the men playing cards. He does not *see* them, he "feels" their physical proximity. Only with an effort does he perceive, out of the corner of his eye, not any one of the men, but merely a disconnected hand: "un éclair rougeaud couvert de poils blancs. C'est une main" (p. 33).

Not only does any single impression appear to him in and by itself, disconnected, isolated, gratuitous, without firmness, without direction, without sense; the same holds true for the sequence in which one impression succeeds another. Roquentin's impression of the card players is repeated, in simple juxtaposition and without any connection after his nauseating impression of Adolphe. Nausea is again engendered by disjointedness, lack of firmness, gratuitousness: the purple suspenders are, at places, buried in the blue of his shirt, and the blue pales while the hesitant purple reappears, or the blue stands out without any relationship against the chocolate-colored wall. Then once again after the impression of the waving arms of the players, the sleepily oscillating Adolphe reappears.

Roquentin finally realizes that it is not a nausea within himself which is projected onto what he perceives, but that his nausea is simply there in the senseless inconsistency that surrounds him; that it is not the sickness of perception, but the perception of sickness:

> Sa chemise de coton bleu se détache joyeusement sur un mur chocolat. Ça aussi ça donne la Nausée. Ou plutôt *c'est*[5] la Nausée. La Nausée n'est pas en moi: je la ressens *là-bas*[6] sur le mur, sur les bretelles, partout autour de moi. Elle ne fait qu'un avec le café, c'est moi qui suis en elle (p. 34).

Unable to stand the nauseating impressions any longer, Roquentin seeks intuitively a significant distraction, one that has been foreshadowed by all the preceding motifs that carried the theme of yearning for firmness, direction, necessity, and for the sense with which those qualities endow an impression. Before the desired record is placed on the phonograph, Roquentin turns his head with great effort to see the players on whose consent his expected relief depends. He notes striking details in their features, but most of all he sees motions and their lack of meaningful direction:

> Les cartes tombent sur le tapis de laine, en tournoyant. Puis des mains au doigts bagués viennent les ramasser, grattant le tapis de leurs ongles.

---

[5] Italics in text.　　　　　　　　　　　　[6] Italics in text.

Les mains font des taches blanches sur le tapis, elles ont [l'air soufflé et poussiéreux]. Il tombe toujours d'autres cartes, les mains vont et viennent. Quelle drôle d'occupation: ça n'a pas l'air d'un jeu, ni d'un rite, ni d'une habitude. Je crois qu'ils font ça pour remplir le temps, tout simplement. Mais le temps est trop large, il ne se laisse pas remplir. Tout ce qu'on y plonge [s'amollit et s'étire]. Ce geste, par exemple, de la main rouge, qui ramasse les cartes en trébuchant: il es tout [flasque]. Il faudrait le découdre et tailler dedans (p. 35).

Stripped of even the obviously artificial, arbitrary and imposed consistency of a game, the gestures seem to Roquentin to be vainly attempting to fill time. In this dimension, with no intrinsic necessity to sustain them, gestures "stretch" senselessly and become "soft" and "flabby." To be meaningful by virtue of their own intrinsic consistency, the gestures would have to be completely redone: "Il faudrait le (the gesture) découdre et tailler dedans." Juxtaposed to this, we find the most significant passage carrying the theme of intrinsic consonance, consistency, necessity, and firmness, which is correlative by contrast (1) to the theme of vagueness, inconsistency, persistence, and gratuitousness of whatever is seen as existing in and by itself, and (2) equally correlative to the theme of extrinsic, imposed, preconceived coherence of the familiar world in which men live together confidently and complacently:

Tout à l'heure viendra le refrain: c'est lui surtout que j'aime et [la manière abrupte] dont il se jette en avant, comme une falaise contre la mer. Pour l'instant, c'est le jazz qui joue; *il n'y a pas de mélodie,* juste des notes, [une myriade de petites secousses]. *Elles ne connaissent pas de repos,* [un ordre inflexible] *les fait naître et les détruit, sans leur laisser jamais le loisir de se reprendre,* [d'exister pour soi]. Elles courent, elles se pressent, *elles me frappent au passage d'un coup sec et s'anéantissent.* J'aimerais bien les retenir, mais je sais que, si j'arrivais à en arrêter une, il ne resterait plus entre mes doigts qu'un son canaille et [languissant]. Il faut que j'accepte leur mort; cette mort, je dois même la *vouloir*[7]: je connais peu d'impressions [plus âpres ni plus fortes] (p. 36).

The abrupt manner of the refrain, the myriad of jolts, the inflexible order all point to the rigorous intrinsic cohesion of the tune. This impression is produced with even greater purity by the mere notes that precede the refrain because they do not even have as much as a melody which might, by virtue of its foreseeable development, suggest a semblance of duration and thus conceivably belong to our time. These impressions of order in music

---

[7] Italics in text.

are free from any notion of existence for itself because of the perceived necessity of consistency and because of the evanescence of each impression. These conditions preclude even the perception of the very *order in time as existing*. All one is left with is a fleeting recognition of order as a *quality that is, but does not exist*. Roquentin wishes to hold back, to keep, each sharp impression, but he knows that for it to be sharp and firm, and for its necessity to be experienced, he must not only accept its death, he must *want* it, lest its duration in human time become an oppressively weighty and familiar presence.

In the course of the development of the broad composite theme of nausea, we have noted motifs carrying the theme of vagueness, inconsistency, and gratuitousness. We have also seen the emergence of a contrasting correlative theme of yearning for firmness, cohesion, and necessity. The theme of bourgeois stability, confident complacency, secure self-satisfaction, or at least the painful pretense thereof (presented by Lucie, the maid), was introduced for contrast from the very beginning to depict a world in which nausea is shut out by practical and orderly purposefulness, by functional considerations, and by the consciousness of one's collective approval. Because of these particular aspects, this theme is structured on plausible coherence, firmness, cohesion, and even necessity which, however, are extrinsically imposed and which are justified by mere expediency. It might be expected that Roquentin, yearning for at least some of these qualities, living "on the surface of solitude," and resolved to seek refuge if necessary in the plausible world of men, should wish to satisfy his yearning and free himself of nausea by taking refuge. Yet we know that he does not and cannot, exactly because he fails to recognize in the world around him the special qualities of intrinsic cohesion and necessity he is seeking. He is succumbing to the most acute experience of nausea because he sees either inconsistency or an extrinsic consistency around him. In a flash of insight he has recognized in the imperturbable duration of disconnected details in time the seat of his nausea. He will soon discover that what constitutes the apparent firmness of the order that surrounds him is the firmness of arbitrary purposes; in its apparent cohesion, he will discover an imposed pattern of forced juxtapositions; and in seeming necessity, he will discover gratuitous rigidity.

However, Roquentin is already aware of that unique aspect of the "inflexible order" of music which consists of never allowing any note to last long enough to assume an existence in and by itself, to become distended in *"our"* time." In the sequence of evanescent notes time is experienced in the uninterrupted births and deaths of impressions. The necessity of each note is determined by the death of its immediate antecedent and the emergence of the note that follows. Each note proves also the necessity of its antecedent, and is the audible cohesive link to the note that follows. Intrinsic structural coherence and necessity, and time measured by constant renewals, constitute the inflexible order. This order has the firmness, the necessity, and the cohesion Roquentin seeks in order to free himself of nausea. However, firmness, necessity, and cohesion of an order do not suffice unless they conquer existence in human time, unless they preclude the perception of duration in which details last long enough to be seen by themselves, without necessary coherences, and gratuitously at what Sartre calls "the bottom of the viscous puddle, at the bottom of our time." It is this short conquest of existence in human time, this conquest of duration in time, that creates the "small happiness of nausea," that familiar happiness during which one is lifted out of the oppressive present by a fleeting experience of the uniqueness of a passing moment. Roquentin experiences, however, yet another happiness: his life suddenly enters into the time of music. In music inevitable cohesion and intrinsic consonance may be broken, destroyed by any occurrence in our time, but as long as their manifestations last no happening in our time can interrupt them:

> Quelques secondes encore et la négresse va chanter. Ça semble [inévitable, si forte est la nécessité] de cette musique: rien ne peut l'interrompre, rien qui vienne de ce temps où le monde est affalé; [elle cessera d'elle-même, par ordre]. Si j'aime cette belle voix, c'est surtout pour ça: ce n'est ni pour son ampleur ni pour sa tristesse, c'est qu'elle est l'événement que tant de notes ont préparé, de si loin, en mourant pour qu'il naisse. Et pourtant je suis inquiet; il faudrait si peu de chose pour que le disque s'arrête: qu'un ressort se brise, que le cousin Adolphe ait un caprice. Comme il est étrange, comme il est émouvant que cette [dureté] soit si fragile. Rien ne peut l'interrompre et tout peut la briser (pp. 36–37).

At the most intense moments of nausea Roquentin felt it "sur le mur, sur les bretelles, partout autour de moi. Elle ne fait qu'un avec le café, [c'est moi qui suis en elle]" (p. 34). When under the impact of music Roquentin suddenly realizes that he is finally freed of nausea, he exclaims: "Je suis *dans*[8] la musique" (p. 37). The linking phrase of "being in" either nausea or music points with special emphasis to the correlative nature of the themes both carry. The other motifs used in connection with these two themes point to their contrasting nature. In his state of nausea everything was stretched, disintegrating. Now, within the time of music everything hardens, the room assumes a metallic transparency, and the glass of beer shrinks and appears dense. Even sleepy

---

[8] Italics in text.

Adolphe, who could barely stand on his feet and who sickened Roquentin because of his utterly meaningless expression, now provides an occasion for happiness derived from Roquentin's perception of intrinsic cohesion and necessity:

> Le visage d'Adolphe est là, posé contre le mur chocolat; il a l'air tout proche. Au moment où ma main se refermait, j'ai vu sa tête; [elle avait l'évidence, la nécessité d'une conclusion]. Je presse mes doigts contre le verre, je regarde Adolphe: je suis heureux (p. 37).

The game of cards, which before did not look like a game at all but merely like a gratuitous sequence of fumbling and flabby gestures stretching senselessly in a vain effort to let time pass, is now seen as a sequence of gestures and moves, as necessary consequences of combinations conceived long before their occurrence. The change in the vision is due to a change from perceiving each move and gesture individually and without connection with anterior and posterior moves, from a limited vision of each move in and by itself, to one that recognizes in each move the last point in a line of necessary progression. Each occurrence in time becomes in its ephemeral manifestation the culmination in a "rigorous succession of circumstances." Each event becomes the focal point from which antecedents reveal in the perspective of retrospection a sequence the "necessity" of which is secured by their immutable past. Events seen in that perspective derive their meaning from such a necessity and only in the course of a retrospective perception do they acquire the quality of adventures the vision of which alone may turn each minute of one's life into a meaningful culmination:

> La silhouette du roi de cœur paraît entre des doigts crispés, puis on le retourne sur le nez et le jeu continue. Beau roi, venu de si loin, préparé par tant de combinaisons, par tant de gestes disparus. *Le voilà qui disparaît à son tour, pour que naissent d'autres combinaisons et d'autres gestes, des attaques, des répliques, des retours de fortune, une foule de petites aventures.*
>
> Je suis ému, je sens mon corps comme une machine de précision au repos. Moi, j'ai eu de vraies aventures. Je n'en retrouve aucun détail, mais *j'aperçois l'enchaînement rigoureux des circonstances.* J'ai traversé les mers, j'ai laissé des villes derrière moi et j'ai remonté des fleuves ou bien je me suis enfoncé dans des forêts, et j'allais toujours vers d'autres villes. J'ai eu des femmes, je me suis battu avec des types; et jamais je ne pouvais revenir en arrière, pas plus qu'un disque ne peut retourner à rebours. *Et tout cela me menait où?*[9] *A cette minute-ci, à cette banquette, dans cette bulle de clarté toute bourdonnante de musique* (p. 38).

---

[9] The word "*où*" is italic in the text.

When he steps out of the café into the cold air to take a walk, he hesitates about which direction to take. He does not feel tempted by the lights of the main streets leading into the heart of the city where dogs, men, and "toutes les masses molles" move with senseless spontaneity. Instead he sinks into the dark hole, the Boulevard Noir, where an icy wind, stones, and earth give him again the sensation of firmness and hardness he has just experienced in freeing himself from nausea which, by contrast, was accompanied by sensations of flabbiness, softness, floating, and the feeling of being "dazed by luminous fogs." Again in contrast to the firm, dark, motionless stones of the boulevard which he wishes to reach, there is a tedious stretch: "Il y a un bout de chemin ennuyeux: sur le trottoir de droite, une masse gazeuse, grise avec des traînées de feu" (pp. 39–40). Before reaching the blackness of the deserted and lifeless part of the street, he steps into a puddle. Although his "sock is soaked through," he is obviously determined to continue his walk: "la promenade commence." Soon he steps with both feet into the gutter, but he goes on in pursuit of exhilaration:

J'ai froid, les oreilles me font mal; elle doivent être toutes rouges. Mais je ne me sens plus; *je suis gagné par la pureté de ce qui m'entoure;* rien ne vit; *le vent siffle, des lignes raides fuient dans la nuit.* Le boulevard Noir n'a pas la mine indécente des rues bourgeoises, qui font des grâces aux passants. Personne n'a pris soin de le parer: c'est tout juste en envers. L'envers de la rue Jeanne-Berthe-Cœuroy, de l'avenue Galvani. Aux environs de la gare, les Bouvillois le surveillent encore un petit peu; ils le nettoient de temps en temps, à cause des voyageurs. Mais, tout de suite après, ils l'abandonnent et *il file tout droit,* aveuglément, pour aller *se cogner* dans l'avenue Galvani. La ville l'a oublié. Quelquefois, un gros camion couleur de terre le traverse à toute vitesse, *avec un bruit de tonnerre.* On n'y assassine même pas, faute d'assassins et de victimes. Le boulevard Noir est *inhumain.* Comme un *minéral.* Comme un *triangle* (p. 41).

All the above motifs (which I have italicized) carry essentially the same theme of stiffness, firmness, hardness, solidity, and *being* like that of a triangle or like that of the tones to which, he thought, an inflexible order gave birth while dispelling his nausea. The cold purity of the darkness has the same effect on Roquentin as the music did; it penetrates him, it is in him as he is in it:

La Nausée est restée là-bas, dans la lumière jaune. Je suis heureux: ce froid est si pur, si pure cette nuit; ne suis-je pas moi-même une vague d'air glacé? N'avoir ni sang, ni lymphe, ni chair. Couler dans ce long canal vers cette pâleur là-bas. N'être que du froid (p. 42).

While Roquentin was living within the time of music, gestures, faces, and things assumed individually an inner cohesion and the previously disparate phenomena combined into a unified pattern of a whole. Similarly, surrounded by the almost tangibly firm darkness of the street, under the beams of a single gaslight, the torn pieces of a poster, whose originally simple, intended, and unified features have disappeared, assume in Roquentin's eyes a new unity. Again, a similar correlative theme recurs in the darkness of the night when Lucie's suffering achieves the purity of unity and authenticity, for she does not slide into the false and vain pretense of overcoming her grief by evasion. Her "face is shining with pain." Roquentin envies her for being able to give herself at last fully to her pain, to experience it without the self-consciousness and calm resignation that rob him of the genuine and total oneness and unity of emotion:

> Oui, c'est elle, c'est Lucie. Mais transfigurée, hors d'elle-même, souffrant avec une folle générosité. Je l'envie. *Elle est là, toute droite, écartant les bras,* comme si elle attendait les stigmates; elle ouvre la bouche, elle suffoque. *J'ai l'impression que les murs ont grandi,* de chaque côté de la rue, qu'ils se sont rapprochés, qu'elle est au fond d'un puits. J'attends quelques instants: *j'ai peur qu'elle ne tombe raide:* elle est trop malingre pour supporter cette douleur insolite. *Mais elle ne bouge pas, elle a l'air minéralisée comme tout ce qui l'entoure.* Un instant je me demande si je ne m'étais pas trompé sur elle, si ce n'est pas sa vraie nature qui m'est soudain révélée . . .
>
> Lucie émet un petit gémissement. Elle porte la main à sa gorge en ouvrant de grands yeux étonnés. *Non, ce n'est pas en elle qu'elle puise la force de tant souffrir. Ça lui vient du dehors . . . c'est ce boulevard.* Il faudrait la prendre par les épaules, l'emmener aux lumières, au milieu des gens, dans les rues douces et roses: *là-bas, on ne peut pas souffrir si fort; elle s'amollirait, elle retrouverait son air positif et le niveau ordinaire de ses souffrances.*
>
> Je lui tourne le dos. Après tout, elle a de la chance. Moi je suis bien trop calme, depuis trois ans. *Je ne peux plus rien recevoir de ces solitudes tragiques, qu'un peu de pureté à vide.* Je m'en vais (p. 43).

Thus we see the correlative nature of the themes carried by the motifs of the music and of the Boulevard Noir. We also see the componence of the motifs depicting the card players, Adolphe, the objects in the café with the motifs depicting Lucie on the dark street. In spite of great material differences, the affinity of the themes these two sets of component motifs carry is striking. In retrospect we may also note the correlative nature of the themes carried by the scene in which we see Lucie in the hotel and by the scene immediately preceding Roquentin's attack of nausea in the café. He does not feel nausea when he sees Lucie in the hotel, but he notes her lack of authenticity and her evasion at the time he is preoccupied with this new experience. The contrast between her lack of authenticity at the hotel and her authentic despair on the boulevard, and the contrast between Roquentin's nausea and his liberation, some aspects of which he is savoring in the darkness of the street where he finds Lucie, clearly relate spuriousness thematically to nausea.

Disconnectedness, lack of firmness, lack of intrinsic consonance, of decisiveness and direction, gratuitousness or mere functional expediency, lack of intrinsic structural necessity, persistent existence in and by itself in time (as opposed to the evanescent phenomenon that emerges as a culmination of a necessary succession of equally ephemeral phenomena), confident complacency and spuriousness constitute a cluster of themes with which the experience of nausea is associated. Subsequent variations on these themes, the purpose of which is a further exploration and clarification of Roquentin's disgust with existence and of his anxious search for a meaningful being, lead us first from the statue of Gustave Impétraz, to the Self-Taught Man, and to the revelation of the "voluminous and insipid idea" that repelled him at Hanoi.

The statue of Gustave Impétraz is bourgeois stability, respectability, and authority cast in bronze. On his pedestal that "bronze giant" is the trustworthy guardian of propriety, of transmitted ideals and of commonly held beliefs. Like M. Fasquelle at his café Mably, Gustave Impétraz too looks positive and reassuring to the citizens of Bouville who can hold on to their beliefs with the confident complacency of knowing that they are right and that all is in order. Just as the people in the café spend their time "happily realizing that they are all of the same opinion," attaching great importance to "thinking the same things all together," so the ladies in the little court happily realize the same:

Il tient son chapeau de la main gauche et pose la main droite sur une pile d'in-folio: c'est un peu comme si leur grand-père était là, sur ce socle, coulé en bronze. Elles n'ont pas besoin de le regarder longtemps pour comprendre qu'il pensait comme elles, tout juste comme elles, sur tous les sujets. Au service de leurs petites idées étroites et solides il a mis son autorité et l'immense érudition puisée dans les in-folio que sa lourde main écrase. Les dames en noir se sentent soulagées, elles peuvent vaquer tranquillement aux soins du ménage, promener leur chien: les saintes idées, les bonnes idées qu'elles tiennent de leurs pères, elles n'ont plus la responsabilité de les défendre; un homme de bronze s'en est fait le gardien (p. 44).

Thanks to this symbol of stability, they do not need to feel the responsibility of scrutinizing their ideas, of ever questioning their justification. Their ideas are safely persisting in immutable existence. Although Roquentin does not feel nauseated, he does find that the little court has "quelque chose de sec et de mauvais, une pointe délicate d'horreur. Ça vient de ce bonhomme, là-haut, sur son socle. En coulant cet universitaire dans le bronze, on en a fait un sorcier" (p. 44). He feels repelled by Imprétaz, who gives him the impression of wanting to drive him away for not belonging, for being unwanted and excluded. But instead of succumbing to nausea, this time Roquentin's repugnance elicits at least a little resistance:

> Je regarde Impétraz en face. Il n'a pas d'yeux, à peine de nez, une barbe rongée par cette lèpre étrange qui s'abat quelquefois, comme une épidémie, sur toutes les statues d'un quartier. Il salue; son gilet, à l'endroit du cœur, porte une grande tache vert clair. Il a l'air souffreteux et mauvais. Il ne vit pas, non, mais il n'est pas non plus inanimé. Une sourde puissance émane de lui: c'est comme un vent qui me repousse: Impétraz voudrait me chasser de la cour des Hypothèques. Je ne partirai pas avant d'avoir achevé cette pipe (p. 45).

An even more significant reaction can be observed in Roquentin's encounter with the Self-Taught Man. Although he "smells of tobacco and stagnant water" and his "souffle empesté" causes Roquentin to throw himself back in order to avoid it, there is no sign of nausea. Roquentin is slightly annoyed but at the same time amused by this caricature of studiousness and erudition. While the motifs pertaining to Impétraz carry primarily the themes of persistent existence, confident complacency, bourgeois stability, gratuitousness, and spuriousness, the motifs pertaining to the Self-Taught Man emphasize in particular some of the other aspects of the cluster of themes we have mentioned.

To some extent the Autodidacte, as he is called, reflects attitudes which Roquentin has already recognized or is recognizing in himself. In objectifying them, he has treated them with irony. We remember his reflections on his materials on Rollebon, and on his attempts at unifying them in a coherent system which, as he discovered, had to be imposed on them. Hence the structure imposed on his materials was extraneous to them—to that extent artificial—and did not achieve the rigor of an intrinsic order. The Autodidacte's system of self-instruction offers a parallel component motif: "il s'instruit dans l'ordre alphabétique." It is the theme of artificiality and gratuitousness carried by these motifs that reveals their component nature. The Autodidacte's method offers in exaggerated form an imposed system of unification of knowledge which substitutes for the rigor of an intrinsic order the rigidity of the alphabet without any concern for any coherence in the subject matter of the books he studies. This approach is rigid, mechanistic, preposterous, and therefore comical. But it has another, more serious aspect as well. The Autodidacte's knowledge is necessarily scrappy, subject to confusion, without purpose; and his pursuit is a gratuitous progression into the future with every assurance of its retaining the same aspect as the past, for the alphabetical quantitative advance in knowledge does not affect the disproportion between what the Autodidacte already knows and what will remain to be explored:

Il a tout lu; il a emmagasiné dans sa tête la moitié de ce qu'on sait sur la parthénogénèse, la moitié des arguments contre la vivisection. Derrière lui, devant lui, il y a un univers. Et le jour approche où il se dira, en fermant le dernier volume du dernier rayon d'extrême gauche: "Et maintenant?" (p. 47).

Under a new entry in the diary and without any material connection, the same theme of gratuitous progression into the future is re-emphasized. An old woman, whom Roquentin watches from his window, is passing by. He can foresee her movements and the direction she will take. The time of transition from the present to the future makes itself felt by its duration because the future is without surprise, for its manifestation can be foreseen. Persistent duration, experienced in the course of perceiving predictable transitions from one stage of existence to another barely altered stage, is hardly less repugnant than that of oppressive immutability in the present:

Je ne distingue plus le présent du futur et pourtant ça dure, ça se réalise peu à peu; la vieille avance dans la rue déserte, elle déplace ses gros souliers d'homme. C'est ça le temps, le temps tout nu, ça vient lentement à l'existence, ça se fait attendre et quand ça vient, on est écœuré parce qu'on s'aperçoit que c'était déjà là depuis longtemps. La vieille approche du coin de la rue, ce n'est plus qu'un petit tas d'étoffes noires. Eh bien, oui, je veux bien, c'est neuf, ça, elle n'était pas là-bas tout à l'heure. Mais c'est du neuf terni, défloré, qui ne peut jamais surprendre (p. 48).

The image of the old woman, which not merely foreshadows the future for Roquentin but permits him to foresee it, is a link between the persistent gratuitous existence of the spirit of Impétraz, whose statue will remain a symbol of erudition protecting narrow-mindedness, and the Autodidacte, whose erudition will never free him from his own limitations. Both Impétraz and the Autodidacte will continue perpetuating the present. The questions Roquentin raises as he watches the woman apply equally to Impétraz and the Autodidacte: "Je *vois*[10] l'avenir. Il est là, posé dans la rue, à peine plus pâle que le présent. Qu'a-t-il besoin de se réaliser? Qu'est-ce que ça lui donnera de plus?" (p. 47). That both represent a sort of stagnant and nauseating eternity, just as the old woman does, may be seen from a passage that follows immediately the reflections just mentioned:

> Elle va tourner le coin de la rue, elle tourne—pendant une éternité.
>
> Je m'arrache de la fenêtre et parcours la chambre en chancelant; [je m'englue au miroir, je me regarde, je me dégoûte]: encore une éternité (p. 48).

The linking phrase clearly alludes to an earlier impression—"une impression de déjà vu qui m'engourdit" (p. 31). Thus the vision of the future as devoid of all surprises, as the foreseeable recurrence of the known, is re-emphasized.

There is a thematic correlation between the Autodidacte and Roquentin. We have already noted the lack of purpose and the confusion that mark the Autodidacte's erudition, and that becomes quite evident while he is looking at Roquentin's photographs of his travels. The derivative nature of his knowledge is emphasized by the use of materially different motifs the thematic correlation of which is, however, obvious. Despite their material difference, these motifs perform the function of repetitious labels:

> [Si ce qu'on dit est vrai], les voyages sont la meilleure école (p. 51).
>
> [J'ai lu] qu'il y a des voyageurs qui ont tellement changé ... (p. 51).
>
> [Il y a un livre] bien curieux, monsieur, sur ces statues en peau de bête ... (p. 51).
>
> [Peut-on dire, avec Pascal], que la coutume est une seconde nature? (p. 52).
>
> [Mais j'ai lu un livre] sur Ségovie (p. 52).

The confusion and the uncertainties which deform his amassed knowledge also receive emphasis:

> Et la Vierge noire? Elle n'est pas à Burgos, elle est à Saragosse? Mais il y en a peut-être une à Burgos? Les pèlerins l'embrassent, n'est-ce pas?—je veux dire: celle de Saragosse (p. 51).

---

[10] Italics in text.

Mais je me défie tant de moi-même; il faudrait avoir tout lu (p. 52).

Monsieur, je ne me rappelle plus le nom de son auteur. J'ai parfois des absences. No ... No ... Nod ... (p. 52).

On parle de la magie des aventures. Cette expression vous semble-t-elle juste? (p. 53).

Through learning he has acquired scraps of knowledge that fill his head, but he feels their insufficiency: "... j'aimerais aussi qu'il m'arrivât de l'inattendu, du nouveau, des aventures pour tout dire" (p. 53). For him an adventure is a single unusual event:

> "Quelle espèce d'aventures?" lui dis-je étonné.
> "Mais toutes les espèces, monsieur. On se trompe de train. On descend dans une ville inconnue. On perd son portefeuille, on est arrêté par erreur, on passe la nuit en prison. Monsieur, j'ai cru qu'on pouvait définir l'aventure: un événement qui sort de l'ordinaire, sans être forcément extraordinaire (p. 53).

The parallelism of component motifs becomes striking when we realize that Roquentin is also looking at some photographs; not those he keeps in a box under the table, but those he has preserved in his memory. He, too, experiences the elusiveness of images that belong in the past, but the difference between himself and the Autodidacte is that he knows it and does not merely experience it:

> Meknès. Comment donc était-il ce montagnard qui nous fit peur dans une ruelle, entre la mosquée Berdaine et cette place charmante qu'ombrage un mûrier? Il vint sur nous, Anny était à ma droite. Ou à ma gauche?
> Ce soleil et ce ciel bleu n'étaient que tromperie. C'est la centième fois que je m'y laisse prendre. Mes souvenirs sont comme les pistoles dans la bourse du diable: quand on l'ouvrit, on n'y trouva que des feuilles mortes (p. 49).

He knows the difference between remembering experiences and the mere knowledge of their past existence, a knowledge that deprives them of their reality:

> Ce Marocain était grand et sec, d'ailleurs je l'ai vu seulement lorsqu'il me touchait. Ainsi je *sais*[11] encore qu'il était grand et sec: certaines connaissances abrégées demeurent dans ma mémoire. Mais je ne *vois*[12] plus rien: j'ai beau fouiller le passé je n'en retire plus que des bribes d'images et je ne sais pas très bien ce qu'elles représentent, ni si ce sont des souvenirs ou des fictions (p. 49).

---

[11] Italics in text.   [12] Italics in text.

He knows how mere words displace or destroy past images, past occurrences, and how the present obliterates the past. Just as the Autodidacte wishes to be moved by some adventure, so Roquentin, too, likes to be able to conjure up and relive some extraordinary past occurrences which words have not yet cast into a rigid mold and which are still alive as perceptible images. He realizes, however, that these are merely dull memories, not of living but of stiff and lifeless verbal formulations. Single past experiences become disconnected incoherent shreds which when recalled are just as repulsive as all the vague and incoherent manifestations that caused his nausea. It was that sort of feeling that filled him with disgust at Hanoi—the feeling that any number of single experiences do not by themselves constitute an adventure:

> D'ordinaire, en effet, je suis plutôt fier d'avoir eu tant d'aventures. Mais aujourd'hui, à peine ai-je prononcé ces mots, que je suis pris d'une grande indignation còntre moi-même: il me semble que je mens, que de ma vie je n'ai eu la moindre aventure, ou plutôt je ne sais même plus ce que ce mot veut dire. En même temps pèse sur mes épaules ce même découragement qui me prit à Hanoï, il y a près de quatre ans, quand Mercier me pressait de me joindre à lui et que je fixais sans répondre une statuette khmère. Et l'IDÉE est là, cette grosse masse blanche qui m'avait tant dégoûté alors: je ne l'avais pas revue depuis quatre ans (p. 53).

. . . .

> Il y a encore cette idée, devant moi, qui attend. Elle s'est mise en boule, elle reste là comme un gros chat; elle n'explique rien, elle ne bouge pas et se contente de dire non. Non, je n'ai pas eu d'aventures (p. 54).

The recurring reminiscence of the nauseating "IDÉE," which occurs for the first time in connection with the change in his vision of objects and his reaction to them (pp. 16–17), and in the course of his reflections on the jerky, incoherent aspect of his life, now finally reveals—at least in the form of a negation—that any single experience, however extraordinary, becomes insipid unless it falls into some such context as that of an inevitable and necessary succession of evanescent firm notes of music, unless it acquires a place in a rigorous order:

> Je suis ému, je sens mon corps comme une machine de précision au repos. *Moi, j'ai eu de vraies aventures.* Je n'en retrouve aucun détail, *mais j'aperçois l'enchaînement rigoureux des circonstances.* J'ai traversé les mers, j'ai laissé des villes derrière moi et j'ai remonté des fleuves ou bien je me suis enfoncé dans des forêts, et j'allais toujours vers d'autres villes. J'ai eu des femmes, je me suis battu avec des types; et jamais je ne pouvais revenir en arrière, pas plus qu'un disque ne peut tourner à rebours. Et tout cela me

menait *où?*[13] A cette minute-ci, à cette banquette, dans cette bulle de clarté toute bourdonnante de musique (p. 38).

But now, having had time to reflect on what it is that differentiates an extraordinary event from an adventure, Roquentin also realizes what it is that turns an event into an adventure:

Je n'ai pas eu d'aventures. Il m'est arrivé des histoires, de événements, des incidents, tout ce qu'on voudra. *Mais pas des aventures.* Ce n'est pas une question de mots; je commence à comprendre. Il y a quelque chose à quoi je tenais plus qu'à tout le reste—sans m'en rendre bien compte. Ce n'était pas l'amour, Dieu non, ni la gloire, ni la richesse. C'était . . . Enfin je m'étais imaginé qu'a de certains moments ma vie pouvait prendre une qualité rare et précieuse. *Il n'était pas besoin de circonstances extraordinaires: je demandais tout juste un peu de rigueur.* Ma vie présente n'a rien de très brillant: mais de temps en temps, par exemple quand *on jouait de la musique dans les cafés, je revenais en arrière et je me disais: autrefois, à Londres, à Meknès, à Tokio j'ai connu des moments admirables, j'ai eu des aventures.* C'est ça qu'on m'enlève, à présent. Je viens d'apprendre, brusquement, sans raison apparente, que *je me suis menti pendant dix ans. Les aventures sont dans les livres.* Et naturellement, tout ce qu'on raconte dans les livres peut arriver pour de vrai, *mais pas de la même manière. C'est à cette manière d'arriver que je tenais si fort* (pp. 54–55).

Although Roquentin's statement clearly indicates that what matters is the manner in which events occur, and although that is true, it is equally true that under the impact of music in the café everything, including Adolphe, the card players, and his memories, all fell into the firm and inevitable "enchaînement rigoureux" of time and circumstance. It is then not only the manner in which events occur that endows them with the quality of adventures, but also the particular vision that permits that manner to be perceived. The manner manifests itself through a clear beginning, quite like the abrupt manner in which the refrain of the song "throws itself forward, like a cliff against the sea."

Il aurait fallu d'abord que les commencements fussent de vrais commencements. Hélas! Je vois si bien maintenant ce que j'ai voulu. De vrais commencements, apparaissant comme une sonnerie de trompette, comme les premières notes d'un air de jazz, brusquement, coupant court à l'ennui, raffermissant la durée . . . (p. 55).

The manner also manifests itself by the end of each occurrence. Just as he accepts the death of each tone and must want it in fact, Roquentin

---

[13] Italics in text.

must also want the death of each moment that carries the adventure to its end:

> Quelque chose commence pour finir: l'aventure ne se laisse pas mettre de rallonge; elle n'a de sens que par sa mort. Vers cette mort, qui sera peut-être aussi la mienne, je suis entraîné sans retour. Chaque instant ne paraît que pour amener ceux qui suivent. A chaque instant je tiens de tout mon cœur: je sais qu'il est unique; irremplaçable—et pourtant je ne ferais pas un geste pour l'empêcher de s'anéantir. Cette dernière minute que je passe—à Berlin, à Londres—dans les bras de cette femme, rencontrée l'avant-veille—minute que j'aime passionnément, femme que je suis près d'aimer—elle va prendre fin, je le sais. Tout à l'heure je partirai pour un autre pays. Je ne retrouverai ni cette femme ni jamais cette nuit. Je me penche sur chaque seconde, j'essaie de l'épuiser; rien ne passe que je ne saisisse, que je ne fixe pour jamais en moi, rien, ni la tendresse fugitive de ces beaux yeux, ni les bruits de la rue, ni la clarté fausse du petit jour: et cependant la minute s'écoule et je ne la retiens pas, j'aime qu'elle passe (pp. 55–56).

The haunting "IDÉE" emerges again: not as before denying his having had any adventures, but denying the possibility of anybody's actually experiencing an adventure. Roquentin reflects on the reason for there not being any adventures: the reason is that in the process of living we are lacking the vision that renders perceptible the manner in which adventures occur. That is the vision that encompasses each moment simultaneously from two perspectives: from the point of view of the actual moment of evanescent perception and, at the same time, from an a posteriori point of view in which each fleeting moment suggests a promise of an inevitable conclusion and each revealed conclusion draws toward itself each preceding moment. This rigorous intrinsic order in which all events allude simultaneously to antecedent and posterior events, he thinks, can be perceived only in the course of reminiscing or in telling a story. In the process of living, except for what Roquentin called before "un petit bonheur de Nausée," and what he now calls the occasional "total partiel," life is an "interminable and monotonous" piling up of random occurrences. Such, he feels, is the truth, the reality of living. Stories cannot be true, for the truth in living lies in its nauseating lack of perceiving in it the intrinsic order which music has revealed for him, and which, he now believes, the point of view from which a story is told may also reveal:

> Quand on vit, il n'arrive rien. Les décors changent, les gens entrent et sortent, voilà tout. Il n'y a jamais de commencements. Les jours s'ajoutent aux jours sans rime ni raison, c'est une addition interminable et monotone.

De temps en temps, on fait un total partiel: on dit: voilà trois ans que je voyage, trois ans que je suis à Bouville. Il n'y a pas de fin non plus: on ne quitte jamais une femme, un ami, une ville en une fois. Et puis tout se ressemble: Shanghaï, Moscou, Alger, au bout d'une quinzaine, c'est tout pareil. Par moments—rarement—on fait le point, on s'aperçoit qu'on s'est collé avec une femme, engagé dans une sale histoire. Le temps d'un éclair. Après ça, le défilé recommence, on se remet à faire l'addition des heures et des jours. Lundi, mardi, mercredi. Avril, mai, juin. 1924, 1925, 1926.

Ça, c'est vivre. Mais quand on raconte la vie, tout change; seulement c'est un changement que personne ne remarque: la preuve c'est qu'on parle d'histoires vraies. Comme s'il pouvait y avoir des histoires vraies; les événements se produisent dans un sens et nous les racontons en sens inverse (pp. 57–58).

A seemingly incidental exploration of the themes with which the experience of nausea is associated, but in particular a further exploration of the theme of adventure, the theme of a rigorous intrinsic order, occurs in a set of motifs describing Sunday at Bouville. Although sequentially again unrelated to preceding motifs, the motifs now encountered do relate thematically to previous ones, and from a certain point on they do so explicitly. Having at first doubted having had any adventures, and later having believed that adventures evade direct experience and belong only in the realm of reminiscence or of a story, Roquentin nevertheless recalls an incident (p. 57) in a café in San Pauli that brought an actual experience of adventure for a brief moment to his awareness. It is true that for him to experience it, he had first to recall it: "Je me suis mis à me raconter ce qui s'était passé depuis mon débarquement." Nevertheless, the incidents he recalled brought him to the very present: "Alors, j'ai senti avec violence que j'avais une aventure." However, it is also true that the moment Erna returned and reminiscing yielded to an actual life experience, the impression of adventure faded. But at the end of the Sunday he is describing, the impression of an adventure persists for some time, and it is free of such stimulants as reminiscing or the impact of music under which a momentary perception of interdependence and coherence seemingly endowed experience with the quality of an adventure.

In his reflections on his Sunday experience, made on the following day, Roquentin remarks in a sober mood that he is disgusted with himself for having been "sublime the previous evening." He seems ashamed of his brief excitement, like a man who, tricked by illusions, has found his past happiness to have been based upon mistaken notions of reality. But

145

this awakening is a device whereby Sartre achieves greater emphasis for Roquentin's sober reflections. In these reflections the notion of the *manner* in which incidents are linked, a notion he had previously emphasized, is modified, and the particular vision *in time* necessary to make the manner perceptible constitutes the modification:

> Hier, je n'avais même pas l'excuse de l'ivresse. Je me suis exalté comme un imbécile. J'ai besoin de me nettoyer avec des pensées abstraites, transparentes comme de l'eau.
>
> Ce sentiment d'aventure ne vient décidément pas des événements: la preuve en est faite. *C'est plutôt la façon dont les instants s'enchaînent.* Voilà, je pense ce qui se passe: brusquement on sent que le temps s'écoule, que chaque instant conduit à un autre instant, celui-ci à un autre et ainsi de suite; que chaque instant s'anéantit, que ce n'est pas la peine d'essayer de le retenir, etc., etc. Et alors on attribue cette propriété aux événements qui vous apparaissent *dans*[14] les instants; *ce qui appartient à la forme, on le reporte sur le contenu.* En somme, ce fameux écoulement du temps, on en parle beaucoup, mais on ne le voit guère. On voit une femme, on pense qu'elle sera vieille, seulement on ne la *voit*[15] pas vieillir. Mais, par moment, il semble *qu'on la voie*[16] *vieillir et qu'on se sente vieillir avec elle: c'est le sentiment d'aventure.*
>
> On appelle ça, si je me souviens bien, l'irréversibilité du temps. *Le sentiment de l'aventure serait, tout simplement, celui de l'irréversibilité du temps.* Mais pourquoi est-ce qu'on ne l'a pas toujours? Est-ce que le temps ne serait pas toujours irréversible? Il y a des moments où on a l'impression qu'on peut faire ce qu'on veut, aller de l'avant ou revenir en arrière, que ça n'a pas d'importance; et puis d'autres où l'on dirait que les mailles se sont resserrées et, dans ces cas-là, il ne s'agit pas de manquer son coup parce qu'on ne pourrait plus le recommencer (pp. 77–78).

The particular vision is conditioned (*a*) by an awareness of the irreversibility of time, of the uniqueness of each moment and of its unavoidable evanescence; (*b*) by an acute consciousness of any incident's simultaneous interrelatedness with other incidents, and (*c*) by the sequential coherence of incidents perceived in prospect and in retrospect. The scope of this vision transcends considerably that within which the perception of the rigorous intrinsic order in music occurred.

Roquentin knows the Sundays in Bouville. Although this entry in his diary is supposed to be a report, it is in great part presented—as was his walk on the Boulevard Noir—as an immediate description of experienced occurrences. First, however, before the "black columns invade

---

[14] Italics in text. [15] Italics in text. [16] Italics in text.

the streets that pretend to be dead," Roquentin, the historian, describes the historical background of the Rue Tournebride and of the church of Sainte Cécile. Then he takes us along Rue Tournebride from store to store and includes a sketch of "an impudent little shop" which was torn down but which recalled "avec insolence les droits de la vermine et de la crasse, à deux pas de l'église la plus coûteuse de France." This sketch of the shop, which Roquentin used to like very much, places the entire preceding account into perspective and points to the themes of bourgeois pretentiousness, assumed respectability, and vanity.

These same themes, already foreshadowed by those we have encountered in connection with the statue of Impétraz, are now complemented by themes of shallowness and of gratuitous conventions carried by the motifs described during the Sunday morning walk of the elegant and dignified crowd of the "little Prado." With Roquentin's observing eyes we witness a ritual of bourgeois propriety. The random occurrences on the Rue Tournebride assume a pattern, a unity shown in the present but grasped with its historical antecedents. Later, at noon, we find Roquentin at the brasserie Vézelize. There the social panorama is supplemented by the little bourgeois who come there to eat their Sunday sauerkraut. The Rue Tournebride offered random sketches of insignificant but ceremonious occurrences; the conversation at the table next to his offers the same insignificant random tidbits, except that ceremoniousness is, in view of the difference in class, reduced almost to coarseness.

While waiting to be served, Roquentin opens "at random" *Eugénie Grandet:* "J'ouvre le livre au hasard: la mère et la fille parlent de l'amour naissant d'Eugénie" (p. 67). In spite of a fortuitous selection, the page in the novel offers a carefully ordered, tightly knit conversation in which all details contribute to the perception of an incomplete yet coherent sketch. Compared to the conversation at the table next to Roquentin's, that in the novel is unrealistic because the real is clearly marked by contingency, vagueness, a lack of ordered succession and a degree of incoherence. It seems that the passage from Balzac's novel has thematically the particular function of showing by contrast the disconnectedness of details in the conversation at the restaurant, and incidentally also alludes to the haphazard bits of conversation on the Rue Tournebride. Since these characteristics of experience have contributed to his nausea previously, we may infer that what Roquentin witnessed at the Sunday parade and at lunch at the brasserie Vézelize was at least potentially nauseating, and yet we do not find in connection with those descriptions any allusion to nausea.

After lunch he feels, as if it were his own experience, all the Bouvillois leave their tables, dress, and go out. He goes with them, in his imagination, to the movies. He watches the members of a family leave their house to go to the cemetery, or to visit relatives, or to go for a walk on the jetty. He joins again the crowd and walks along the seashore. He remarks on the breakdown of the social stratification he had witnessed earlier. Now everybody is anybody's neighbor. He recognizes the faces he saw in the morning, but they are more relaxed:

> Pour l'instant ils voulaient vivre avec le moins de frais, économiser les gestes, les paroles, les pensées, faire la planche: ils n'avaient qu'un seul jour pour effacer leurs rides, leurs pattes d'oie, les plis amers que donne le travail de la semaine. Un seul jour. Ils sentaient les minutes couler entre leurs doigts; auraient-ils le temps d'amasser assez de jeunesse pour repartir à neuf le lundi matin? Ils respiraient à pleins poumons parce que l'air de la mer vivifie: seuls leurs souffles, réguliers et profonds comme ceux des dormeurs, témoignaient encore de leur vie. Je marchais à pas de loup, je ne savais que faire de mon corps dur et frais, au milieu de cette foule tragique qui se reposait.
>
> La mer était maintenant couleur d'ardoise; elle montait lentement. Elle serait haute à la nuit; cette nuit la Jetée-Promenade serait plus déserte que le boulevard Victor-Noir. En avant et sur la gauche un feu rouge brillerait dans le chenal (p. 73).

Just as in the morning, Roquentin's experiences occur simultaneously on two levels: he is "in the midst of this tragic crowd" but is standing above it at the same time. Similarly, the present and the future fuse in a single experience: while he is watching the crowd on the shore and on the jetty, he already visualizes the high tide and the deserted jetty as they will appear in the darkness of the night. Finally at sunset, and while the expressions on the faces change, the already foreseen light of the lighthouse goes on and a little boy near him murmurs with an air of ecstasy, "Oh, the lighthouse!" Thereupon Roquentin remarks: "Alors, je sentis mon cœur gonflé d'un grand sentiment d'aventure" (p. 74).

He cannot quite understand what has caused this experience of adventure:

> Rien n'a changé et pourtant tout existe d'une autre façon. Je ne peux pas décrire; c'est comme la Nausée et pourtant c'est juste le contraire: enfin une aventure m'arrive et quand je m'interroge, je vois qu'*il m'arrive que je suis moi et que je suis ici; c'est moi*[17] qui fends la nuit, je suis heureux comme un héros de roman (p. 75).

---

[17] Italics in text.

148

All he knows is that he has an adventure and that he is in fact in the process of experiencing it. He recognizes himself in the role of a fictional hero whose life is not only evolving, but whose every move is felt to relate to some future event toward which he is progressing:

> Quelque chose va se produire: dans l'ombre de la rue Basse-de-Vieille, il y a quelque chose qui m'attend, c'est là-bas, juste à l'angle de cette rue calme, que ma vie va commencer. Je me vois avancer, avec le sentiment de la fatalité (p. 75).

It does not especially matter what particular direction he will take nor toward what particular event he is moving; what does matter is that upon reaching it, a plausible and necessary existence of incidents will become apparent:

> Je ne sais si le monde s'est soudain resserré ou si c'est moi qui mets entre les sons et les formes une unité si forte: je ne puis même pas concevoir que rien de ce qui m'entoure soit autre qu'il n'est (p. 75).

He is enchanted with the consciousness of his present experience being relatable to previous experiences and with the awareness of his life being simultaneous with life elsewhere:

> Je repars. Le vent m'apporte le cri d'une sirène. Je suis tout seul, mais je marche comme une troupe qui descend sur une ville. Il y a, en cet instant, des navires qui résonnent de musique sur la mer; des lumières s'allument dans toutes les villes d'Europe; des communistes et des nazis font le coup de feu dans les rues de Berlin, des chômeurs battent le pavé de New York, des femmes, devant leurs coiffeuses, dans une chambre chaude, se mettent du rimmel sur les cils. Et moi je suis là, dans cette rue déserte et chaque coup de feu qui part d'une fenêtre de Neukolln, chaque hoquet sanglant des blessés qu'on emporte, chaque geste précis et menu des femmes qui se parent répond à chacun de mes pas, à chaque battement de mon cœur (pp. 75–76).

Finally, stopping in front of the café Mably and looking through the window, he is thrilled with his consciousness of the necessary succession of all the incidents of the day, and with the unity of his existence:

> La salle est bondée. L'air est bleu à cause de la fumée des cigarettes et de la vapeur que dégagent les vêtements humides. La caissière est à son comptoir. Je la connais bien: elle est rousse comme moi; elle a une maladie dans le ventre. Elle pourrit doucement sous ses jupes avec un sourire mélancolique, semblable à l'odeur de violette que dégagent parfois les corps en décomposition. Un frisson me parcourt de la tête aux pieds: c'est . . . elle qui m'attendait. Elle était là, dressant son buste immobile au-dessus du comptoir, elle souriait. *Du fond de ce café quelque chose revient en arrière sur les moments épars de ce dimanche et les soude les uns aux autres, leur*

donne un sens: j'ai traversé tout ce jour pour aboutir là, le front contre cette vitre, pour contempler ce fin visage qui s'épanouit sur un rideau grenat. Tout s'est arrêté; ma vie s'est arrêtée: cette grande vitre, cet air lourd, bleu comme de l'eau, cette plante grasse et blanche au fond de l'eau, et moi-même, nous formons un tout immobile et plein: je suis heureux (pp. 76–77).

Once the exaltation has passed, however, Roquentin is left with the bitter regret of not being able to sustain his consciousness of adventure:

Quand je me retrouvai sur le boulevard de la Redoute il ne me restait plus qu'un amer regret. Je me disais: "Ce sentiment d'aventure, il n'y a peut-être rien au monde à quoi je tienne tant. Mais il vient quand il veut; il repart si vite et comme je suis sec quand il est reparti! Me fait-il ces courtes visites ironiques pour me montrer que j'ai manqué ma vie?" (p. 77).

The elusiveness of the experience of adventure is a cause for his regrets, but the intensity of his consciousness of "adventure" makes life without such consciousness appear insignificant and worthless. Roquentin does not yearn for anything so much as he does for that experience, but he must soon recognize that its elusiveness and evanescence are not alone in revealing to him the irony of his condition in that most of his life appears wasted to him. The final discovery of the illusory nature of the experience itself, the final realization of existence, is still merely suspected but not yet confirmed.

Roquentin's reflections on the irreversibility of time lead thematically to Anny's ability to exploit her awareness of the evanescence of significant moments in life. He is to meet with Anny again, and he hopes to relive those intense moments her ingenuity may conjure up and from which he expects to draw the strength for life. The entries in his diary prior to his departure are filled with reflections in the course of which his exhilarating adventure proves to be an illusion. From the point of view of thematic correlation, it is interesting to note that the later entries record a gradually intensified feeling of nausea which, at its height, is illumined by so intense an insight into its nature that Roquentin experiences an exultation akin to that occasioned by his adventure.

On the same day Roquentin felt disgusted with himself for having felt elated the previous evening, on the same day he realized that not the events themselves but rather the vision of their irreversible succession in time or of their ephemeral manifestation had caused his experience of adventure, he has two additional entries in his diary. Both are materially unrelated to one another as well as to the previous entry, but their thematic relatedness needs to be pointed out. The first pertains to Rollebon, the second to the Patronne of the "Rendez-vous des Cheminots."

150

Rollebon has already shown himself elusive because of the inconsistencies Roquentin had noted. It is not Rollebon's pompousness and the mystery with which he surrounds his life that annoy Roquentin; it is rather the historian's inability to uncover significance behind the mystery, to discover the making of a life as interesting as Rollebon's. Rollebon is not a man who thinks, plans, and acts; rather, he reacts appropriately: "Il pense peu, mais, en toute occasion, par une grâce profonde, il fait exactement ce qu'il faut" (p. 80). Rollebon appears as much a rascal as he does a virtuous man, but it is impossible to ascribe his life to any genuinely pursued concern: "Que sais-je de lui? On ne peut rêver plus belle vie que la sienne: mais l'a-t-il faite?" (p. 79). Rollebon is not the maker of his life. Behind the façade, behind the public image over which he is concerned, an historian would look in vain for historically significant reality: the concealed intention, the purpose, behind action. Rollebon, as Roquentin realizes, would lend himself better to becoming the hero of a novel for whom the author's imagination could furnish consistency, whereas the historian is allowed to detect only demonstrable reality. Hence no incident in Rollebon's life has the quality derived from irreversibility in time, nor does any incident in his life reveal the quality of "perfect moments" such as those for which Anny used to set the stage. Therefore Rollebon, Roquentin's "only justification of existence," creeps understandably into the nauseating dream described in the last entry of that day (pp. 80–81). Rollebon's disconcerting and to Roquentin nauseating concern for appearance without a discernibly underlying reality is even more shocking when seen in the light of the contrasting concerns of Anny which Roquentin cherished in her:

> Je sors; je tiens l'enveloppe entre mes doigts, je n'ose pas l'ouvrir; Anny n'a pas changé son papier à lettres, je me demande si elle l'achète toujours dans la petite papeterie de Piccadilly. Je pense qu'elle a conservé aussi sa coiffure, ses lourds cheveux blonds qu'elle ne voulait pas couper. Elle doit lutter patiemment devant les miroirs pour sauver son visage: ce n'est pas coquetterie ni crainte de vieillir; elle veut rester comme elle est, tout juste comme elle est. C'est peut-être ce que je préférais en elle, cette fidélité puissante et sévère au moindre trait de son image (p. 82).

If Anny does not reveal her feelings in her letter, Roquentin fully appreciates her reasons, whereas he condemns Rollebon for the same effect. He knows that Anny's lack of revelations is a prelude to what may become a meeting to which they would bring their sensitivity, their attentive disponibilité, and in which they would unite in filling time with ephemeral outbursts of created consonance:

Je prends sa lettre dans mon portefeuille. Elle n'a pas écrit "mon cher Antoine". Au bas de la lettre, il n'y a pas non plus de formule de politesse: "Il faut que je te voie. Anny." Rien qui puisse me fixer sur ses sentiments. Je ne peux m'en plaindre: je reconnais là son amour du parfait. Elle voulait toujours réaliser des "moments parfaits". Si l'instant ne s'y prêtait pas, elle ne prenait plus d'intérêt à rien, la vie disparaissait de ses yeux, elle traînait paresseusement, avec l'air d'une grande fille à l'âge ingrat (p. 84).

Earlier in his considerations, Roquentin spoke of the order the historian imposes on the materials he uncovers in his research, and he bewailed the lack of intrinsic cohesion he was seeking to determine in his study of Rollebon. His realization of Rollebon's evasions, inconsistencies, lies, and pretense resumes the theme of his frustration as an historian whose failure is due to the imperfections of the materials with which he is supposed to deal. But when he is faced with the task of *creating* intrinsic cohesion in brief moments of his life, Roquentin's failure is due to his own inability to bring his mind and his emotions into an imaginative accord with a reality that awaits a creative act:

Elle m'expliquait, d'une voix basse et rapide, ce qu'elle attendait de moi.
"Ecoute, tu veux bien faire un effort, n'est-ce pas? Tu as été si sot, la dernière fois. Tu vois comme ce moment-ci pourrait être beau? Regarde le ciel, regarde la couleur du soleil sur le tapis. J'ai justement mis ma robe verte et je ne suis pas fardée, je suis toute pâle. Recule-toi, va t'asseoir dans l'ombre; tu comprends ce que tu as à faire? Eh bien, voyons! Que tu es sot! Parle-moi."
Je sentais que le succès de l'entreprise était dans mes mains: l'instant avait un sens obscur qu'il fallait dégrossir et parfaire; certains gestes devaient être faits, certaines paroles dites: j'étais accablé sous le poids de ma responsabilité, j'écarquillais les yeux et je ne voyais rien, je me débattais au milieu de rites qu'Anny inventait sur le moment et je les déchirais de mes grands bras comme des toiles d'araignée. A ces moments-là elle me haïssait (p. 85).

Neither Roquentin the historian nor Roquentin the man can find "adventure" accessible. Rollebon's history does not have the necessary quality to be seen as an adventure, and life requires one to be especially attuned in order to experience at times the illusion of adventure as a fleeting reality. Roquentin has recognized his experience of adventure as illusory and wishes to cleanse his mind and remove confusion: "Je me suis exalté comme un imbécile. J'ai besoin de me nettoyer avec des pensées abstraites, transparentes comme de l'eau" (p. 77). But if, as he supposed, adventures could be perceived and experienced at least in perspective, a posteriori, could they be conjured up at will? He knew that they would have to depend on memories; but these were "comme les pistoles dans la bourse du diable, quand on l'ouvrit, on n'y trouva que des feuilles mortes" (p. 49). He knew their evanescence and how difficult it was to preserve in one's memory the reality of an experience. He knew that he had to reconstruct the past with the help of the present: "Je construis mes souvenirs avec mon présent. Je suis rejeté, délaissé dans le présent. Le passé, j'essaie en vain de le rejoindre: je ne peux pas m'échapper" (p. 50). And he knew that the present obliterated the past when he tried to recall memories after the Autodidacte's visit in his hotel room.

The same sobering thoughts occur to him again as he tries to recall his past life with Anny, although in this case he ascribes the loss of recollection to the burden of each past moment that both of them had carried, for three years, to each succeeding moment, until they felt crushed:

> Je glisse la lettre d'Anny dans mon portefeuille: elle m'a donné ce qu'elle pouvait; je ne peux pas remonter à la femme qui l'a prise dans ses mains pliée, mise dans son enveloppe. Est-il seulement possible de penser à quelqu'un au passé? Tant que nous nous sommes aimés nous n'avons pas permis que le plus infime de nos instants, la plus légère de nos peines se détachât de nous et restât en arrière. Les sons, les odeurs, les nuances du jour, même les pensées que nous ne nous étions pas dites, nous emportions tout et tout restait à vif: nous n'avons pas cessé d'en jouir et d'en souffrir au présent. Pas un souvenir; un amour implacable et torride, sans ombres, sans recul, sans refuge. Trois années présentes à la fois. C'est pour cela que nous nous sommes séparés: nous n'avions plus assez de force pour supporter ce fardeau. Et puis, quand Anny m'a quitté, d'un seul coup, d'une seule pièce, les trois ans se sont écroulés dans le passé. Je n'ai même pas souffert, je me sentais vide. Ensuite le temps s'est remis à couler et le vide s'est agrandi (p. 86).

His past is nothing but "un trou énorme," and it occurs to him that whatever one retains in one's memory is as if it had been learned from books, and even sights from the past disappear: "Le tramway qui passe devant l'hôtel Printania n'emporte pas, le soir, à ses vitres, le reflet de l'enseigne au néon; il s'enflamme un instant et s'éloigne avec des vitres noires" (pp. 86–87).

Yet if only he were able to recall his memories, those might be of the sort that lend themselves to being seen in the perspective from which he supposed adventures might be perceptible. His memories are those one cannot associate with the things one accumulates; they are memories

153

that are embedded in the perceptions, feelings, and emotions of a man who lives without the permanence of things around him. Ironically those are also the very memories whose reality cannot be preserved, that turn into names or become altered when recalled.

Thus in the process of cleansing his mind, Roquentin has proved to himself that he could not use his past-lived experiences in order to perceive them in perspective and experience them again as a cohesive adventure. If he could not recall memories of his experiences, how could others succeed when their scattered memories cling to a random collection of things?

> Douce lumière; les gens sont dans les maisons, ils ont allumé aussi, sans doute. Ils lisent, ils regardent le ciel par la fenêtre. Pour eux . . . c'est autre chose. Ils ont vieilli autrement. Ils vivent au milieu des legs, des cadeaux et chacun de leurs meubles est un souvenir. Pendulettes, médailles, portraits, coquillages, presse-papiers, paravents, châles. Ils ont des armoires pleines de bouteilles, d'étoffes, de vieux vêtements, de journaux; ils ont tout gardé. Le passé, c'est un luxe de propriétaire.
>
> Où donc conserverais-je le mien? On ne met pas son passé dans sa poche; il faut avoir une maison pour l'y ranger. Je ne possède que mon corps; un homme tout seul, avec son seul corps, ne peut pas arrêter les souvenirs; ils lui passent au travers. Je ne devrais pas me plaindre: je n'ai voulu qu'être libre (p. 88).

Nor do such memories acquire the quality of uniqueness in evanescence because they are endowed with the durability of the things to which they cling.

There is a rational and analytical transition from the treatment of the perception and experience of intrinsic necessity in adventures to the realization of the futility of aspiring to such experiences. There is an interesting thematic transition from Roquentin's recognition of his delusion to the more or less unconscious self-deception by which others conceal their lack of remembered experiences. The first motifs which carry that thematic transition are the things with which people surround themselves in the hope of conjuring up memories by association and thereby of perpetuating their delusion. This thematic transition leads at the same time from the theme of authenticity to the theme of spuriousness, from the exploration of the experience of adventure to that of nausea.

The next motif cluster, which carries the thematic transition, again materially largely unrelated to antecedents but thematically clearly correlative, pertains to the chance meeting of M. Achille and Dr. Rogé.

What M. Achille has in common with Roquentin is his solitude and perhaps also a sort of nausea:

> Il est seul comme moi, mais plus enfoncé que moi dans la solitude. Il doit attendre sa Nausée ou quelque chose de ce genre. . . . Les familles sont dans leurs maisons, au milieu de leurs souvenirs. Et nous voici, deux épaves sans mémoire (p. 88).

Dr. Rogé, whose very features bear the signs of a full life and of "experience," is able to impress and to intimidate M. Achille. Observing this encounter, Roquentin feels the humiliation to which Achille is exposed. In his silent reflections the doctor's experience (and hence his perspective) is unmasked as vain and presumptuous:

> Ils voudraient nous faire croire que leur passé n'est pas perdu, que leurs souvenirs se sont condensés, moelleusement convertis en Sagesse (p. 92).

In Roquentin's eyes, the doctor's wise and useful experience is the last spurious self-justification of failure:

> La vérité m'apparaît brusquement: cet homme va bientôt mourir. Il le sait sûrement; il suffit qu'il se soit regardé dans une glace: il ressemble chaque jour un peu plus au cadavre qu'il sera. Voilà ce que c'est que leur expérience, voilà pourquoi je me suis dit, si souvent, qu'elle sent la mort: c'est leur dernière défense. Le docteur voudrait bien y croire, il voudrait se masquer l'insoutenable réalité: qu'il est seul, sans acquis, sans passé, avec une intelligence qui s'empâte, un corps qui se défait. Alors il a bien construit, bien aménagé, bien capitonné son petit délire de compensation: il se dit qu'il progresse. . . . Et ce terrible visage de cadavre, pour en pouvoir supporter la vue dans les miroirs, il s'efforce de croire que les leçons de l'expérience s'y sont gravées (pp. 93–94).

Thereupon the thematic treatment reverts to Roquentin's final scrutiny of his exultation. To be cleansed completely of his delusion, Roquentin is made to experience the vanity of the last illusion that contributed to his intoxication. In his imagination he believed himself to be at one with life and incidents that were happening elsewhere. In a vast encompassing simultaneous perception he perceived the cohesion and unity of life everywhere and recognized himself to be part of it. Sartre uses, with what appears to be calculated consistency, a device which may be considered as a linking phrase. Although the variations in wording are manifold, the theme carried by them is more or less the same. The entry in the diary under "Friday" (p. 94) begins in the following manner: "Le brouillard était si dense." Most of this entry is devoted to Roquentin's assumption that M. Fasquelle of the café Mably is dead. The following entry under "Saturday morning" (p. 107) begins thus: "Un soleil charmant, avec une brume légère qui promet du beau temps pour la journée." During breakfast at the café Mably Roquentin finds out that M. Fasquelle has a bad cold. Roquentin imagines Fasquelle's death only because the latter has not come down from his room at the usual hour of his appearance in the café. Only two of the twelve bulbs are lit and, furthermore, the waiter forces Roquentin to take a table in a dark corner. While the waiter goes for the coffee, Roquentin notes: "J'avais de l'ombre jusqu'aux yeux, une sale ombre glaciale" (p. 95). Shortly thereafter the telephone rings for M. Fasquelle. The waiter explains that his patron is not yet in the café: ". . . Le patron n'est pas là. . . . Oui, il devrait être descendu. . . . Ah, par ces temps de brouillard" (p. 95). As soon as he hangs up the receiver, Roquentin notes: "Le brouillard pesait sur les vitres comme un lourd rideau de velours gris" (pp. 95–96).

A man and a woman, who have had breakfast at a table next to Roquentin's, get up and leave. The waiter explains who they are:

> Ce sont des artistes, me dit le garçon en m'apportant mon café, c'est eux qui ont fait le numéro d'entr'acte au Ciné-Palace. La femme se bande les yeux et elle lit le prénom et l'âge des spectateurs. Ils s'en vont aujourd'hui parce que c'est vendredi et qu'on change les programmes (p. 96).

Soon the waiter turns off the light completely because the use of electricity for a single customer is unjustified.

Thereupon the following note:

> [La pénombre envahit le café]. Une faible clarté, barbouillée de gris et de brun, tombait maintenant des hautes vitres (p. 97).

Then an old woman enters with a message from Mme Florent, the cashier, who is sick. It is the old woman who wonders whether M. Fasquelle might be dead. Roquentin is sensitive to the remark: "C'est bien le genre d'idées qu'on se fait par ces temps de brouillard" (p. 97). He is thinking of his own room which, he believes, the fog would already have filled. From that moment M. Fasquelle occupies Roquentin's mind:

> M. Fasquelle dormait encore. Ou bien il était mort au-dessus de ma tête. Trouvé mort dans son lit, [un matin de brouillard].—En sous-titre: dans le café, des clients consommaient sans se douter . . .
>
> Mais était-il encore dans son lit? N'avait-il pas chaviré, entraînant les draps avec lui et cognant de la tête contre le plancher?
>
> Je connais très bien M. Fasquelle; il s'est enquis parfois de ma santé. C'est

un gros réjoui, avec une barbe soignée: s'il est mort c'est d'une attaque. Il sera couleur aubergine, avec la langue hors de la bouche. La barbe en l'air; le cou violet sous le moutonnement du poil.

L'escalier privé se perdait dans le noir. A peine pouvais-je distinguer la pomme de la rampe. *Il faudrait traverser cette ombre.* L'escalier craquerait. En haut, je trouverais la porte de la chambre . . .

Le corps est là, au-dessus de ma tête. Je tournerais le commutateur: je toucherais cette peau tiède, pour voir.—Je n'y tiens plus, je me lève. Si le garçon me surprend dans l'escalier, je lui dirai que j'ai entendu du bruit (pp. 97–98).

Roquentin suggests to the waiter that M. Fasquelle may actually be dead:

"Oui, mais je crois que ca ne va pas: on aurait dit des râles et puis il y a eu un bruit sourd."

Dans cette salle obscure, [avec ce brouillard derrière les vitres], ça sonnait tout à fait naturel. Je n'oublierai pas les yeux qu'il fit (p. 98).

The fog lifts a little and Roquentin hurries toward the Rue Tourne-bride, for he needs its lights. But even there the notion of M. Fasquelle's death pursues him. Away from the café Mably and even with the partial lifting of the fog, Roquentin remains the victim of his imagined perception of simultaneously occurring events:

Je m'arrêtai devant la charcuterie Julien. De temps à autre, je voyais à travers la glace une main qui désignait les pieds truffés et les andouillettes. Alors une grosse fille blonde se penchait, la poitrine offerte, et prenait le bout de chair morte entre ses doigts. Dans sa chambre, à cinq minutes de là, M. Fasquelle était mort.

Je cherchai autour de moi un appui solide, une défense contre mes pensées. Il n'y en avait pas: peu à peu, [le brouillard s'était déchiré], mais quelque chose d'inquiétant restait à traîner dans la rue. Peut-être pas une vraie menace: c'était effacé, transparent. Mais c'est justement ce qui finissait par faire peur. J'appuyai mon front contre la vitrine. Sur la mayonnaise d'un œuf à la russe, je remarquai une goutte d'un rouge sombre: c'était du sang. Ce rouge sur ce jaune me soulevait le cœur.

Brusquement, j'eus une vision: quelqu'un était tombé, la face en avant et saignait dans les plats. L'œuf avait roulé dans le sang; la rondelle de tomate qui le couronnait s'était détachée, elle était tombée à plat, rouge sur rouge. La mayonnaise avait un peu coulé: une mare de crême jaune qui divisait la rigole de sang en deux bras.

"C'est trop bête, *il faut que je me secoue.* Je vais aller travailler à la bibliothèque" (p. 99).

He knows that he is a victim of his own imagination, a victim of the fog and the darkness that surround him and of that other fog which he later describes in the library:

> Le brouillard avait envahi la pièce: pas le vrai brouillard, qui s'était dissipé depuis longtemps—l'autre, celui dont les rues étaient encore pleines, qui sortait des murs, des pavés. Une espèce d'inconsistance des choses (p. 101).

He knows that M. Fasquelle has become an obsession and that he does not actually believe the patron of the Mably to be dead:

> Au fond, je ne croyais pas trop à sa mort et c'est précisément ce qui m'agaçait! c'était une idée flottante dont je ne pouvais ni me persuader ni me défaire (p. 101).

He is quite aware of the difference between the actual and the potential, of the limitations actuality imposes on potentiality, of the degree to which actuality determines the limits of plausibility ("Ainsi ces objets servent-ils au moins à fixer les limites du vraisemblable" [p. 101]), but he also realizes the degree to which imagination enables potentiality to arrest actuality in time, in a pause, before almost unlimited yet reasonable thrusts into the future.

Thus Roquentin recognizes that his notion of perceived simultaneity (which incidentally contributed to his exaltation at experiencing his adventure), however plausible, is yet a mere assumption. The linking image of the woman at the Mably breakfast table is Sartre's first though rather inconspicuous comment on Roquentin's notion. She plays the entr'acte at movie where she blindfolds herself and tells the name and age of the people in the audience. When the program changes, the spurious performance is at an end. The other and more obvious comment is in the next entry: M. Fasquelle is not dead; he merely has the flu, and a "charming sun" is shining in the sky.

With sarcasm turned against himself, with the realization of the tenuous nature of imagination, the last support of his thrilling adventure is removed and his recent experience of adventure is relegated to the status of all past experience which the present obliterates. First, though only ephemerally, music succeeded in relieving nausea. Then the vision of rigorous succession and simultaneity held out the promise of adventure's being within reach and call until critical reflection proved the vanity of mere illusions. Roquentin had seemingly overcome his nausea but only so long as his delusion was spared by his swift and conspicuous scrutiny. The theme of the vision of coherence, cohesion, intrinsic necessity, and unity having reached the apex of the material structure of the work, the theme of nausea and its thematic substructure is resumed. Inconsistency, secure and confident bourgeois complacency, spuriousness, unrelatedness, gratuitousness, and oppressive existence in human time emerge again, but without Roquentin's perplexity at their occurrence and without his hope of ever escaping into illusions of adventure. From this point on these themes are no longer carried by fortuitously introduced and seemingly inconsequential motifs as before. Instead, previously used motifs, or at least similar motifs recur; they appear in dense and heavy clusters with repeated and therefore familiar overtones. What before were mere suggestions, now become analytical and increasingly significant expressions.

With memories that recall the employees in the café, the men who live with others in a familiar world where each man plays his part and moves confidently from one stage of his existence to the next in a purposeful or at least in a habitual order; with memories of Impétraz whose statute symbolizes the stability of bourgeois values, civic unanimity on what matters, and common purposes whose achievement fills the passage of time; with memories of the Sunday morning promenade on the Rue Tournebride where men pay homage to their interdependence, to their relative status and to the importance of rank, we are led with Roquentin to the Musée de Bouville and to the gallery of portraits of the city's famous citizens. With a few exceptions all the men portrayed were embodiments of a stage of human existence, received and transmitted from generation to generation; they were carriers or even creators of a heritage, conscious of their duties and conscious of their rights to which their accomplishments entitled them. By contrast the painting depicting the death of a bachelor portrays solitude as the severe and deserved punishment of the man who decided to live by himself:

Cet homme n'avait vécu que pour lui-même. Par un châtiment sévère et mérité, personne, à son lit de mort, n'était venu lui fermer les yeux. Ce tableau me donnait un dernier avertissement; il était encore temps, je pouvais retourner sur mes pas. Mais, si je passais outre, que je sache bien ceci: dans le grand salon où j'allais entrer, plus de cent cinquante portraits étaient accrochés aux murs; si l'on exceptait quelques jeunes gens enlevés trop tôt à leurs familles et la mère Supérieure d'un orphelinat, aucun de ceux qu'on avait représentés n'était mort célibataire, aucun d'eux n'était mort sans enfants ni intestat aucun sans les derniers sacrements. En règle, ce jour-là comme les autres jours, avec Dieu et avec le monde, ces hommes avaient glissé doucement dans la mort, pour aller réclamer la part de vie éternelle à laquelle ils avaient droit.

Car ils avaient eu droit à tout: à la vie, au travail, à la richesse, au commendement, au respect, et, pour finir, à l'immortalité (pp. 108–9).

The death of the bachelor carries the theme of society's condemnation of the solitary man who refuses to exist together with other men. This then is a correlative theme to that found early in the diary. The rejection of the outsider who is a challenge to collective confidence in common sense and whose views escape collective approval, occurred also in the form of an impression Roquentin gained when he felt that the statue of Impétraz was driving him out of the little court. The same theme recurs in the museum as he watches the portrait of Jean Parrottin, a man possessed with the notion of his rights:

Cet homme avait la simplicité d'une idée. Il ne restait plus en lui que des os, des chairs mortes et le Droit Pur. Un vrai cas de possession, pensai-je. Quand le Droit s'est emparé d'un homme, il n'est pas d'exorcisme qui puisse le chasser; Jean Parrottin avait consacré toute sa vie à penser son Droit: rien d'autre. A la place du léger mal de tête que je sentais naître, comme à chaque fois que je visite un musée, il eût senti à ses tempes le droit douloureux d'être soigné. Il ne fallait point qu'on le fît trop penser, qu'on attirât son attention sur des réalités déplaisantes, sur sa mort possible, sur les souffrances d'autrui. Sans doute, à son lit de mort, à cette heure où l'on est convenu, depuis Socrate, de prononcer quelques paroles élevées, avait-il dit à sa femme, comme un de mes oncles à la sienne, qui l'avait veillé douze nuits: "Toi, Thérèse, je ne te remercie pas; tu n'as fait que ton devoir." Quand un homme en arrive là, il faut lui tirer son chapeau.

Ses yeux, que je fixai avec ébahissement, me signifiaient mon congé. Je ne partis pas, je fus résolument indiscret. Je savais, pour avoir longtemps contemplé à la bibliothèque de l'Escurial un certain portrait de Philippe II, que, lorsqu'on regarde en face un visage éclatant de droit, au bout d'un moment, cet éclat s'éteint, qu'un résidu cendreux demeure: c'était ce résidu qui m'intéressait (pp. 115–16).

These correlative themes do not have merely an affinity of similarity; seen together they show that the reasons for which Roquentin feels rejected expand the theme and make it more specific. At first Roquentin feels merely odd in the midst of confident and complacent people who simply distrust a man who cannot share the comfort of belonging, of enjoying life as others do by common accord. Then he feels that Impétraz is driving him away partly for the same reasons, but he also feels rejected for not accepting conformity in thought, for not being able to relegate the right of forming his own ideas, for not recognizing, in blind confidence, the moral and intellectual preeminence of a leader. Finally he feels rejected because he

160

cannot recognize anybody's assumed right to impose respect and submission on the basis of inherited or even acquired social pre-eminence. Roquentin's feeling of rejection is the feeling of the free and independent mind—a trait the later Meursault shares with his predecessor.

The portrait gallery is primarily an exhibit of bourgeois rights, and the examination of the portraits is a scrutiny of justifications. As Roquentin moves from portrait to portrait he describes the rights he feels each portrayed man reflects. These were men who maintained order, checked the parties of disruption, built the economy, broke strikes, sent their sons to war, recognized in themselves the élite, demanded by virtue of their heredity, education, and experience the right to command, and exhorted each other to practice that right as an obligation:

> Ce que ces toiles sombres offraient à mes regards, c'était l'homme repensé par l'homme, avec, pour unique parure, la plus belle conquête de l'homme: le bouquet des Droits de l'Homme et du Citoyen. J'admirai sans arrière-pensée le règne humain (p. 117).

These men knew their obligations and carried them out with what could be recognized as gracious benevolence. However, Sartre's sarcasm is made quite obvious by the order in which he presents the seemingly random enumeration of bourgeois achievements and virtues:

> Ils ont fait de Bouville le port commercial français le mieux outillé pour le déchargement des charbons et des bois. L'allongement et l'élargissement des quais a été leur œuvre. Ils ont donné toute l'extension désirable à la gare Maritime et porté à 10 m. 70 par des dragages persévérants, la profondeur d'eau de mouillage à marée basse. En vingt ans de tonnage des bateaux de pêche, qui était de 5.000 tonneaux en 1869, s'est élevé, grâce à eux, à 18.000 tonneaux. Ne reculant devant aucun sacrifice pour faciliter l'ascension des meilleurs représentants de la classe travailleuse, ils ont créé, de leur propre initiative, divers centres d'enseignement technique et professionnel qui ont prospéré sous leur haute protection. Ils ont brisé la fameuse grève des docks en 1898 et donné leurs fils à la Patrie en 1914.
>
> Les femmes, dignes compagnes de ces lutteurs, ont fondé la plupart des Patronages, des Crèches, des Ouvroirs. Mais elles furent, avant tout, des épouses et des mères. Elles ont élevé de beaux enfants, leur ont appris leurs devoirs et leurs droits, la religion, le respect des traditions qui ont fait la France (pp. 109–10).

Magnanimity is heavily coated with self-interest. Even in the home, in the family, the pretense of self-abnegation is all too apparent under the barely concealed authority of the grandfather, an authority rendered indisputable by the unquestionable weight of experience and honorable durability:

Au soir de la vie, il répandait sur chacun son indulgente bonté. Moi-même s'il me voyait—mais j'étais transparent à ses regards—je trouverais grâce à ses yeux: il penserait que j'avais eu, autrefois, des grands-parents. Il ne réclamait rien: on n'a plus de désirs à cet âge. Rien sauf qu'on baissât légèrement le ton quand il entrait, sauf qu'il y eût sur son passage une nuance de tendresse et de respect dans les sourires, rien, sauf que sa belle-fille dît parfois: "Père est extraordinaire; il est plus jeune que nous tous"; sauf d'être le seul à pouvoir calmer les colères de son petit-fils en lui imposant les mains sur la tête et de pouvoir dire ensuite: "Ces gros chagrins-là, c'est le grand-père qui sait les consoler", rien, sauf que son fils, plusieurs fois l'an, vînt solliciter ses conseils sur les questions délicates, rien enfin sauf de se sentir serein, apaisé, infiniment sage. La main du vieux monsieur pesait à peine sur les boucles de son petit-fils: c'était presque une bénédiction. A quoi pouvait-il penser? A son passé d'honneur, qui lui conférait le droit de parler sur tout et d'avoir sur tout le dernier mot. Je n'avais pas été assez loin l'autre jour: l'Expérience était bien plus qu'une défense contre la mort; elle était un droit: le droit des vieilliards (pp. 112–13).

Except for Parottin, the doctor, whose congenial character portrait, it would seem, is described primarily to offer a contrast to the subsequent description of his brother's portrait personifying "Pure Right," all the portraits to which Roquentin pays attention represent above all else the confidence of superiority and the insolence of self-righteous existence—both unassailable and at the same time offensively censorious:

Je compris alors tout ce qui nous séparait: ce que je pouvais penser sur lui ne l'atteignait pas; c'était tout juste de la psychologie, comme on en fait dans les romans. Mais son jugement me transperçait comme un glaive et mettait en question jusqu'à mon droit d'exister. Et c'était vrai, je m'en étais toujours rendu compte: je n'avais pas le droit d'exister. J'étais apparu par hasard, j'existais comme une pierre, une plante, un microbe. Ma vie poussait au petit bonheur et dans tous les sens. Elle m'envoyait parfois des signaux vagues; d'autres fois je ne sentais rien qu'un bourdonnement sans conséquences.

Mais pour ce bel homme sans défauts, mort aujourd'hui, pour Jean Pacôme, fils du Pacôme de la Défense Nationale, il en avait été tout autrement: les battements de son cœur et les rumeurs sourdes de ses organes parvenaient sous forme de petits droits instantanés et purs. Pendant soixante ans, sans défaillance, il avait fait usage du droit de vivre. Les magnifiques yeux gris! Jamais le moindre doute ne les avait traversés. Jamais non plus Pacôme ne s'était trompé.

Il avait toujours fait son devoir, tout son devoir, son devoir de fils, d'époux, de père, de chef. Il avait aussi réclamé ses droits sans faiblesse: enfant, le droit d'être bien élevé, dans une famille unie, celui d'héritier d'un nom sans tache, d'une affaire prospère; mari, le droit d'être soigné, entouré d'affection tendre; père, celui d'être vénéré; chef, le droit d'être obéi sans murmure. Car un droit n'est jamais que l'autre aspect d'un devoir (pp. 110–11).

Under the crushing impact of these monuments to meritorious existence, under the impressive gaze of men who succeeded in creating order, stability, security, and meaning for themselves and others; whose lives led to honors and respect; who by making themselves useful and necessary never dreamed of their purposes appearing arbitrary and their existence gratuitous, Roquentin is led to question the justification of his own existence:

Et les soldats? J'étais au centre de la pièce, point de mire de tous ces yeux graves. Je n'étais pas un grand-père, ni un père, ni même un mari. Je ne votais pas, c'était à peine si je payais quelques impôts: je ne pouvais me targuer ni des droits du contribuable, ni de ceux de l'électeur, ni même de l'humble droit à l'honorabilité que vingt ans d'obéissance confèrent à l'employé. Mon existence commençait à m'étonner sérieusement. N'étais-je pas une simple apparence? (p. 113).

Roquentin's scrutiny, however, reveals that the dignitaries of Bouville did not avoid presumptuousness or spuriousness. They considered themselves, their enterprise, and their continuity as important, rightful, and necessary. It never occurred to them to think of their existence as fortuitous and gratuitous. Thematically they foreshadow Roquentin's experience of gratuitous existence, but in his immediate reaction contempt and derision save him from an attack of nausea:

J'avais traversé le salon Bordurin-Renaudas dans toute sa longueur. Je me retournai. Adieu beaux lis tout en finesse dans vos petits sanctuaires peints, adieu beaux lis, notre orgueil et notre raison d'être. Adieu. Salauds (pp. 122–23).

When we consider the visit in the portrait gallery from the point of view of the subsequent entry in which Roquentin relates his reasons for abandoning his research on M. de Rollebon, and describes his confrontation with existence on a more conscious level than before, we realize that those men of Bouville took their rights to a certain kind of existence for granted. We see that they were, just as Roquentin himself had been, completely unaware of what the raw material of life—sheer existence—really was. They did not know its obsessive powers; they did not even suspect it, as Roquentin did when it appeared as an illusive and insipid idea that beset him suddenly and forced him to uproot himself in what he later recognized to be a disgust caused by the accumulation of unrelatable incidents that gave his life its jerky and incoherent aspect. Their lives were built on forethought guided by clearly conceived and highly approved purposes. Their lives assumed the shape of largely pre-established coherences. They did not have to think of creating coherence within existence, for they were born with patterns to follow. Their aim was to impress themselves and others that they had done their duty in unerringly following those patterns, and they enjoyed the pleasure of exercising their right to follow them, and thereby the right to live honored and respected. The fact of their falling into ready-made patterns, their pretense of having accomplished their tasks successfully, and their consequent presumptuousness made them repugnant to Roquentin and earned them his designation as "Salauds." In an almost delirious obsession with existence Roquentin describes a gentleman who believes in his right to existence and sees no need to think of anything except his rights. This sketch is thematically related to the portraits in the gallery by the use of the designation "Salauds":

> Le monsieur. Le beau monsieur existe. Le monsieur sent qu'il existe. Non, le beau monsieur qui passe, fier et doux comme un volubilis, ne sent pas qu'il existe. S'épanouir; j'ai mal à la main coupée, existe, existe, existe. Le beau monsieur existe Légion d'honnheur, existe moustache, c'est tout; comme on doit être heureux de n'être qu'une Légion d'honneur et qu'une moustache et le reste personne ne le voit, il voit les deux bouts pointus de sa moustache des deux côtés du nez; je ne pense pas donc je suis une moustache. Ni son corps maigre, ni ses grands pieds il ne les voit, en fouillant au fond du pantalon, on découvrirait bien une paire de petites gommes grises. Il a la Légion d'honneur, les Salauds ont le droit d'exister: "j'existe parce que c'est mon droit." J'ai le droit d'exister, donc j'ai le droit de ne pas penser: le doigt se lève (p. 131).

It was exactly the feeling of sheer existence that caused him to leave suddenly for France, to escape from himself, from the incoherent and meaningless mass of fading incidents that crowded without form in his past. It was in the hope of being able to ignore himself that he turned to his historical investigation, that he searched in the life of another man for the coherence he could not find in his own:

> Il y a quelques années, à Shanghaï (actually at Hanoi), dans le bureau de Mercier, je suis soudain sorti d'un songe, je me suis réveillé. Ensuite j'ai fait un autre songe, je vivais à la cour des Tsars, dans de vieux palais si froids que des stalactites de glace se formaient, en hiver, au-dessus des portes. Aujourd'hui, je me réveille, en face d'un bloc de papier blanc. Les flambeaux,

les fêtes glaciales, les uniformes, les belles épaules frissonnantes ont disparu. A la place il reste *quelque chose*[18] dans la chambre tiède, quelque chose que je ne veux pas voir.

M. de Rollebon était mon associé: il avait besoin de moi pour être et j'avais besoin de lui pour ne pas sentir mon être. Moi, je fournissais la matière brute, cette matière dont j'avais à revendre, dont je ne savais que faire: l'existence, *mon*[19] existence. Lui, sa partie, c'était de représenter. Il se tenait en face de moi et s'était emparé de ma vie pour me *représenter*[20] la sienne. Je ne m'apercevais plus que j'existais, je n'existais plus en moi, mais en lui; c'est pour lui que je mangeais, pour lui que je respirais, chacun de mes mouvements avait son sens au dehors, là, juste en face de moi, en lui; je ne voyais plus ma main qui traçait les lettres sur le papier, ni même la phrase que j'avais écrite—mais, derrière, au delà du papier, je voyais le marquis, qui avait réclamé ce geste, dont ce geste prolongeait, consolidait l'existence. Je n'étais qu'un moyen de le faire vivre, il était ma raison d'être, il m'avait délivré de moi. Qu'est-ce que je vais faire à présent (pp. 126–27).

With his own existence within his consciousness and after the vain attempts to find coherence and self-obliteration in M. de Rollebon's life, Roquentin's research becomes repugnant to him. This is so partly because of the lack of intrinsic cohesion in his materials, and partly because he discovers in M. de Rollebon the same pretentiousness and spuriousness he found in the lives of the portrayed dignitaries of Bouville.

Again, materially there is no apparent connection between Roquentin's visit to the gallery and the immediately following entry in his diary from which we learn that he has given up writing his book on M. de Rollebon. Yet in view of his reasons for giving up his work on a man who has been his raison d'être, one cannot leave unnoticed the thematic correlation and the textual contiguity between the end of the entry pertaining to the portraits and the beginning of the subsequent entry:

Adieu beaux lis tout en finesse dans vos petits sanctuaires peints, adieu beaux lis, notre orgueil et notre raison d'être. Adieu. Salauds.

LUNDI.

Je n'écris plus mon livre sur Rollebon; c'est fini, je ne *peux*[21] plus l'écrire. Qu'est-ce que je vais faire de ma vie? (pp. 122–23).

Roquentin, the historian, is an honest portraitist. He is unable and unwilling to lend a pleasing appearance to his subject, to use his skill in order to falsify nature, as it is, for the sake of pleasing effects and at the price of

---

[18] Italics in text.
[19] Italics in text.
[20] Italics in text.
[21] Italics in text.

deception—of others and particularly of himself. After all, Roquentin undertook the task in order to find that sense of a rigorous order that was lacking in his own life. To become a "Renaudas" or a "Bordurin" would mean to insist on self-deception which he was unwilling to endure even when his illusions of adventure were proving rapturously gratifying. Roquentin refuses to find a purpose in his life by following the examples of the gallery portraitist; he refuses to endow the historical portrait of Rollebon with a superimposed clarity and firmness of features:

> On les avait peints très exactement; et pourtant, sous le pinceau, leurs visages avaient dépouillé la mystérieuse faiblesse des visages d'hommes. Leurs faces, même les plus veules, étaient nettes comme des faïences: j'y cherchais en vain quelque parenté avec les arbres et les bêtes, avec les pensées de la terre ou de l'eau. Je pensais bien qu'ils n'avaient pas eu cette nécessité, de leur vivant. Mais, au moment de passer à la postérité, ils s'étaient confiés à un peintre en renom pour qu'il opérât discrètement sur leur visage ces dragages, ces forages, ces irrigations, par lesquels, tout autour de Bouville, ils avaient transformé la mer et les champs. Ainsi, avec le concours de Renaudas et de Bordurin, ils avaient asservi toute la Nature: hors d'eux et en eux-mêmes (p. 117).

Nor does he want to follow the example of M. Achille who, unable to trust his own experience, trusted the experience of another. Roquentin knows that experiences are supposed to be made of a preserved past, but he has learned that the past, as an experience, evades conservation:

> Je revis soudain la grosse bonne de "Chez Camille", la tête hagarde de M. Achille, la salle où j'avais si nettement senti que j'étais oublié, délaissé dans le présent. Je me dis avec lassitude:
> "Comment donc, moi qui n'ai pas eu la force de retenir mon propre passé, puis-je espérer que je sauverai celui d'un autre?" (p. 123).

Since there is no genuine memory of any past event, and therefore no genuine experience, it follows that there is also no genuine past that can be recaptured, no historian's shelter in which to take refuge. The present alone, the immediate moment of perception or thought, is life; its counterpart is not an existence laid to rest for us to behold, to contemplate, to relive; its counterpart is obliteration:

> Je jetai un regard anxieux autour de moi: du présent, rien d'autre que du présent. Des meubles légers et solides, encroûtés dans leur présent, une table, un lit, une armoire à glace—et moi-même. La vraie nature du présent se dévoilait: il était ce qui existe, et tout ce qui n'était pas présent n'existait pas. Le passé n'existait pas. Pas du tout. Ni dans les choses

ni même dans ma pensée. Certes, depuis longtemps, j'avais compris que le mien m'avait échappé. Mais je croyais, jusqu'alors, qu'il s'était simplement retiré hors de ma portée. Pour moi le passé n'était qu'une mise à la retraite: c'était une autre manière d'exister, un état de vacances et d'inaction; chaque événement, quand son rôle avait pris fin, se rangeait sagement, de lui-même, dans une boîte et devenait événement honoraire: tant on a de peine à imaginer le néant. Maintenant, je savais: les choses sont tout entières ce qu'elles paraissent—et *derrière*[22] elles . . . il n'y a rien (p. 124).

This is the insight that causes Roquentin to feel the "immense écœurement" and to drop his pen. However, this is not an attack of nausea, for this time he understands not only what it is that besets him with its oppressive presence, but also the reasons for that presence. He understands that the past is dead and that it was for that reason that "M. de Rollebon had just died a second time."

Roquentin's situation is similar to and yet markedly different from what it was in Mercier's office at Hanoi. From there he fled, for he did not know what that "insipid idea"—that threat of nausea—was that caused him to seek refuge in planned and perceptible coherence—intuitively, and one may say instinctively, since it was an act of self-preservation. What he now fears more than an attack of nausea is yet another flight, a knowingly senseless flight that may ultimately lead him back to the same point where he finds himself now and where he was before: to the oppressive and nauseating presence and thingness of living experience. That insipid idea still stares at him, but at last he has unlocked its secret and has recognized it as the dreadful and nauseating lack of cohesion, of rigorous coherence, of the elation he later found within music, that insipid idea, that thing that lay in wait for him was the thingness of his own existence: "La chose, qui attendait, s'est alertée, elle a fondu sur moi, elle se coule en moi, j'en suis plein.—Ce n'est rien: la Chose, c'est moi. L'existence, libérée, dégagée, reflue sur moi. J'existe" (p. 127). The existence of his limbs, of his body, invades his consciousness. It does not matter what he does with his hand, it continues existing because he remains aware of its weight, its warmth, its sensations, its persistent and independent presence. He *thinks* his existence: "J'existe. Je pense que j'existe" (p. 129). Even if he tried, he could not eradicate his consciousness, his thought of existence. The horror and disgust he feels in this confrontation reinforce his awareness of existence—of ubiquitous existence, of the contiguity of existing things. Even the voice on the record exists, for existence pervades every-

---

[22] Italics in text.

thing, fills the present and crowds the conscious mind that yearns for a perception of an intrinsic rigorous order:

> La voix, grave et rauque, apparaît brusquement et le monde s'évanouit, le monde des existences. Une femme de chair a eu cette voix, elle a chanté devant un disque, dans sa plus belle toilette et l'on enregistrait sa voix. La femme: bah! elle existait comme moi, comme Rollebon, je n'ai pas envie de la connaître. Mais il y a ça. On ne peut pas dire que cela existe. Le disque qui tourne existe, l'air frappé par la voix, qui vibre, existe, la voix qui impressionna le disque exista. Moi qui écoute, j'existe. Tout est plein, l'existence partout, dense et lourde et douce. Mais, par delà toute cette douceur, inaccessible, toute proche, si loin hélas, jeune, impitoyable et sereine il y a cette . . . cette rigueur (pp. 132–33).

This rigorous order for which he yearns is really inaccessible, however. It remains a concept and does not penetrate existence nor lived experience. Roquentin has now convinced himself of the illusory nature of that experience within which he believed that his sense of existence was relieved and nausea conquered.

These are the reflections in the entry of his diary placed between the visit to the gallery and the relinquishing of his research on the one hand, and his meeting with the Autodidacte on the other.

The portrayed citizens of Bouville were completely unaware of existence. They felt no need for a relief of existence. Convinced of their importance and of their rights, they found in life proof of their indispensability, and evidence of their self-justification. The Autodidacte who was not born with a notion of his right to life, who did not inherit the belief in his importance, who knew what solitude and melancholy could mean, had to seek his self-justification, and he found it. He found it in the fellowship of men, or rather in his illusion of such a fellowship. His self-justification differs considerably from that of the men in the portraits, but they all had this in common: ignorance of existence and faith in their usefulness, in their mission. Life, they believed, was meaningful and had a purpose, regardless of whether the notion of the purpose was taken for granted or arbitrarily chosen. Living meant fulfilling the purpose. This theme relates closely the two separated entries of the diary in spite of their striking material difference. From the point of view of the entry that separates them, from the point of view of the consciousness of existence which Roquentin has reached, yet another thematic affinity links the motifs of the gallery with those that constitute the meeting with the Autodidacte. Not only do the dignitaries and the Autodidacte fail to realize that there is no reason for the conservation of their precious existence, no reason for existence at all, they also produce equally spurious though different reasons for their self-justification. The men of Bouville gratified only their own ruthless egocentrism in relating their functions with the interests of the city and the country; and the Autodidacte found in his socialistic humanism a basis for loving mankind without having to look at the repugnant side of any individual. They were all lying to themselves but without knowing that they had to resort to falsehood and illusions so that the deeper layers of living, those that touch gratuitous existence, may remain concealed; so that one may remain safely ignorant of one's own insignificance and superfluousness.

Clearly, Sartre does not discount the significance, the usefulness, even the seeming necessity of some human relationships, and Roquentin's hope and wish to be able to have Anny stay with him is by itself sufficient evidence of this. But there is more important contextual evidence in the fact that Roquentin's reflections on Anny stand at the beginning of his account of the meeting with the Autodidacte. The motif introducing the meeting is obviously an allusion to the subsequently developed theme of the gratuitousness and uselessness of existence:

MERCREDI.

Il y a un rond de soleil sur la nappe en papier. Dans le rond, une mouche se traîne, engourdie, se chauffe et frotte ses pattes de devant l'une contre l'autre. Je vais lui rendre le service de l'écraser. Elle ne voit pas surgir cet index géant dont les poils dorés brillent au soleil.

"Ne la tuez pas, monsieur!" s'écrie l'Autodidacte.

Elle éclate, ses petites tripes blanches sortent de son ventre; je l'ai débarrassée de l'existence. Je dis sèchement à l'Autodidacte:

"C'était un service à lui rendre."

Pourquoi suis-je ici?—Et pourquoi n'y serais-je pas? Il est midi, j'attends qu'il soit l'heure de dormir. (Heureusement, le sommeil ne me fuit pas.) Dans quatre jours, je reverrai Anny: voilà, pour l'instant, ma seule raison de vivre. Et après? Quand Anny m'aura quitté? Je sais bien ce que, sournoisement, j'espère: j'espère qu'elle ne me quittera plus jamais. Je devrais pourtant bien savoir qu'Anny n'acceptera jamais de vieillir devant moi. Je suis faible et seul, j'ai besoin d'elle (p. 133).

The unconscious falsehood of the Autodidacte, his unawareness of shutting out knowledge of existence from his range of perception, and Roquentin's witnessing—with knowledge of what existence entails—this blind act of bad faith, cause the latter to experience nausea again:

"Vous m'excuserez, mais quand je pense à la profondeur de mon amour pour les hommes, à la force des élans qui m'emportent vers eux et que je nous vois là, en train de raisonner, d'argumenter . . . cela me donne envie de rire."

Je me tais, je souris d'un air contraint. La bonne pose devant moi une assiette avec un bout de camembert crayeux. Je parcours la salle du regard et un violent dégoût m'envahit. Que fais-je ici? Qu'ai-je été me mêler de discourir sur l'humanisme? Pourquoi ces gens sont-ils là? Pourquoi mangent-ils? C'est vrai qu'ils ne savent pas, eux, qu'ils existent. J'ai envie de partir, de m'en aller quelque part où je serais vraiment *à ma place,*[23] où je m'emboîterais. . . . Mais ma place n'est nulle part; je suis de trop.

L'Autodidacte se radoucit. Il avait craint plus de résistance de ma part. Il veut bien passer l'éponge sur tout ce que j'ai dit. Il se penche vers moi d'un air confidentiel:

"Au fond, vous les aimez, monsieur, vous les aimez comme moi: nous sommes séparés par des mots."

Je ne peux plus parler, j'incline la tête. Le visage de l'Autodidacte est tout contre le mien. Il sourit d'un air fat, tout contre mon visage, comme dans les cauchemars. Je mâche péniblement un morceau de pain que je ne me décide pas à avaler. Les hommes. Il faut aimer les hommes. Les hommes sont admirables. J'ai envie de vomir—et tout d'un coup ça y est: la Nausée (p. 155).

C'est donc ça la Nausée: cette aveuglante évidence? Me suis-je creusé la tête? En ai-je écrit! Maintenant je sais: J'existe—le monde existe—et je sais que le monde existe. C'est tout. Mais ça m'est égal. C'est étrange que tout me soit aussi égal: ça m'effraie. C'est depuis ce fameux jour où je voulais faire des ricochets. J'allais lancer ce galet, je l'ai regardé et c'est alors que tout a commencé: j'ai senti qu'il *existait.*[24] Et puis après ça, il y a eu d'autres Nausées; de temps en temps les objets se mettent à vous exister dans la main. Il y a eu la Nausée du "Rendez-Vous des Cheminots" et puis une autre, avant, une nuit que je regardais par le fenêtre; et puis une autre au Jardin public, un dimanche, et puis d'autres. Mais jamais ça n'avait été aussi fort qu'aujourd'hui (p. 156).

Although his feeling of nausea is stronger than ever before, he finds the experience itself a matter of indifference. He seems to have reached a perspective, an intellectual distance, and is able to cope even with an unusually strong attack. His original uneasiness that accompanied nausea was largely due to the fact that he could not fathom its nature. Now, with increased knowledge about its nature and increasing knowledge about its

---

[23] Italics in text.   [24] Italics in text.

cause, his anxiety is sufficiently allayed to permit indifference to mitigate its effects. Insight, however, does not eliminate the experience; in fact insight causes the crushing burden of the experience to be perceived with all its oppressive and besetting properties. Insight leads Roquentin so far as to make him realize that his nausea is part of himself, that it is even identifiable with himself as the perceiver of the thingness of the world, of existence stripped of attributed meaning and utility:

> Je ne peux pas dire que je me sente allégé ni content; au contraire, ça m'écrase. Seulement mon but est atteint: je sais ce que je voulais savoir; tout ce qui m'est arrivé depuis le mois de janvier, je l'ai compris. La Nausée ne m'a pas quitté et je ne crois pas qu'elle me quittera de sitôt; mais je ne la subis plus, ce n'est plus une maladie ni une quinte passagère: c'est moi.
>
> Donc j'étais tout à l'heure au Jardin public. La racine du marronnier s'enfonçait dans la terre, juste au-dessous de mon banc. Je ne me rappelais plus que c'était une racine. Les mots s'étaient évanouis et, avec eux, la signification des choses, leurs modes d'emploi, les faibles repères que les hommes ont tracés à leur surface (p. 161).

He has penetrated the surface of designations, classifications, functions, and superficial diversities. He has pierced the surface upon which human perception moves in the realm of color and motion in the blissful illusion of enchanting variety without suspecting the nauseating abundance and ubiquity of the sameness of existence, without realizing its superfluousness and basic unrelatedness. What brings forth his nausea when the Autodidacte speaks to him in the restaurant is exactly the realization of human delusions based on lack of perception. This is the realization of man's intuitive self-deception in the face of the *absolute absurdity* of existence, of the recognition of man's successful endeavor to deceive himself by concealing absolute absurdity in attributing to the surface of existence purposes, functions, significance, even necessity, and thereby attributing to himself an importance that breeds security and self-satisfaction. This full insight into existence and into man's world of misconceptions is bound to maintain the state of nausea and to keep Roquentin in its grip, but the insight itself, the understanding of the relation between existence and human delusions, fills him with an "extase horrible." Contrary to the ecstasy he felt in recognizing the rigorous order within music, where every tone was in a necessary and fleeting relationship to another tone, the world of existence, by virtue of its contingency, permanence, and absurdity, is the cause of a "horrible" ecstasy. In the first instance ecstasy is due to an insight into *being,* in the latter it is due to an insight into *existence.* It is at this stage that the two contrasting themes of existence and being become perceptible from a single focus and reveal to us simultaneously through Roquentin's recognition of the essential differences of the particular cohesions of existence and of being. From this point on *La Nausée* explores through various motifs, and seemingly only incidentally, the deceptive correspondence between existence and being.

Anny who no longer plays her favorite game of perfect moments, who has given up setting the stage for them in what she called "privileged situations," explains to Roquentin how she once believed that existence may achieve the quality of being and that she had thought it her duty to achieve it:

> "Oui, dis-je, j'ai compris. Dans chacune des situations privilégiées, il y a certains actes qu'il faut faire, des attitudes qu'il faut prendre, des paroles qu'il faut dire—et d'autres attitudes, d'autres paroles sont strictement défendues. Est-ce que c'est cela?"
>
> "Si tu veux . . ."
>
> "En somme, la situation c'est de la matière: cela demande à être traité."
>
> "C'est cela, dit-elle: il fallait d'abord être plongé dans quelque chose d'exceptionnel et sentir qu'on y mettait de l'ordre. Si toutes ces conditions avaient été réalisées, le moment aurait été parfait."
>
> "En somme, c'était une sorte d'œuvre d'art."
>
> "Tu m'as déjà dit ça, dit-elle avec agacement. Mais non: c'était . . . un devoir. Il *fallait*[25] transformer les situations privilégiées en moments parfaits. C'était une question de morale. Oui, tu peux bien rire: de morale" (p. 187).

However, just as Roquentin had analyzed his thrilling experience of adventure and found that it was based on illusions, that there was nothing in the incidents themselves and that his experience of adventure was due to his vision of coherences superimposed by himself, Anny, too, was struck by the same realization. She, too, knew the same discouragement and the same despair deriving from man's inability to impose upon existence a future rigorous course. Not even the illusion of adventure held out a promise of survival under the weight of existence constantly ready to encroach upon man's visions (just as, in a subsequent linking image, Roquentin sees nature ready to engulf the city):

> "Qu'il n'y a pas de situations privilégiées?"
>
> "Voilà. Je croyais que la haine, l'amour ou la mort descendaient sur nous, comme les langues de feu du Vendredi saint. Je croyais qu'on pouvait rayonner de haine ou de mort. Quelle erreur! Oui, vraiment, je pensais que ça existait "la Haine", que ça venait se poser sur les gens et les élever au-dessus d'eux-mêmes. Naturellement il n'y a que moi, moi qui hais, moi

---

25 Italics in text.

qui aime. Et alors ça, moi, c'est toujours la même chose, une pâte qui s'allonge, qui s'allonge . . . ça se ressemble même tellement qu'on se demande comment les gens ont eu l'idée d'inventer des noms, de faire des distinctions."

Elle pense comme moi. Il me semble que je ne l'ai jamais quittée (p. 189).

"Eh bien, mais tu ne penses pas du tout les mêmes choses que moi. Tu te plains parce que les choses ne se disposent pas autour de toi comme un bouquet de fleurs, sans que tu te donnes la peine de rien faire. Mais jamais je n'en ai tant demandé: je voulais agir. Tu sais, quand nous jouions à l'aventurier et à l'aventurière: toi tu étais celui à qui il arrive des aventures, moi j'étais celle qui les fait arriver. Je disais: "Je suis un homme d'action." Tu te rappelles? Eh bien, je dis simplement à présent: on ne peut pas être un homme d'action."

Il faut croire que je n'ai pas l'air convaincu, car elle s'anime et reprend avec plus de force:

"Et puis il y a un tas d'autres choses que je ne t'ai pas dites, parce que ce serait beaucoup trop long à t'expliquer. Par exemple, il aurait fallu que je puisse me dire, au moment même où j'agissais, que ce que je faisais aurait des suites . . . fatales. Je ne peux pas bien t'expliquer . . ." (pp. 189–90).

What, in view of the defeat inflicted by such a realization, can Anny and Roquentin make of their lives? Anny leaves to merge apathetically with existence, and Roquentin, "alone and free," envisages the same fate for himself, the fate of the victim who succumbs to his existence which he has vainly tried to justify in his work on Rollebon's existence, and to which he has vainly tried to give the quality of adventure, the aura of being:

Toute ma vie est derrière moi. Je la vois toute entière, je vois sa forme et les lents mouvements qui m'ont mené jusqu'ici. Il y a peu de choses à en dire: c'est une partie perdue, voilà tout. Voici trois ans que je suis entré à Bouville, solennellement. J'avais perdu la première manche. J'ai voulu jouer la seconde et j'ai perdu aussi: j'ai perdu la partie. Du même coup, j'ai appris qu'on perd toujours. Il n'y a que les salauds qui croient gagner. A présent, je vais faire comme Anny, je vais me survivre. Manger, dormir. Dormir, manger. Exister lentement, doucement, comme ces arbres, comme une flaque d'eau, comme la banquette rouge du tramway.

La Nausée me laisse un court répit. Mais je sais qu'elle reviendra: c'est mon état normal. Seulement, aujourd'hui mon corps est trop épuisé pour la supporter. Les malades aussi ont d'heureuses faiblesses qui leur ôtent, quelques heures, la conscience de leur mal. Je m'ennuie, c'est tout. De temps en temps je bâille si fort que les larmes me roulent sur les joues. C'est un ennui profond, profond, le cœur profond de l'existence, la matière même dont je suis fait (p. 197).

Only illusion can graft being upon existence and only for as long as the illusion is allowed to persist through ignorance maintained by the comfort and the security of institutions within a "belle cité bourgeoise." At the beginning of his diary, at the first signs of nausea, Roquentin consoled himself in his own ignorance with the notion that he must have been the victim of "une petite crise de folie" and with the comfort of being "bien bourgeoisement dans le monde." At the end of his diary a contrasting yet materially similar theme is developed as he stands on a hill overlooking Bouville for the last time:

> Comme je me sens loin d'eux, du haut de cette colline. Il me semble que j'appartiens à une autre espèce. Ils sortent des bureaux, après leur journée de travail, ils regardent les maisons et les squares d'un air satisfait, ils pensent que c'est *leur*[26] ville, une "belle cité bourgeoise." Ils n'ont pas peur, ils se sentent chez eux. Ils n'ont jamais vu que l'eau apprivoisée qui coule des robinets, que la lumière qui jaillit des ampoules quand on appuie sur l'interrupteur, que les arbres métis, bâtards, qu'on soutient avec des fourches. Ils ont la preuve, cent fois par jour, que tout se fait par mécanisme que le monde obéit à des lois fixes et immuables. Les corps abandonnés dans le vide tombent tous à la même vitesse, le jardin public est fermé tous les jours à seize heures en hiver, à dix-huit heures en été, le plomb fond à 335°, le dernier tramway part de l'Hôtel de Ville à vingt-trois heures cinq. Ils sont paisibles, un peu moroses, ils pensent à Demain, c'est-à-dire, simplement, à un nouvel aujourd'hui; les villes ne disposent que d'une seule journée qui revient toute pareille à chaque matin. A peine la pomponne-t-on un peu, les dimanches. Les imbéciles. Ça me répugne, de penser que je vais revoir leurs faces épaisses et rassurées. Ils légifèrent, ils écrivent des romans populistes, ils se marient, ils ont l'extrême sottise de faire des enfants. Cependant, la grande nature vague s'est glissée dans leur ville, elle s'est infiltrée, partout, dans leur maison, dans leurs bureaux, en eux-mêmes. Elle ne bouge pas, elle se tient tranquille et eux, ils sont en plein dedans, ils la respirent et ils ne la voient pas, ils s'imaginent qu'elle est dehors, à vingt lieues de la ville. Je la *vois*,[27] moi, cette nature, je la *vois*[28] ... Je sais que sa soumission est paresse, je sais qu'elle n'a pas de lois: ce qu'ils prennent pour sa constance ... Elle n'a que des habitudes et elle peut en changer demain (pp. 198–99).

Between the first and the last component motif carrying the theme of bourgeois security and complacency there lies Roquentin's conquest of ignorance through insights into the gratuitousness and the fortuitousness of existence, and into the vanity of man's seeking to overcome existence with his optimism nurtured by science, humanism, and thought, all of which

---

[26] Italics in text.   [27] Italics in text.   [28] Italics in text.

are founded on the consoling assumption of the immutability and controllability of nature:

> Je m'adosserai à un mur et je leur crierai au passage: "Qu'avez-vous fait de votre science? Qu'avez-vous fait de votre humanisme? Où est votre dignité de roseau pensant?" Je n'aurai pas peur—ou du moins pas plus qu'en ce moment. Est-ce que ce ne sera pas toujours de l'existence, des variations sur l'existence? ... C'est de l'existence que j'ai peur (p. 200).

While his mind is still gripped by his insight into existence, and by particularized variations of existence as they appear to him from the hill, and as they later elicit his fascination, horror, and anger in the library, where the Corsican's and the watchful woman's indignation drive the Autodidacte into solitude, Roquentin takes his final leave of Bouville. However, his impending physical separation from the particular existence of the city allows him to see himself already divorced from its sights and its people, freed from his habits and his tenuous ties, and freed from even his recent hope of a life with Anny. There is nothing left but consciousness within which even his identity as Antoine Roquentin becomes objectified. He enters for the last time the "Rendez-vous des Cheminots" and Madeleine plays for him his favorite record. With his consciousness turned toward his wasted life, in the sight of familiar ugliness, stains, and dirt that surround him, he listens to the music, but cannot, as he once did, perceive existence in the glow of the tune. In contrast to people in concert halls who imagine that their sufferings turn to music, Roquentin listening to the music feels ashamed: ashamed of existence, of his superfluousness, and of his self-pity: "j'ai honte pour moi-même et pour se qui existe *devant* elle" (p. 218). At the height of consciousness, he realizes that the music does not exist, that it has its intrinsic necessity, that it has being:

> *Elle*[29] n'existe pas. C'en est même agaçant; si je me levais, si j'arrachais ce disque du plateau qui le supporte et si je le cassais en deux, je ne l'atteindrais pas, *elle*.[30] Elle est au delà—toujours au delà de quelque chose, d'une voix, d'une note de violon. A travers des épaisseurs et des épaisseurs d'existence, elle se dévoile, mince et ferme et, quand on veut la saisir, on ne rencontre que des existants, on bute sur des existants dépourvus de sens. Elle est derrière eux: je ne l'entends même pas, j'entends des sons, des vibrations de l'air qui la dévoilent. Elle n'existe pas, puisqu'elle n'a rien de trop: c'est tout le reste qui est trop par rapport à elle. Elle *est*[31] (p. 218).

With keenest awareness and fullest knowledge, purged of delusions and self-deceptions, he realizes again, but this time desperately, that existence

---

[29] Italics in text. [30] Italics in text. [31] Italics in text.

cannot be turned into being, that being cannot even alter existence except during fleeting illusions:

> Et moi aussi, j'ai voulu *être*.[32] Je n'ai même voulu que cela; voilà le fin mot de ma vie: au fond de toutes ces tentatives qui semblaient sans liens, je retrouve le même désir: chasser l'existence hors de moi, vider les instants de leur graisse, les tordre, les assécher, me purifier, me durcir, pour rendre enfin le son net et précis d'une note de saxophone. Ça pourrait même faire un apologue: il y avait un pauvre type qui s'était trompé de monde. Il existait, comme les autres gens, dans le monde des jardins publics, des bistrots, des villes commerçantes et il voulait se persuader qu'il vivait ailleurs, derrière la toile des tableaux, avec les doges du Tintoret, avec les braves Florentins de Gozzoli, derrière les pages des livres, avec Fabrice del Dongo et Julien Sorel, derrière les disques de phono, avec les longues plaintes sèches des jazz. Et puis, après avoir bien fait l'imbécile, il a compris, il a ouvert les yeux, il a vu qu'il y avait maldonne: il était dans un bistrot, justement, devant un verre de bière tiède. Il est resté accablé sur la banquette; il a pensé: je suis un imbécile. Et à ce moment précis, de l'autre côté de l'existence, dans cet autre monde qu'on peut voir de loin, mais sans jamais l'approcher, une petite mélodie s'est mise à danser, à chanter: "C'est comme moi qu'il faut être: il faut souffrir en mesure" (pp. 218–19).

As he thinks of the composer and the singer who have created the music, it occurs to him that they may have at least partially "washed themselves of the sin of existence"—not by changing their existence in which they probably felt drowned, but by creating *being*. To that extent they have succeeded in justifying their own existence, and have taught him to seek a justification of his own:

> Est-ce que je ne pourrais pas essayer . . . Naturellement, il ne s'agirait pas d'un air de musique . . . mais est-ce que je ne pourrais pas, dans un autre genre? . . . Il faudrait que ce soit un livre: je ne sais rien faire d'autre. Mais pas un livre d'histoire: l'histoire, ça parle de ce qui a existé—jamais un existant ne peut justifier l'existence d'un autre existant. Mon erreur, c'était de vouloir ressusciter M. de Rollebon. Une autre espèce de livre. Je ne sais pas très bien laquelle—mais il faudrait qu'on devine, derrière les mots imprimés derrière les pages, quelque chose qui n'existerait pas, qui serait au-dessus de l'existence. Une histoire, par exemple, comme il ne peut pas en arriver, une aventure. Il faudrait qu'elle soit belle et dure comme de l'acier et qu'elle fasse honte aux gens de leur existence (pp. 221–22).

---

[32] Italics in text.

6

Conclusion

Only by following the development of the themes of existence and being in *La Nausée* can one actually determine a coherent linear succession of any sort. There is no story in *La Nausée*. The sequence of incidents is plausible in time but hardly any segment of incidents is a development of the previous segment. Contiguous segments, for the most part, are materially in no relationship to one another and frequently even incidents within a segment differ materially from one another. Contingency and mere contiguity mark the linear succession of incidents. In *La Nausée* this structural feature is of considerable significance, for it reflects one of the most important aspects of one of the pervasive themes of the work: existence. On the other hand, the cohesion of themes carried by materially different segments of incidents is a reflection of one of the significant aspects of another pervasive theme: being.

Nor is there any real plot in *La Nausée*. True, Roquentin is motivated to seek the cause and to determine the nature of his nausea, but he does not undertake any action in order to achieve that purpose. He reacts reflectively to contingent incidents but does not initiate any moves directed toward his purpose. He does reveal one single yearning, however: the hope and the desire to be reunited with Anny; but again reaction rather than effort marks his conduct during their brief meeting. Finally, his purpose to write a history of the life of M. de Rollebon is given up when his effort proves intellectually futile. Roquentin's is a reflective mind, and *La Nausée* is the record of an increasingly deepening insight into the nature of existence and being.

La Symphonie pastorale had a clear linear progression and a complex plot structure. Generic thematic coherence depended largely upon the cohesion of the themes of story and plot. Where that was not the case, various leitmotifs were often used to allude to the thematic relatedness of sequentially frequently separated component motif clusters.

In *L'Etranger* the story rests largely on clusters of contingent incidents in the first part, and contingency is only partly veiled by court procedures

177

and prison routine in the second part. The plot structure, too, is more similar to that in *La Nausée* than to that in *La Symphonie pastorale,* although Meursault's motivations and purposes are far more pronounced if we compare him with Roquentin, who is almost bereft of any. With story and plot relatively underemphasized, the generic coherence of themes constitutes a more important factor in the unity of the thematic fabric.

La Nausée has no story and no plot. Here the unity of the thematic fabric is based almost exclusively upon the generic coherence of themes. While Camus made considerable use of leitmotifs in relating correlative themes, Sartre relied primarily upon variations of certain motif clusters to establish the cohesion of the thematic fabric.

We may conclude by stating that the more story and plot are underemphasized, the more does the unity of the structure of the work depend upon the generic coherence of its themes. Abstraction of themes was the key to analysis in this study, but it was an abstraction with a constant regard for motifs and their variations in the text and for the complex correlations of the themes in the entire fabric. Textual manifestations were the basis for abstraction; recognition of cohesion and unity was its aim.

Index

Similarity; see Affinity

Story, 5, 6, 7, 21, 178; incidents in, 24–25; see also Themes

Symphonie pastorale, La: central themes of the story, 33–36, 37, 42–43, 45; generic coherence of themes, 45–51, 177; linear coherence of incidents, 30–31; thematic units of segments, 31–33; themes of the plot, 36–45

Taine, Hippolyte, 25

Thematic units of segments: in *L'Etranger,* 83–84; in *La Symphonie pastorale,* 31–33, 83

Thematism, xi, xii, xiii, xvi, xx

Themes, xii, xiii, xv, xvii, xix, xx, 1, 2, 15, 25, 26; correlative, 8, 20, 45; in iconography and iconology, 21 ff.; as message, 3; of the plot, 26–27, 36–45, 79–83, 84, 177, 178; of the story, 26–27, 33–36, 37, 41, 42–43, 45, 52–78, 79, 83, 84, 117–18, 177; as topic, 2, 3, 24

Tolstoy, Lev Nikolaevich, 1

Topic; see Themes

Topos, xiii

Wagner, Richard, 1

Walzel, Oskar, 2, 10

Zola, Emile, 1

180